Unfinished Business

UNFINISHED BUSINESS

IN NEIGHBORHOOD
AND NATION

Helen Hall

THE MACMILLAN COMPANY New York, New York
COLLIER-MACMILLAN LIMITED London

Dedicated to my husband

PAUL KELLOGG

in loving memory

The Macmillan Company
866 Third Avenue, New York, N.Y. 10022
Collier-Macmillan Canada Ltd., Toronto, Ontario
Library of Congress Catalog Card Number: 76-114325

First Printing

PRINTED IN THE UNITED STATES OF AMERICA

Contents

(Photographs follow pages 64, 128, 192, and 256)

INTRODUCTION: *Unfinished Business*   ix

PART ONE
The Depression Years, 1928–1939

I   From Schuylkill to the Lower East Side   3
II   Public Relief   10
III   The Dutchman's Farm   15
IV   The Coming of Fiorello La Guardia   22
V   The New Deal Initials   29
VI   Settlement Studies of Unemployment   40
VII   Social Security   53

PART TWO
The Anatomy of a Settlement

VIII   A General Practitioner   61
IX   Residents and Visitors   77
X   The Board   84
XI   The Staff   92
XII   Personal Service   96

XIII   Young Neighbors   *100*

XIV   Health or Lack of It   *108*

XV   The Playhouse   *114*

XVI   The Music School   *120*

XVII   The Art Department   *125*

XVIII   Our Credit Union, A People's Bank, Young People's
        Cooperatives, and Buying Clubs   *139*

XIX   From Community Studies to Community Action   *144*

XX   The Aged Are People   *158*

XXI   Cooperation with the Public Schools   *167*

XXII   The National Federation of Settlements and the
        United Neighborhood Houses   *173*

PART THREE

The War Years, 1940–1945

XXIII   The Shadow of War   *181*

XXIV   A Leave of Absence in the South Pacific   *190*

XXV   The Promise of the United Nations   *207*

PART FOUR

The Postwar Years, 1945–1955

XXVI   Disruption of Neighborhoods and
        Gang Warfare   *219*

XXVII   Heightened Gang Warfare and the Predelinquent
        Gang Project   *226*

XXVIII Postwar Unemployment   *231*

XXIX   More New Housing   *235*

XXX   The Beginning and the Slow Understanding of Nar-
        cotics Abuse   *245*

XXXI The Founding of the Lower Eastside Neighborhoods Association (LENA) 254

XXXII The Beginning of Mobilization for Youth 269

XXXIII Still Unfinished Business and Chaos 277

XXXIV An Unfinished Story of a Community's Fight for Its Hospital 288

XXXV Some Beginnings of the Consumer Movement 318

XXXVI Consumers in World War II—Price Control and Rationing 337

XXXVII Low-Income Study and the Poor Pay More 349

A Last Word 354

Acknowledgments 355

Index 357

Introduction:
UNFINISHED BUSINESS

In this book I am allowing myself to approach the subject of unfinished business largely by way of neighborhood work and the many national concerns which grew out of it, as well as through my own personal experiences from childhood on. That must of necessity be the route by which all of us come to understanding, whether consciously or not.

My father was a manufacturer and my mother a painter. As I grew up it became part of the family planning that I was to be a sculptor. Not, as I look back on it, so much because I showed such marked talent in that direction, but because my mother and father took it for granted that women as well as men should have purposeful lives.

However, while in the process of pursuing the Arts, I decided that I wanted to stop and find out what was done for people when they were very poor, and in trouble. It was not that we were always well off ourselves, but there was enough comfort and plenty of love to go round.

As with most of us, my concern had sprung from small things that are hard to trace today. But I suppose my first glimpse of a whole people being persecuted came when, at fourteen, my mother in some way found living near us an Armenian family just escaped from the Turkish massacres. She had me take chicken broth to the young girl my own age in the family, when she was ill. This girl's senseless plight and that of the younger brothers and sisters standing around the bed, obviously hungry, too, not only aroused my sympathy but my indignation.

Later I came to know some of the children living in the little houses on the way to my father's factory in Port Chester, a small town outside of New York City. While I knew my father was having a hard time meeting the factory payroll, I saw their poverty at close hand. I knew my father was paying good wages for those days and yet I could see that it did not seem to be enough for a good life for those children.

Something else that stands out clearly from those days, so vividly in fact that it taught a conscious lesson, was the night my father's factory burned. It happened to be the building where the expensive, and hard-come-by machinery had just been set in operation. It was such a big blaze that crowds gathered to watch the fun. My younger sister, my mother, my father, and I stood together and apart from the crowd, watching, too, but we didn't cheer the beauty of the spectacle as the others did, when the flaming roof caved in. I think, even then, I knew that that cheer was not meant to be cruel but just came from lack of awareness. As I have gone along, I've come to see that lack of awareness is back of so much cruelty, and that is why I have always felt that a settlement's job of interpretation is a primary one. As a matter of fact I feel that this is true of anyone in social work. Whenever in later years I allowed myself to waver in this belief, I was always strengthened by the understanding of my husband, Paul Kellogg, the editor of *The Survey*, whose work for fifty years was one of interpretation.

Again, what that fire, and many other things, did to our family fortunes brought home to me the realization that no child, however sheltered, entirely escapes sharing in any searing worry that may beset its parents.

So when we look back and realize what deep impressions the incidents of our own youth can make on the fresh film of a young mind, we should be eternally rebellious against the myriad forms of ugliness and insecurity that slum neighborhoods have to offer as first impressions to the children starting life there. I remember discussing this once with a group of settlement girls, and one of them said bitterly, "There's so much dirt here, Miss Hall, you just have to keep walking away from it every minute of your life." And she added reflectively, "Some just can't seem to walk away." It is not that all ugliness is centered in the slums, but that is where its inescapability is the greatest.

As we grow older, single impressions, or even a climate of love or of fear, lose much of their power either to lift or to destroy. Emotional impact is blurred by all that has gone before, and characters have been set. But while we have found no way to measure it in exact terms, experience points in no uncertain way to the devastating impact of unfavorable circumstances on the human personality as it takes shape.

I remember so well a night years ago in my Philadelphia settlement neighborhood when a drunken family quarrel spilled over into our street. A husband and wife rolled in the gutter while a crowd collected. Our settlement staff darted into the fray and between us all we stopped it quickly. However, it was a hot summer night and neighbors stayed around gossiping, the fight soon forgotten by the grownups. But as I said goodnight an hour later to two fathers who during this time happened to be holding a small girl and a little boy on their respective shoulders, the fathers responded cheerfully enough, but one small child, looking at me still wide-eyed and startled, said, not good night, but, "The man and the lady was fightin', wasn't they?" And the other, in much the same questioning voice said, "The man hit the woman, didn't he?" I'll warrant that impression was indelible and that no succeeding years would completely wipe out the hateful sight.

So to understand neighborhood work you must understand this background where early impressions can be so ugly, and then you can better know why we struggle so to bring beauty, affection, and understanding to compete in children's lives for first place in their secret minds. That is one of the reasons why we feel that music, dancing, drama, painting, pottery, clubs, or anything we have to choose from should be creatively led. In other words, a settlement should be a place where adventure may build and not destroy. And what we do must hold its own in competition with so many neighborhood factors that tear the child apart. And this is basic to the Settlement philosophy—to win out, our work must not only be good but within easy reach.

Too, it isn't the tenements and the street corners alone that tend to make life a sort of obstacle race for the young. The tensions and pressures inside the home can be worse than the streets they battle or the stairs they climb. It can be the parents' lack of understanding—neglect or much worse—that builds a barrier between the young and what they need. That is why we feel that the whole family is our job if we are to be really effective. Take a twelve-year-old boy in our pottery workshop. That was where he was happy, and that was where he was good, and it was home to him. But, and this is a dreadful "but" to most children, his father thought he was wasting his time. Our teacher in the workshop knew that sculpture was only part of her job, and that the mind should be at reasonable rest as the hands build. As this boy's story gradually came out, she decided to go and see the father, but first she put some of the boy's work in our exhibition case. Finally, after some visiting, she was able to persuade the father to come back to the settlement with her. Here he saw to his surprise that his son could make something that other people thought worth putting under a strong light, and looking at it. His attitude toward our whole setup changed and the child dropped, for the time being, anyway, the albatross of family disapproval.

To go back: when I finished a year at what in those days was the New York School of Philanthropy, now the Columbia University School of Social Work, I was caught beyond all recall in the enthrallment of social work. First I organized a small settlement in Westchester County, then worked at child placement and with widows' pensions in the Westchester Department of Child Welfare; afterward I did a stint in the First World War with the Red Cross running recreation huts in hospitals in France, and organized a Foyee des Allies* for the Y.W.C.A. in Alsace. Shortly after coming home, the Army sent me out to the Philippines and China to establish service clubs for enlisted men in that Corps Area. Upon returning a year and a half later, I decided to go into the settlement field.

At this point I met some resistance. "Settlements are old-fashioned," I was told. While brief, my experience had already

---

* Girls club.

given me other ideas about that. Many of my reactions were, of course, nebulous, but one of the things that I did think out quite clearly at that time was that, as I saw it, no matter how much responsibility you might assume in the settlement you never got away from friendship with the people around you. No amount of work with staff, board, committees could come between you and the folks with whom you were working. I am pleased that I thought this out so long ago, for I know now that it is one of the constants, and one of the strengths, of the settlements. Personal encounter is a great spur to action. It helps keep you throughout the years from taking other people's misery for granted, as something bad but unavoidable, something you can treat but not cure. And, of course, to get at the roots of evil in city slums is what the settlement is all about.

I remember writing the stories of unemployed neighbors during the Depression until the words seemed to have no meaning and the task hopeless. At this point I would put down my pencil and go out and talk to a family where there was unemployment, and I would come back determined that if it killed me I was going to make others understand.

However, at the time I came to Henry Street in 1933 from University House in Philadelphia, there was again talk about the settlements being unnecessary, this time because, it was said, slum neighborhoods were becoming a thing of the past. Those of us living and working in such neighborhoods knew this was nonsense and that neighborhood life was circumscribed by the many factors inherent in poverty.

We knew that centralization of social and health services, both public and private, had been steadily increasing, and that while it may have meant saving of overhead, too often it was at the expense of being where, and when, your services were needed most. This meant that neighborhood work had an increasingly important role to play, for the neighborhood is where vulnerability is highest, where observations should be keenest, and services most ready.

We knew, of course, that specialization was essential in the profession of social work as in any other profession, but if our social services were to be more and more specialized, then there would be more need than ever before for general practitioners in our neighborhoods.

It is important for someone to see the so-called "closed" cases after they are closed—to see the child on his *way* to trouble, the family on its *way* to breaking up, the old people caught on the sixth-floor walk-ups, the defeated, the shy, the defiant. I have often seen children standing on a tenement stoop, looking tentatively up and down our rugged street, and I think, what a place it is for the timid child to face alone. To hold their own they must hide their diffidence, learn to put on a brave front, to yell as loudly, or preferably louder than the next one, kick over the garbage can if need be, and be ready with fists, which no one must ever guess are reluctant. These children we see along with all the others, the average, the ambitious, the hostile, the gifted; all whose chances of success may be enhanced by having opportunities for development within easy reach. Our intake policy, if you could call anything so informal by that name, must be bent to the pressures of our neighbors' special needs, which defy all categories. That does not need to mean that there is chaos at our front doors, either.

And I would hope it would mean that we were working to get some of these—to us, essentials—into the school buildings, to become a part of public education. Every family in neighborhoods such as ours should, through some form of local agency have access to the kind of services offered at Henry Street and other settlement houses and community centers in the city. Just not knowing where to turn when in trouble is a misery too often allied with poverty.

I have found it hard to tell of life in a settlement in an orderly fashion. Looking back, one can see a pattern of change and growth. But it is the day-by-day events that build the pattern, and they are anything but orderly. It is hard to hold to chronological terms also because date lines cut confusingly into threads of work that run over periods of years.

Because the settlement is such a flexible tool, responding not to set patterns but to changing needs, the people who take major responsibility for administration must be equipped temperamentally to build new patterns as they go along. During my years at Henry Street I was fortunate in having three such associates—Franklin Harbach for my first ten years, and Ralph Tefferteller and his wife Ruth, for the twenty-one years after the war. These partnerships added immeasurably to the welfare of the settlement, as well as to my own.

As I look back, I do see the years divided by different overriding problems. And, except for the four years of war, the problems of most concern to the people of slum neighborhoods such as mine have seemed to last approximately a decade, with each ten years producing a new concern. So I have divided the following account into this pattern as nearly as seemed reasonable, with the exception of two pieces of very unfinished business— Health and Consumers—which are each treated as one narrative.

The Depression years between 1929 and 1939 lasted until the four years of war which, of course, presented their own special pattern of time and tragedy.

At the end of the war in 1945, began ten years when the disruption of neighborhoods and its concomitant of gang warfare was of top concern.

Then from 1955 to approximately 1965, drug addiction and individual violence became most disturbing to neighborhood life.

By the mid-sixties changed aspects of the civil rights movement from nonviolent to violent and the rebellion of youth from slums, to suburbs, to universities, had added mass violence to our still rising individual crime rate, which is still related to the increase in the use of drugs—all of which has changed the pattern of neighborhood life. With muggings in the offing, evening meetings take on a different aspect!

In pointing up what were overriding concerns in the decades, I am counting on the reader's understanding that all through this time the problems of decent housing, health care, steady employment, and better education were the basic and continuous needs of the neighborhoods, and that they are the very unfinished business of today should go without saying. That there has been progress made over the years is obvious, but when what has been done is matched against the need, it should stir the most sluggish conscience.

I retired in 1967 after thirty-four years at Henry Street. Bertram Beck took my place as director of Henry Street, and continued to head Mobilization for Youth, plans for which had started at Henry Street in 1957. His background as deputy director of the National Association of Social Workers had brought him in touch with national problems, as did his five years with the United States Children's Bureau during the gang years, when he was in charge of their Juvenile Delinquency Project. His friendliness and appreciation of people especially fit him for neighborhood work, and he and his wife, Deborah, who is also a social worker, with their two baby girls are living at the settlement. The second baby was born after the Becks moved to Henry Street, so, to use a presently popular term describing neighborhood people, she is truly indigenous.

I am sure the years ahead will continue to bear down hard on our neighborhoods, and on those working to change them. But the coming years should be determining ones, for it seems as though slums have at last reached the consciousness of the upper echelons. From mayors, to governors, to the Congress, the state of our deteriorated cities has become a part of political talking and I hope this will mean political doing as well. Perhaps it will, because the people themselves are fighting for change; often using violence, but also coming to use the ballot as well.

At Christmas time I used to crowd a group of small next-door neighbors into my car and we would go to visit the big tree at Rockefeller Center. On one of these occasions, as we came to Park Avenue and the brightly lighted parts of the city, eight-year-old Arturo piped up from the back seat, "Oh, Miss Hall, I like this city." I explained that this was New York, and the answer was, "Oh, no! Where we live is New York."

Arturo had not seen that part of New York before, and I think most people have never really seen the slums where he lived. They talk about the slums but they never really see them, for if enough of them did, the slums would have gone long ago.

One morning the Commissioner of Health was on the radio, telling people how dangerous rats were and for people to be sure to put their covers on their garbage cans tightly. I have had quite a bit of experience with rats—bitten babies, scared children, and rat epidemics. When the tenements across the street were torn down, Henry Street had an epidemic of them in the cellar, and the way you got rid of them was not just to put the garbage can cover on more tightly. As I listened, I thought of the filthy tenement back yards where garbage had not been collected; the often garbage-laden airshafts of the new-law tenements, and of the old, delapidated garbage cans in front of tenement-lined streets. This well-meant plea seemed so typical: Not the Sanitation Department really collecting the garbage; not the Health Department destroying the rats; just telling people to keep them out of their garbage cans so the rats might be so hungry they would die.

It does not seem very nice to start a book talking about rats; but maybe it is to the point, as I have known so many children who have had to start their life in close association with these dangerous and disgusting rodent slum dwellers. And perhaps it is appropriate, as last winter the Congress refused to pass a rat control bill. Even rats are unfinished business when we live in the slums.

PART ONE

The Depression Years
1928 - 1939

I

From Schuylkill to the Lower East Side

In 1933 as you looked down Henry Street you saw as a backdrop to the tenements the tall buildings of the Wall Street section of New York, and at sunset it was one of the most beautiful views in the city. For a short time each day the tenements were clothed in beauty and became a part of New York's magnificence. But without the glamour of the sunset there was little of magnificence about our neighborhood but its people.

The sun was just setting on a hot August first when I arrived at Henry Street, and I saw it at its best. As I drove down the street toward "265," where I was to live, the firehouse on the corner was running a sprinkler, and its spray caught the rays of the sun. I saw the dancing bodies of the children through a sparkle and behind them all Henry Street aglow from the sun. As I pulled up, an eight-year-old boy, Sammy by name, came to open the car door and started dragging out the luggage. He had a serious speech defect which I was to hear for many years, for Sammy's early position at the firehouse almost became permanent, not replaced by any of the remedial plans we tried to get his family to accept for him. He stood there, an errand runner for the firemen, and a kind of loud-voiced incomprehensible boss of his particular corner. From the very beginning, if I forgot my key, it was Sammy who climbed the iron grille at the sidewalk and got in the never locked front windows, running around to let me in at the door with the gesture of a host. And it was Sammy, grown large and fat, who late at night after closing hours handed out our front door key from the fire house where an extra one is still kept for emergencies.

That afternoon the men residents at Henry Street quickly supplemented the little boy's efforts and I was settled in. As I faced the new "settlement family" at dinner that evening the sense of high adventure was somewhat obscured by home-sickness for my University House family in Philadelphia and the neighborhood of which I had felt so much a part. The little one-family houses of Schuylkill in Philadephia, where I had lived for eleven years, seemed so much more friendly and less forbidding than the tenements. And a ready-made staff and residents certainly were less cozy than the familiar faces I had left, where our strengths and weaknesses were already known to each other and an affectionate rapport had been established.

I had chosen to start my work at Henry Street in August so that I could get a sense of the neighborhood and the settlement before the pressures of the fall set in, and I was looking forward with zest as well as some trepidation to the new opportunities ahead.

No adult clubs were meeting in August but this was 1933 and there was a very active group of unemployed men and women that had as headquarters a small store—it would be known as a "store front" today—for which Henry Street was paying the rent. It was diagonally opposite our 301 Henry Street buildings, the three buildings where the gym and most of our clubrooms were situated.

A headquarters of their own lent more dignity to the unemployed than the usual street corner. While unemployment brought to the mother the agony of trying to feed a family on nothing a week, her hands at least were busy with some of her accustomed tasks; but the man of the family, when the early morning job-hunting was done, had the long hours of the day to kill, time laden with the sense of being unneeded. And we found leisure-time activities very hard to make absorbing when such leisure was enforced. It was only later, when we were able to call on the man- and woman-power of the Works Progress

Administration (WPA) that we were able to set up more adequate programs to hold worried minds.

I remember one of the most ardent members of a dramatic group in Philadelphia, whose night work had never given him enough time for rehearsals, saying, in answer to my question as to why he did not come to the group while he was unemployed, "It's funny, but now that I've got the time, I don't seem to have the heart." Sure enough, when he finally did get a job, he was back eager as ever.

It takes a special kind of self-discipline to reorganize your time well and get some kind of fun or learning out of it. This was why the organized groups of unemployed of those days served a valuable psychological purpose aside from the pressure they could exert—it was something you belonged to where everyone was in the same boat. And you were imbued with the broad general purpose of getting consideration for the problems of the unemployed in whatever quarter possible, and through many different means.

In my first week at Henry Street I attended a meeting of our unemployed group in our gymnasium. It was a hot night, and I could sense that the temperature of the meeting was going to be even hotter. I came and sat in a corner, hoping not to be recognized, just to observe the proceedings. The League for Industrial Democracy had been the first to help organize the unemployed on a city-wide basis, and Mary Fox, was there that night, representing them. The question was, should our group join a "United Front" with the Communist-sponsored Unemployed Councils.

This proposition was fought over violently. Voices rose to shouts over "points of order" and the two sergeants-at-arms were busy pushing people back into their seats. No blood was shed, however, to my surprise, because I had just come from an Irish neighborhood where fists followed angry words in quick succession. After a couple of hours of din, I heard the chairman insistently pounding his gavel, and when semiquiet prevailed, I was startled to hear him saying, "It is for a shame that the first night we have our new woman with us we have this little disagreement!" I decided then that if this was only a little disagreement, life on Henry Street was going to be exciting.

Coming from the Philadelphia neighborhood where I knew everyone from babies to grandmothers, what I minded most about those first days was being in a neighborhood of strangers. So as soon as I went out to our camps and began to meet the clubs in town, I asked them to say "hello" to me in the street, because I was lonely and missed having friends all around me. Thrown on their mettle, to make me feel at home became a cause; children and grownups alike speeded the job of friendship as I came and went in my new neighborhood. Some years afterward a young girl recalled: "Do you remember when you told us at camp to speak to you on the street because you were lonely? Well, I always did," she added proudly.

I had one bit of luck at my own door. In those days the general guardian at the entrance of "301," where we had our gym and club rooms, was Stanley Schlein, a man who had grown up on Henry Street. Years before, he had happened to show my father and me around Henry Street when we were on a casual visit and this seemed to give him a sense of responsibility for my settling in, a feeling he carried over all the years we worked together until his sudden death in 1952.

But while the people were different, the problems of my new neighborhood were not: unemployment was the overpowering, ever-present concern against which everything else was insignificant. How to keep a roof over your head and get food enough to live on not only takes precedence, but brings in its wake all the dreary concomitants of strain, family breakdown, and personal disintegration. Coming home a failure every day after an unsuccessful job-hunt seldom helps a man to build personality or cement family relationships.

The settlement and the Visiting Nurse Service were under one administration when I came to Henry Street. The nursing service was generally regarded as the most important of the many things that had sprung from the "House on Henry Street." Lillian Wald herself was a nurse, and with her young partner, Mary Brewster, had come to the East Side with the idea of giving and teaching bedside nursing to the poor of that district. The first group of visiting nurses had their office at 265 Henry Street, and were still there when I came. By that time the service had extended to three boroughs, with seventeen offices and 265 nurses. Lillian Wald had developed visiting nurses into a world-wide movement through her imagination and initiative. She was a nurse, social worker, and social reformer in one, and set the early pattern for visiting nursing, bringing into it social objectives beyond the techniques involved in nursing itself.

The administration of the Henry Street Settlement and the Henry Street Visiting Nurse Service was separated in 1937. Miss Wald died in 1940, and in 1944 separate corporations were formed—Henry Street Settlement keeping its original name and the nursing service becoming the Visiting Nurse Service of New York.

Miss Wald had been seriously ill and had lived at her home in Westport for two years before I came to Henry Street as the director of what by that time had grown to be two separate functions. Karl Hesley had been in charge of the settlement and Margaret Wales in charge of the nursing service. Mr. Hesley had resigned that fall, but before he left he had done his best to start me off well with the various groups. However, despite his efforts, at the end of the first few months, one of the young men's club members came to me and said that he felt he owed it to me to tell me that his group had all planned to dislike me very much in spite of the nice things Mr. Hesley had said about me. They had loved Miss Wald so much and they were so devoted to Mr. Hesley that they had felt that they just couldn't like me. Happily, the upshot of the conversation was, as I got it, that they were finding me acceptable and, I judge, were having to give up the luxury of disliking me, to which apparently they had looked forward with so much zest!

It would be foolish to suggest that it was as easy as that all along the line. But I can say that the neighborhood people showed me the warmest friendliness from the moment I came; and working in the Henry Street neighborhood continued to be an infinite satisfaction throughout the years.

Taking over from pioneers is a delicate operation, often conducted on everyone's part with more emotion than understanding. I was told that one resident cried herself to sleep every night at the thought of having my furniture moved into what had been Miss Wald's apartment. To her it seemed desecration; to me it just seemed my old furniture! So far apart is the newcomer from the strong emotional ties often inherent in long associations.

I am sure I trod unnecessarily on many toes in the process of my own adjustment. But, in later years, I came to feel that the change from Miss Wald's long and distinguished administration of what was her own creation was accomplished with reasonable success on all our parts, thanks, of course, to the many persons who wanted it to work as much as I did. Rita Wallach Morgenthau and Hyman Schroeder, both board members and two of Miss Wald's oldest friends and associates, knew the organization from the ground up, and had much to do with helping make the change easier for me.

Hyman Schroeder himself had been in the first boys' club at Henry Street, which Miss Wald herself led and which was called the "American Heroes." He eventually became successful in business, but Henry Street never lost his devotion and his deep understanding, all touched with the special gentleness of his personality. His sympathy has stretched unwaveringly from the Jewish children of his own beginnings to the Negro and Puerto Rican youngsters of today as they too try to find security and happiness in our kind of neighborhood.

Mrs. Morgenthau had helped Miss Wald persuade me to come to Henry Street so she felt a special responsibility toward me. Miss Wald, of course, had much to do with the caliber of the board and was the builder of the liberal tradition that I inherited at Henry Street. At a preliminary meeting with the Henry Street Board of Directors when I was considering coming, I said I felt that much of my work would have to be outside the organization and in the community. Did they agree? Their answer was that that was why they were asking me to come.

This attitude has held throughout the years. I think it was because we were all agreed on the settlement's basic responsibility to the larger community that smaller things fell into place.

Risking changes in a staff of long standing is one of the most difficult tasks that faces any new administrator. I made none that first winter. I was only too glad to have many staff members stay on—among them Franklin Harbach, who, years later, went on to do distinguished work as the head of the leading settlement in Houston, Texas.

Fighting for change has been to me one of the settlement's primary jobs, but the settlement's continuity and stability are also important to those whose lives have been unstable from babyhood on. One of the most important contributions Henry Street has made to an ever-changing neighborhood has been this sense of stability.

I was reminded of how important long association in neighborhood work can be when three young, just-discharged soldiers from the Korean War came to get some advice from me as to their future work. They talked over their past and future, jobs, war experiences, and neighborhood changes. Meanwhile I was thinking that my knowledge of two of the boys had been slight, and with the other one I had had only problems as he had gone through his particularly obstreperous teens. But I was first on his calling list and he took it for granted I'd be glad to see him. I had been a part of his growing up—an association to which you come back as you do to home, taking welcome for granted.

I was aware of this important coming-back business, so when I came to Henry Street I did not make any changes for a long time in our two little parlors. Even if returned visitors had to see a new head, they could at least feel at home in the parlor—that was my thought.

Yet I should have known that it is not the decorations that matter as much as a sense of "belonging," in the visitor's mind. The sitting room at University House in Philadelphia had been so unattractive to me that I had at once enlisted my mother's artistic hand in its complete redoing. Yet a returned resident of a very early vintage had settled down for a talk, saying, "So good to be back in the old room! Not a thing has changed. I'd know it anywhere." At Henry Street, I reversed the process, for sentiment's sake keeping unchanged rooms which I disliked heartily, only to overhear an old resident say to Miss Wald at a reunion, "These rooms were never dark like this in our day, were they?"

II

Public Relief

Public relief in American cities, at the outset of the Depression, was not only wickedly inadequate but was archaic in its methods. In Philadelphia, the early development of case-work techniques by private agencies had played an unfortunate part in Philadelphia's almost total lack of public welfare when the city was faced with mass unemployment. Public relief methods had been so poor when Mary Richmond was developing methods of family case work in Philadelphia between 1900 and 1909 that it was felt that private administration of relief was the only way to handle the situation.

The result was that Philadelphia faced the collapsed households of the unemployed with practically no money to spend and a firm tradition of no public responsibility. It was, of course, a task that private agencies were in no position to undertake, either financially or in terms of policy. Psychiatry was well entrenched in social work, and cases were accepted largely where it was hoped that the solving of emotional difficulties would put the family back in a position of self-dependence.

Sometimes, to those of us in neighborhoods where there was no escape from the daily sight of hungry, anxious people, the intense preoccupation with psychiatry of those days seemed an escape on the part of social workers themselves from the hard economic facts around them. Even though we were in a city with a United Fund, the board of University House continuously raised special funds to deal with the most pressing family needs in the neighborhood. I remember once being so desperate at hearing—"We don't take unemployment cases"—that I decided to start my request for help from a private casework agency with a past sex-problem which had come out as a mother pleaded for money to pay her rent. The case was accepted, and the mother came in later to tell me that the "nicest" lady came and paid her rent. I felt a little sheepish but very relieved!

While the atmosphere of misery and discouragement on the Lower East Side was no different from that of the University House neighborhood of Schulylkill in Philadelphia, I found New York further advanced in accepting the relief of mass unemployment as a public responsibility, however chaotic it still was. In New York, as in Philadephia and other American cities, efforts to meet the situation by private giving had preceded public responsibility. Bread lines, food baskets, and food orders instead of cash generally appeared first, followed by work relief projects. Money was raised by special citizens' groups; responsible people all over the country rallied with private giving to meet the needs of their fellow citizens.

It must be admitted, however, that back of some of these humanitarian efforts was the hope of keeping government out of relief—city and state, if possible, but especially the federal government.

In Philadephia, Karl de Schweinitz, head of the Family Society, and Jacob Billikopf, director of the Jewish Social Service Society, had helped to raise the first private unemployment relief funds in Philadelphia. Both of these men were very much aware of the economic situation, and their organizing gifts helped get relief measures going.

The earliest leadership in this direction on a nationwide basis that I encountered in those days was that of the editor of *The Survey* magazine, Paul Kellogg. His intense awareness made him untiring in his efforts to bring understanding of the plight of his fellow Americans to where it could help most. His genius and his conscience never let him, or those around him, rest as he fought against public apathy and ancient prejudice. He had faith in people, and it was his firm conviction that human mistakes most often spring from lack of understanding. Therefore, it was the social worker's responsibility wherever they were to make the situation clear to those directly removed from suffering. He encouraged us in the settlements when we started to gather the case stories that became a nationwide study in 1928. And it was his editorial skill and guidance that carried them through to their publication and success. When I first started to collect case stories of unemployment, I was discouraged by being told by someone whose opinion I respected that I was not an economist so I could do very little to affect unemployment. I asked Paul Kellogg whether he thought this was true, and I remember his firm rejoinder: "Certainly not, you don't have to be an economist to help make people see what you are seeing every day, and you have an obligation to do it."

All sorts of cruel devices were used to make the money go around. In New York, for instance, one was called "Skip the Feed," by which to save money the monthly food order for every tenth family was arbitrarily skipped by the Home Relief Bureau of the Department of Public Welfare. The "tenth" families in our neighborhood, of course very frightened, appeared continuously at our doors with tales of hunger and distress.

Perhaps one of the worst rulings of those days, in New York, was that which allowed the payment of one month's rent only after the family was evicted and their furniture was on the street. Then the Department of Public Welfare paid one month's rent on a new apartment and no more rent was paid until the family was evicted again and the whole miserable business started over. I knew families who had gone through this so often that their once proudly owned furniture was battered and worthless. As we went around the neighborhood the most pitiful sights we saw were the little piles of evicted furniture on the sidewalks in front of the tenements, often in the rain. And even worse than their destroyed furniture were the faces of the children returning from school to find their homes on the street.

Early one day I came upon an old woman who might have been Mother Machree herself, standing in the rain. Her little huddle of overstuffed furniture at the curb was beginning to get soaked. Drops of rain were blurring the home-relief voucher that she held in her hands. The voucher was for her next month's rent in some other flat, if she could find a landlord who would let her in. A friend of hers who joined us explained her apathy: "She got a dispossess once before and now she don't care where she goes. She won't look no more."

Right across from the settlement, as I looked out one morning, I saw a little pile of furniture on which someone had hung an American flag and beside it a poster of the Blue Eagle of the National Recovery Administration.

When an eviction notice was served, the family often landed at Henry Street as they scurried around to try to raise the rent money. Our limited funds went most often to keep families from being evicted when there was illness, or to help a large family with small children. There was acute misery in the breaking-up of families and their getting together again, for the city was often forced to take the children to one shelter, the parents to another, while the search for a new apartment went on. The furniture had to be stored for the hunt was often long, as the landlords under the circumstances did not want relief cases. Understandably they were reluctant to take in such families; they knew that only one month's rent would be paid unless the family could borrow or beg the rent from family or friend. If not, they had the miserable and expensive business of eviction, or had to carry the family without payment of rent. Landlords and small grocers were often the victims of their own kindness as well as having to share in the economic plight around them.

We took the stories of neighborhood suffering continually to Mayor La Guardia, to the heads of the Department of Public Welfare, to Harry Hopkins in Washington, and on down. But during the long years it took to educate the public to a sense of its responsibility, public officials had to stem the tide of need with hopelessly inadequate funds.

During this time we so often had to start out having to combat a punitive attitude toward the unemployed. I remember one of the largest employers in Philadelphia saying to me that "anyone who really wanted a job could get one," while at the same time he was discharging several hundred men a day. He also sent a detective to University House to see whether the stories of unemployed families I had written about, and which the president of the board of University House, Benjamin West Frazier, had distributed widely, were true. Of course the stories were true but the names had naturally been changed, so his investigator had quite a time!

Social workers were all too timid in asking for sufficient relief appropriations; too often, we feared, if we put the sum closer to reality we would be looked upon as unrealistic. This attitude was mitigated as time went on and as unemployment reached into almost every economic group.

Spending for the relief of unemployment was not popular politics at that time, nor to my mind has it ever been despite much talk to the contrary. I remember that the Unemployment Committee of the United Neighborhood Houses, of which I became chairman in the fall of 1933, went against general social work advice when we put the sum needed for relief in New York City, as I recall it, at $15 million a month.

It was not only hunger that took its toll; joblessness attacks family life from as many angles. The story of a mother from one of the clubs at Henry Street illustrates one of the most serious problems. She sank down in my office and began, "Miss Hall, you've got to do something for me. There's four men sitting in my kitchen all day—my husband and the three boys. They go out early every day looking for jobs and then come home and just sit. I know it's better than the corner but I think I'm going crazy if *one* of them doesn't got a job."

We did get a temporary job for one of them but in all those years of struggle and makeshifts what we could do was so inadequate and what was needed so overwhelming that while your eyes were on the misery and the bit of immediate help you could give, you continually had to be working on the broader picture.

But if you worked in a settlement, you couldn't put off a mother with a sick baby and an eviction notice by saying that you were working at City Hall to get a more humane way of handling rents. It had to be both and at the same time, and if you couldn't help, you listened, which kept your own awareness up to the minute with plenty of emotional urge behind it.

III

The Dutchman's Farm

It is impossible to think of those years except in terms of the Depression, as we moved painfully along from complete chaos to some kind of order in the handling of unemployment and its consequences.

However, along with getting to know my neighbors as quickly as I could, I realized that there were many changes taking place on the East Side and that we ought to know more about them. The tide had turned in population; people were moving away faster than they were moving in. That doesn't mean that we were not crowded; but we were now only the second, instead of the first, most crowded area in the city. East Harlem, we found, had taken over this honor. On the other hand, families had begun to move in from Harlem to get our cheaper rents, and there were still many Irish and Italian families in the neighborhood. But the population was predominately Jewish in 1933.

That first fall we started a Community Studies Department at Henry Street, and Duane Ramsey joined our staff as its director. That first winter we undertook to measure unemployment, wages, and rents, and the racial and religious changes that were taking place around us.

To make our figures measurable, in some respects, against the past, we chose for our study a census tract of eleven blocks right opposite our club building at 299-301-303 Henry Street. The tenements housing the families we called on for two years in succession, were some of the most dilapidated on the Lower East Side, although there was little to choose from among most of the old tenements still standing there or elsewhere in New York City.

Our first job was to measure with some accuracy the extent of unemployment in our neighborhood, to be able to report just what our neighbors there were up against. We were continually asked, "Just how much unemployment is there in your neighborhood?" and our figures from this study were used constantly in the city to bring national statistics down to people.

We discovered that half the wage earners in these families were unemployed, and that half of those employed were earning less than $15 a week. These figures take on added meaning when we visited the same families the second winter and they were a tiny bit worse. As months go into years, the help to which a marginal family normally turns in emergencies dries up and their savings, if any, are gone. The small storekeepers who usually give credit from payday to payday or from job to job, face bankruptcy themselves when half their customers have no payday. They, in turn, are staving off wholesalers who are short of credit themselves. Friends or members of the family who may have helped out in the past now need help themselves.

The material gathered in this two-year study, with later additions, was called *A Dutchman's Farm* after Corlears Hook, which in turn was named after Jacobus Van Curler (or Corlear), whose farm it had once been in 1638 when New Netherlands gave out parcels of land to those who would till them.

Because the Lower East Side of New York City has such a long recorded history and also one somewhat typical in our fast-changing country, I am including here the highlights of the study we made in 1939 of the history of this Dutchman's Farm. Corlears Hook is an older name by three centuries than Times Square or Rockefeller Center. When in 1789 our first Congress met in New York and George Washington came by stage and barge to be inaugurated as our first President, Corlears Hook had already housed settlers and townsfolk for 150 years.

This capsule history of Corlears Hook—the burgeoning of

commerce and trade, the influx of immigrants, the cancerous multiplication of tenements, and particularly the rise and fall of real estate values, unemployment, and poverty—unhappily, was to be for other American cities the pattern for slums which have spewed forth the myriad social problems we face today. It was our first "ghetto," as the slums are referred to today.

In the beginning, Corlears Hook was a sandy point not far from the southern end of a narrow island—later to be called Manhattan—where the Indians landed their canoes on trips over from the long island across the river.

With the coming of the Dutch, the land began to be intensively cultivated. The first farmer, after whom the Hook had been named, Jacobus Van Curler, had been granted seventy-six acres, and started a tobacco plantation. Eight years later another grantee, Edward Marill, built a house on a nearby high hill and set out a garden, erecting a strong stockade of logs to protect his home from the Indians and to ward off wild animals. Today all the buildings of the Henry Street Settlement stand on the old Marill farm.

In 1654 the entire Van Curler farm was sold to William Beekman, seventeenth-century realtor who was buying up New York land. He served the first "dispossess notice" on a Negro tenant, one Anthony Fernando.

In 1664 the Duke of York captured the Dutch colony, and Nieuw Amsterdam became New York. More land was bought up. Philip Van Cortlandt and Isaac Stoutenburgh together owned 259 acres in lower New York. They did not live on their bouweries (farms), but rented out their holdings to tenant farmers.

By 1700 the price of land inched up to 3 cents a square foot. By 1750 shipping had moved up the East River, which was dotted with piers and had a shipbuilding site rented by Everett Bynanek. By 1765 Mount Pitt, long since leveled, and today the site of the Henry Street Settlement Playhouse and Music School, was graced by country houses built by Delanceys and Willetts. Not far away, the first saloon, a seamen's hang-out, opened.

In 1776 British men-of-war anchored in the East River; General George Washington built a series of earthworks along the

Corlears Hook ridge; the British took the fortification and held the Hook for seven years.

As the Revolutionary War drew to a close, business came to the district. A cobblestone street was laid across the Hook to the river, and in 1797 ferries began to cross to Brooklyn. The Lower East Side became fashionable. A club for "rich young men," the Belvedere, overlooked Corlears.

By 1807 the price of land had gone up to 12 cents a square foot. But now the first depression set in: the shipping trade was hard hit by troubles with England. The unemployed demanded "bread and work." The city hired them to fill in swampy places along the East River and to build a bulkhead—the first work relief project.

With the immigration of thousands of Irish, more work relief was needed. In 1814 the hills of Corlears Hook were cut down and more land filled in along the waterfront to make more real estate.

Business revived. Robert Fulton's first steamboat passed up the East River in 1818. Soon the *Savannah*, the first steamboat to cross the Atlantic, would be launched from a shipyard on Corlears Hook.

Former one-family houses became tenements, with six or seven families crowded into one house. But the big fire of 1835 destroyed many of these buildings. More tenements were built as replacements, but with two, three, and four families on a floor.

Business boomed again. Merchants who had been burnt out built new warehouses on the waterfront. As many as 144 Yankee clippers, plying the China trade, lined the wharves every day.

Since fire was a constant threat, firemen's associations were organized and they became strong political clubs. In 1848, Number Six Company, next door to the buildings in which Miss Wald started on Henry Street, boasted a famous red engine with a tiger on its back. Bill Tweed, member of Number Six, carried this symbol with him when he became boss of Tammany Hall.

In 1853 the newly established New York Association for Improving the Condition of the Poor, made the first tenement survey.

By 1860 the price of land in the area rose to $5.71 a square foot. But times were bad after the Civil War. The East River froze over, and plague ran through the city. In the winter of 1867 the first rudimentary housing laws were passed.

By 1870 New York's first shopping center sprang up on Grand Street, where Lord and Taylor, Ridley and Sons, and other merchants served the fashionable trade. The ferries attracted more business to the area.

Now rear tenements were put up in back yards and gardens, their only access to the street through the halls of front tenements. New square brick structures, four, five, and six stories high, brought buildings wall to wall.

Jacob Riis wrote in the *Tribune* about the evils of slums. In 1879, laws were passed requiring indoor toilets and an airshaft at least four feet wide between newly constructed buildings. These were known as new-law tenements. But tenements already standing (old law) were exempt.

With the finishing of the Brooklyn Bridge in 1883, East River ferry business declined and tenements replaced Grand Street's business section. Department stores were moving uptown.

During the 1880s, a wave of new immigrants from Italy, Russia, and Poland supplanted the Irish, who, like the early German immigrants before them, were finding greener pastures.

In 1886 The Neighborhood Guild, later to become the University Settlement, was founded by Stanton Coit. This was the first settlement in the United States. In 1893 Lillian D. Wald came to live and work on the Lower East Side, founding the Henry Street Settlement and starting its Visiting Nurse Service.

In that same year, several blocks were condemned and land cleared for a park at Corlears Hook, but it was not completed for twelve years. Meanwhile Jacob Riis, Miss Wald, and others pressed for housing reform. The reformers, who had grown in number and influence, had some success in their struggle with landlords and real estate interests, and in 1901, New York City, under an enabling state law, set up its first Tenement House Department. The champions of reform under the leadership of the Charity Organization Society won what they hoped would prove "the death warrant of the slums." Yet once again, tenements already built were exempt.

In 1908 the Association of Neighborhood Workers, later called the United Neighborhood Houses, prepared a "congestion exhibit" to bring a realization of the slums to the rest of the city.

Tenement houses proved profitable investments, particularly the old-law tenements, into which more and more families were packed. Some new structures were built, but *none* after 1905. Even so, the price of land skyrocketed in 1910 to $20 a square foot. Immigrants were still flooding into the area.

By 1912 the incoming tide reached its highwater mark. The First World War slowed down the exodus from Europe, and in 1921 the new Quota Law shut off most immigration. In the meantime an outgoing tide carried away to less congested parts of the city a second generation who were making good. By 1920, 100,000 people had left the Lower East Side. Rents and land values dropped.

In 1915 land values had spurted up briefly when Architect Walter Russell pictured Corlears Hook as the future rival of Riverside Drive, citing its waterfront view and nearness to Wall Street. He envisioned an exclusive apartment development, but nothing came of it and land values fell again.

Then by 1928, the Corlears Hook neighborhood was condemned as "the worst slum in the city." A survey made by the Tenement House Department showed that 25 percent of its structures were rear dwellings, accessible only through alleyways or courts which provided their only light and air; 33⅓ percent had unsafe halls or stairways; 17 percent, windowless rooms; 50 percent, insufficient light and ventilation; and 25 percent were more than seventy years old.

It was into one of those rear dwellings that Miss Wald had gone with a little girl to see the child's sick mother. She found the conditions so horrible that this visit became one of the determining factors in her coming to the Lower East Side. That same house which Miss Wald had first visited forty years before was still standing in 1934 when we went to Albany to protest the moritorium on fire retarding halls and having a toilet in every apartment, and I used it as part of my testimony.

It was not until 1934 that the new City Housing Authority and the Works Progress Administration undertook New York's first experiment in public housing. "First Houses" opened at East

Third Street and Avenue A—the first low-income project completed in the country. While dedicating First Houses in bitter December weather, Mayor La Guardia recalled that he had been warned by constitutional lawyers that it would be a cold day before federal funds would go into public housing in New York—and it was! And it was the drop in land values at that time which later made Vladeck Houses possible.

IV

The Coming of Fiorello La Guardia

Fiorello La Guardia was elected mayor in November, 1933, just after I arrived in New York, and New York City in the years to follow was to be dominated by his stormy and amazingly gifted political personality. Not the Republican party alone, but the Fusion forces had put him into office. Over those years I had the feeling that City Hall was an extension of Henry Street, or Henry Street of City Hall; our concerns were so much the same and La Guardia's response to the problems we brought to him so spontaneous. This was to be the case again when Robert F. Wagner became mayor of New York. He was not as flamboyant a mayor but he also cared about people and related to them and their problems with deep concern.

I had known of La Guardia's interest in unemployment while he was serving in Congress in 1932, at the time when we were working to get a Federal Employment Act. I had taken a night train to Washington, when it was to come up for a vote, to talk to Congressman J. Mayhew Wainwright from Westchester County, the father of my girlhood friend, Fonrose Wainwright Condict. I saw Congressman Wainwright at breakfast and went over the two major bills under consideration. He had been ill but was going to the House that morning, against doctor's orders, for this vote. His wife and daughter and I repaired to the gallery armed with sandwiches against a long day. The

Administration bill, known as the Doak Bill, was defended by a congressman from Pennsylvania—a tall gentleman who affected a carnation or some similar decoration in his button-hole. Opposed to him, and speaking for the more adequate bill, was Fiorello La Guardia. As against the other congressman's imposing size, La Guardia's head seemed hardly to come above the rostrum. But it didn't need to come any farther. When he turned to "his friend," Congressman Wainwright, who rose to speak and cast a Republican vote for the more adequate bill, I nearly dropped my sandwich over the railing with excitement. The bill won that day, but it was killed by President Hoover's pocket veto ten days later.

It is hard to pick the qualities most characteristic of La Guardia. Vitality, humor, astuteness, contrariness, brilliance, mimicry, warmth, and a fabulous energy—all these, and so much more, were his. But to my mind, one of Fiorello La Guardia's greatest gifts to New York and his country was his power to make government, causes, politics, even a garbage truck, dramatic. Dullness has killed many a good cause but never one La Guardia took on.

I remember sitting on the edge of my chair for nearly three hours at a meeting of the City Affairs Committee while he told the story of his first year in City Hall and the horrendous conditions he had found in each City Department. On the way out, I remember asking Paul Kellogg if he didn't think it was a wonderful speech. "It certainly was," he replied, "but," he added quizzically with his usual insight, "I noticed that he left Moses in the Bull Rushes." Paul was right, for the mayor had not tackled the Parks Department of which Robert Moses was then head!

When the first plane was to land at La Guardia Airport a few of us went out with La Guardia to see the event, and I shall always remember his squat figure with its broad-brimmed hat, standing alone way out on the field waiting for that first plane to come in. It was a thoroughly appropriate tribute to him and we could feel his excitement and satisfaction in this achievement.

Although in contrast to La Guardia's colorful personality, Stanley Isaacs, elected on the mayor's ticket in his second term as Manhattan borough president, was also a great gift to the city. A lawyer and a man of independent means, he devoted his legal expertise and his encyclopedic knowledge of the city to serving all its people until the day he died in 1962. The settlements shared in the city's good fortune by having Stanley Isaacs as president of United Neighborhood Houses for more than thirty years, and board chairman until his death. He was a great believer in the settlements' first-hand approach, and between Stanley Isaacs and Helen Harris the causes the settlements espoused through United Neighborhood Houses were in extraordinarily skillful hands.

Before his term as Manhattan borough president was over, Stanley Isaacs had a run-in with La Guardia. He refused to dismiss a young man from his staff, a former writer for the Communist party's *Daily Worker*, after attacks made on him, first by the Brooklyn *Tablet*, a Catholic publication, followed by pressures from friends as well as politicians. This caused a tremendous furor at the time. It was typical of Stanley Isaacs to insist that as the young man was doing his job well, he would not be discharged because of his politics. However, La Guardia refused to back his second term as borough president because of it.

For once, I felt that La Guardia was completely wrong and went to see him about it. "Helen," he said, "I'll lose forty-thousand votes in Brooklyn if I back Stanley." I reminded him that he might lose forty thousand votes elsewhere if he didn't. I don't know which of us was right as to numbers, since La Guardia was reelected, but the city lost Stanley Isaacs' services as borough president. It may have been poor political strategy on Stanley's part, but it gave a lift to many of us to see integrity win over strategy in a public servant.

Stanley Isaacs then ran as city councilman where for many years he served as Republican minority leader of the Council until his death. But it did not matter too much what his official position was; his unofficial position as a leader in all that was good in New York was unique. Certainly one, if not the most important contribution was the Sharkey–Brown–Isaacs Bill passed by the City Council, which outlawed racial discrimination in all publicly aided housing in New York City, and set the pattern for future legislation. Stanley Isaacs' kindly way with people must have helped win many causes for him. The East

River Drive, now the Franklin D. Roosevelt Drive, was built when he was borough president, and on a trip along the East River in a small boat, Stanley explained to his guests the many ingenious ways that had to be worked out to get the land for the Drive and not destroy other valuable things along the way which the typical bulldozer mentality so often does.

I remember a small incident in relation to the Drive in its early days. I was driving my mother down to Henry Street and we saw a tall iron fence being put up between the uptown and downtown sides. It was very ugly, and my artist mother was outraged. "Why do you let them do such things, Helen?" she demanded. "They are spoiling the Drive." I modestly reminded her that I wasn't running the city! But she continued, "You must be able to do something!" Anyway, she made me feel guilty, so when I got to Henry Street I telephoned Stanley Isaacs about it and he said at once that he would go home that way. The next morning he called me to say that the fence was dreadful and he had stopped it, but he added, "Why didn't you tell me before they got so much up?" I certainly felt my mother had had the last word, and so did she!

During the 1933 election, many of the young men of the settlement neighborhood joined in watching at the polls, along with residents and staff. You could watch under the aegis of the Honest Ballot Association, which embraced members of all parties: all those who wanted clean politics and a fair vote. There certainly was no such thing in our district at that time, judging by what I saw in that election. I knew something about the ethics of machine politics for I had spent my eleven years in Philadelphia in one of its strongest boss-ridden wards.

I had grown up thinking, by way of my father's New England viewpoint, that political corruption centered in Tammany Hall. Then, of course, I had found the boss-ridden Republican machine in my Philadelphia neighborhood equally corrupt. I remember one of our not-too-bright settlement neighbors in Philadephia coming to me in indignation one election day, saying, "What do you think, Miss Hall, they're only paying fifty cents for an honest woman's vote this year! It's a disgrace." The implication was that I should do something about a wage scale as low as that.

Not because crooked politics are any different in whatever

party you find them, but because this was such a hot election with La Guardia in the ring challenging Tammany, I learned quite a few things that the Republican machine in Philadephia had not shown me. I had never seen a contested election there. During my time, things there went through as machine-planned. But not so in New York that day, although the Lower East Side had been almost as uniformly Democratic as my ward in Philadelphia had been Republican.

Christine Anderson, a resident of the settlement and also one of the Henry Street visiting nurses, had volunteered to watch at one of the polls located across the street from the settlement. Things were under way when we went in a few minutes after 6 A.M., and one of the local politicians, already slightly tipsy, was holding the curtain aside and frankly watching the voter. A policeman, whom we signaled, dodged quickly out of sight, and we were left alone to deal with the hullabaloo that ensued when we protested. One of the assistant district attorneys, sent to circle around the neighborhood that day, finally came back with me to clinch our argument. Miss Anderson, a stalwart fighter for what she believed right, refused to leave her post until the polls closed at night. We fed her at intervals, but budge she wouldn't. "I know their tricks by now," she said, "and someone else would have to learn them."

In one booth I visited, a hole had been burned at the eye-level of the man who operated the curtain. When we protested this, a menacing roar went up. We stood our ground and someone finally got out a needle and thread and sewed up the hole. The fact that the tools were so handy certainly took me by surprise, but it was comforting to feel that at least protests were anticipated.

I hadn't been living on Henry Street long enough to have a vote that year and so I couldn't even be an official poll watcher, but I went around with a group of young men who wanted my encouragement. We had all agreed, in discussions amongst us before election, that no matter what your party, a secret ballot was an elemental American right. It was to insure that right that we circled the neighborhood bringing reinforcements and food to watchers, thereby making ourselves generally disliked. I stopped for a short spell around three o'clock only to hear a knock on my door and a voice saying, "Would you please come out? We just went to that booth on Madison Street [now the site of a housing project], and they say they'll kill us if we bring 'that woman' in here again, so we feel you should come right back." I don't know that I felt quite as eager about it as they did, but off we went again.

This condition cleared up greatly in our neighborhood during the La Guardia Administration, and today there is pride in the obviously decent behavior at our local polls, whatever may go on behind the scenes.

One of the worst results of political corruption was the cynicism among young people regarding government—the taking it for granted that "pull" was the only answer to getting ahead. I recall a session at Henry Street on the operations of civil service following a speaker on the subject, in which a young people's group showed depressing skepticism. Later, I learned of some of the practices employed by the Civil Service Commission during the time these boys had grown up and I realized I had small reason to be surprised.

However, we had to face the fact that the political clubhouse in those days had come to the aid of the poor when in trouble, even if not always for altruistic reasons, when public relief was not being provided. Local politicians are also friends and neighbors, and many have a sincere desire to help people, regardless of politics. They can bring to bear a down-to-earth knowledge of problems and of ways to get things done that social workers do not always have and that can sometimes ably serve our neighbors. When you work with local political leaders, of whatever party, on "causes" rather than "political platforms," you often find yourself aided by very practical partners.

For a number of years we held forums every Monday night at our Playhouse. Many different subjects were discussed, linking Lower East Side audiences with national and international developments. These were followed by long question periods which I often chaired. We had our quota of odd questioners and odder questions having no bearing on the subject of the evening. One large woman almost always brought up the price of chickens. One day Paul Kellogg and I were inspecting the new park on the East River at the foot of Grand Street which we had rejoiced in only at a distance. Our walk led us to a quiet bench right by the water. Suddenly we looked up and saw a big woman purposefully bearing down upon us. As she got in front of me she shook her finger at me accusingly and said, "And for why did you let the price of chickens go up?" I found myself saying hastily, "But I didn't." "Oh, yes you did," said my questioner of the previous Monday's meeting. "They're up!"

Before each election, we always invited representatives from the major political parties to the forums to explain their attitudes on the chief questions involved at the time. I once invited a Republican friend, Richard Scandrett, who was running for Congress at that time, to one of these meetings where Democrats Socialists, Communists, and Republicans held forth. But after the Socialists and Communists had done with each other, he was left with few listeners. It seemed to me that the Communist speakers often had the edge as debaters, but not when Norman Thomas was our Socialist speaker. He may not have won an election, but he certainly won our debates!

V

The New Deal Initials

The first lift in neighborhoods such as ours came with Franklin Roosevelt's election in 1932, while I was still at University House in Philadelphia. I remember one reaction to his first speech about bank failures. Our doorman, known as "Reds," was an ex-painter with a seventeen-year record at one factory without missing a day. For two years after his shop shut down he had put on his work clothes each morning and walked around the neighborhood pretending, mostly to himself, that he had a job. At last he could no longer keep up his spirits that way and he sank into apathy, from which we were able to rescue him, in part, with our doorman's job. After the President's speech he came in elated. "Did you hear the President?" he asked. "Why, it was just like he was talking to me in our kitchen."

It was not just the magic of the Roosevelt voice, but the sense he gave of communication between the President of the United States and his fellow Americans. Later I thought of "Reds" when a refugee from Hitlerism living at Henry Street told me how he had listened to a radio in Germany, placed high on top of a toilet box to avoid detection, and how everybody in the household crowded in when there was any hope of hearing Roosevelt's voice. Even those who couldn't understand felt he cared about them, and were comforted. The gift of communication should not be underrated in a democracy just because it has been perverted by dictators and cheapened by advertising.

After several years of hopeless search for jobs, a leaden sense of failure must be overcome. Jobs needed to be created quickly and on a large scale, while long-term efforts at meeting the "boom and bust" cycle get underway. From the moment Franklin Roosevelt came into office, the weight of misery in our neighborhood seemed to be shared. The moves first to relieve hunger and then to combat unemployment brought an immediate sense of relief.

The Civil Works Administration was the first of the nation-wide work relief projects and gave work to four million unemployed during the winter of 1933–34. Immediately upon its announcement, lines of men and women blocks-long, waited all night in the bitter cold to register for work. We opened our Playhouse, as did the other settlements, the largest rooms they had, to meet the sudden demand for local offices. This did not eliminate the waiting lines, but with us the first four-hundred applicants at least had shelter while they waited. Our staff worked with the CWA in job registering. Applicants registered over and over again when jobs were not quickly forthcoming, as the creation of work projects could not keep pace with the frantic registration.

Later, as the Civil Works Administration turned into the Works Progress Administration—to go down in history as the controversial WPA—the persons engaged on the "white-collar" projects were made available for work in settlements, supplementing our own staffs' efforts. This brought us into close touch with the WPA, not only through the jobs it supplied to the unemployed members of our neighborhood families but because WPA workers themselves were working with Henry Street. Many of them became valuable staff members.

One day, I was suddenly informed that Henry Street had been assigned fifty white-collar workers at one fell swoop. One of the first group turned out to be a pants presser and another a clarinet player. It took a little planning to determine how best to use them. Things were simplified for us somewhat when Grace Gosselin, former headworker of Meinhard Memorial House, became director of the WPA "White-Collar Project." Our pants presser was eventually persuaded that "recreation" was not his forte, and he was transferred to another project.

Our clarinet player served us musically and in many other ways.

The clarinet player I remember for a very charming reason, as well as because of our first startled concern as to what we would do with him full time. Paul Kellogg and I were married in February of 1935, and there were celebrations of many delightful kinds at Henry Street. We were both touched by a request from this WPA clarinetist and his wife, who accompanied his clarinet, that they be allowed to perform for us an original composition created just for the occasion. So they came to dinner at the settlement and afterward they played their "gift" to us.

The welcome that the neighborhood gave to Paul Kellogg was well deserved, even if all the neighbors were not aware of it. He was one of the staunchest and most understanding interpreters of the settlements. For many years he had been in close touch with Jane Addams, Lillian Wald, and all the pioneers of the movement. John Lovejoy Elliott, the founder of Hudson Guild and a leader of the Ethical Culture Society, was one of our closest friends and, with Owen Lovejoy, founder of the National Child Labor Committee, officiated at our wedding.

The clarinet player has led me away from the WPA, against which so much has been said and written. I want to tell something of the WPA workers as we saw them, both as staff members and in relation to our neighborhood families. First the CWA and then the WPA came to relieve the stagnation of relief to employable men and women, for work was a step toward getting back into the current of life. You had somewhere to go when you got up in the morning, and actual cash for the family at the end of the week. It was only after years of failing to get a regular job in private industry that the WPA, which lasted until December, 1942, came to seem a deadend to many. The eternal criticism of boondoggling leveled against it didn't help the WPA worker to maintain self-respect either. Many of the criticisms of the WPA were heartless and very often came from ignorance. One of the most startling came to me in a Red Cross grass hut in New Guinea, in the second year of World War II. A U.S. Air Force general of great distinction, one whom I knew to be enormously concerned with the welfare of the men under him, sank down in the hut exhausted from his flight that morning to direct the Battle of Buna. It was completely airborne and was what finally stopped the Japanese at that time from coming over the Stanley Range unexpectedly into the heart of Australia. I could tell things were bad that morning, but I was startled to hear the general say, "The trouble with Americans is they don't want to die, that's the trouble with them." This was no time for argument, but I did murmur, "Isn't it a credit to a country if its people want to live?" "No," he said sharply, "It's the WPA, that's what it is. They just want to get back to the WPA." Knowing the character of this man and knowing the horrible strain he was under, I did not, for once, take up the cudgels for work relief, but it did bring home to me the great difference in our experiences. It illustrated very sharply why, as we struggled out of the Depression, there was often so little understanding of the many aspects of work relief. I had lived in a settlement and had seen the desperate struggle for jobs first hand. The general had lived his life in one of the most economically sheltered parts of our economy—the Army.

It was said repeatedly that the WPA spoiled men for jobs in industry. Better to say that it was lack of jobs in industry that spoiled workers, not the WPA. When the hunt for a job continued with no success for too many years, skills and spirits grew rusty, just as tools left too long in the rain corrode.

We were not dealing with the unemployment of 1929 or '30 but the unemployed of the middle thirties. Unless you came in contact with them first hand, it was hard to realize how far the slow sapping of both material and spiritual resources had gone on. When there had been unemployment over a long period, the family's ordinary equipment for life was used up. To take a simple illustration, our nurses said at that time: "You can't turn the mattresses in the homes of families on relief because they would fall to pieces and you couldn't put them together again." And more. "Families sleep together because beds have given out and because bed clothes are scanty; they huddle together to keep warm."

More serious than any of their physical discomforts were the discouragements and tensions that held families in the grip of invisible hands. Physicians may tell us how worry relates to illness, but only those who are fortunate enough never to have really worried about something to the point of physical sensation could question the part anxiety played in the health of fear-ridden families.

The resilience and courage of the human spirit is so great that it took some men years to realize that they could not find work. All-night waits so as to be the first in the morning, failure, daily rebuffs, worn-out shoes, shabbier and shabbier clothes, cold, often hunger—still men fought on. Worst of all, I sometimes thought, was the unsuccessful return to the waiting family. I have seen the sense of suspense on the faces of the wife and even little children as they heard the father's returning footsteps. "It seems to me I can tell just from his footsteps whether he has got a job or not," one mother said to me as the father returned and she and the children listened.

The unemployment of young people is of long term psychological importance along with everything else. An older teenage group at Henry Street decided to have a neighborhood meeting about the discouraging unemployment they were facing. One day their President came in to show me a telegram they had just received from Mrs. Roosevelt accepting their invitation to speak.

"What shall we do? We never expected her to come. We wrote lots of people, but no one else even replied. Will you be Chairman?"

I said, "Of course not. You are head of your group." But, he said, he was very much worried "about the embarrassing questions they might ask." That was settled by having questions written so he could select them.

The meeting went off to their great satisfaction and Mrs. Roosevelt answered questions with her usual skill and directness. I remember one of them was, "did she believe in God."

Jobless women were even more nervous and distraught. The other side of this was that one of the unhappy by-products of those days was that it was sometimes easier for the women in the family to get a job than the men. They could be had cheaper. This only served to emphasize the father's failure to provide. Men did not, as a rule, take over the mother's household jobs of cooking, dishwashing, and caring for the children. It generally turned out that the working woman did both. I remember going to see one of these mothers, and when I heard the day and night working hours, I asked the children when their mother slept. "Oh." was the reply. "She puts her head down on the table after supper and sleeps till she goes out at ten."

The WPA workers assigned to us made it possible to do many things that pressingly needed to be done at that time. For instance, our Personal Service office, where neighbors come for information and for help in any kind of trouble, in those days was carrying families until they could get relief, staving off evictions, helping move furniture off sidewalks. We had been so understaffed that these pressures had added to the nightmare of those early years. Now a number of willing, intelligent persons were added to the staff. Our first "paraprofessionals."

Play streets blossomed all around us, manned by our new workers. We had staff to distribute vast quantities of surplus food tickets, on a well-planned basis.

When I first came to Henry Street every inch of space was used for the programs already there. You do not change, or put out, or even ask people to squeeze over, until you are familiar with their activities. As far as possible, changes come with the consent, or at least an understanding, of the people whose programs are involved.

But we did need space to move ahead and so we first rented in 1934 and then purchased 263 Henry Street, adjacent to our two older buildings, 265 and 267, and set up the new programs that the times called for. We were anxious to set up a project in Workers' Education, with help from the WPA, and they in turn were looking for quarters for their Workers'-Education project. They had been put out of their Museum of Natural History headquarters with the dinosaurs, because a reporter from one of the newspapers had found something of a communist nature among their educational material. And so, at Grace Gosselin's request, to save the project we took them into 263 Henry Street until they found permanent quarters. Our own new Community Studies Department needed room, too, so they moved in there also. Our own Workers'-Education project under Emerich Kurtagh's leadership, with WPA teachers, was housed here during the lifetime of this project.

A metal-working shop grew out of the rebirth of an old craftsman—a skilled metal worker from Holland who had found no need for his skills for three years. When the WPA placed him with us, he was so close to breakdown that he couldn't have worked under normal pressure. We found a place for him in our art room, at first with only one child as a pupil, and a well-behaved one at that. He had lost all confidence in himself, but our confidence and assurance that we needed him reached through, and gradually he took more children under his wing. Finally, after a few months, he was given a little basement room at 263 Henry Street which turned into a metal working shop for teen-agers. Here he was able to interest and teach this difficult age in a room crowded with eager workers. These were children whose grandparents had perhaps known this craft abroad, but it had skipped a generation to come to life again happily on Henry Street.

The metal shop went on under Mr. Van's prideful leadership until he came to us one day to say that his skill was now needed in industry, to make precision instruments for the war. Because he had been saved by the WPA he was able to give back his unusual skill where and when it was needed most.

After relief measures became more than temporary initials and began to seep down into neighborhoods such as ours through permanent city agencies, we were still continuously involved with the people who didn't fit into categories and the often painful and wasteful rules set up by the agencies which had come into being to relieve the distress they were sometimes causing. Often the rules were instituted in an effort to save money. But they sometimes grew out of a lack of first-hand knowledge of how they bore down on human beings and, unfortunately, sometimes out of the kind of thinking that makes it more important to protect goods than people.

I shall always see a long line of soldiers reaching around the block in front of our Red Cross Service Club in Townsville, in the suffocating sun of north Australia, waiting to get in for a cold drink of water, as at that moment we had the only ice in town. When I got in, I saw that there was an old milk can fixed up with a spigot and *one* glass. I said, "Haven't you some paper cups?" and the harassed head of the club said, "I couldn't get them out of the storehouse because they said my requisition wasn't made out right, and I haven't had time to go back!"

United Neighborhood Houses had an unemployment committee which beat a path to the Home Relief Office with suggestions of how the "rules" would better fit the needs as we saw them. Some of the rules we complained about may have seemed unimportant, but they were not unimportant by the time they reached the sixth floor of a tenement.

At that time, the Welfare Council in New York had invited a group of the heads of large agencies to discuss how public relief was working. The then head of the Home Relief Bureau reported to us at each meeting as to how things were going and what changes and improvements were being made. I can remember how Mrs. Simkhovitch, the head of Greenwich House, and I, almost in unison, would say at the end of the Home Relief report, "But it really doesn't work that way!" From her standpoint she was giving an honest report, but she was a good many people away from the families getting or not getting relief. Perhaps the directors of all social agencies of any kind should carry a case or two, or a group or two so that their understanding could be kept fresh by the best teachers in the world, the recipients of the service!

Every so often, we at Henry Street conferred with the Department of Welfare on the Lower East Side to bring their attention to what our neighbors found to be road blocks in getting help. I remember one such conference in the late thirties held at Henry Street with the chief of our local welfare office, his assistants, and someone from headquarters. They themselves seemed swamped by the inherent difficulties in their situation, especially untrained personnel and red tape and rulings by the city, state, and federal governments. At the end of our recital of our difficulties in getting help for our neighbors, I remember their saying, "Do you know that we have a 50 percent yearly turnover in our investigators?"

When I look back on the long, hard fight to get public funds from city, state, and especially the federal government, to take on the financial responsibility for people in need, I feel ashamed that social workers and their allies could not have helped with a better development of welfare. Perhaps at first we were too relieved to have money coming into the homes to fight hard enough against the red tape which we saw beginning to strangle

the families as they came for help. I don't mean to imply that
social workers didn't try, but obviously we didn't succeed, for
public welfare has become handicapped not only by red tape,
but by prejudices of one kind or another that have developed
along the way and helped delay its reorganization intolerably.
Today, the recipients of welfare have fought on picket lines
to help get the public attention necessary to be able to make
the drastic changes that are necessary. Almost everybody has
had something against welfare—the recipients along with the
taxpapers!

You really have to have lived through the Depression to know
that, as badly as we may be carrying it out, the acceptance of
federal responsibility for starvation was a monumental step forward and certainly worthy of better next steps.

To name a few stumbling blocks to reform—one element in
the climate of dislike and criticism springs from the feeling that
people are "getting something for nothing" and that they could
all work if they wanted to! No matter how many times figures
are given to show the small percentage of employable people
on relief against the high proportion of children and old people
and disabled, it seems to make little impression. Nor how many
times it is pointed out that lack of preparedness of some kind
has kept able-bodied people out of jobs in our increasingly
mechanized and unionized economy, and how much more difficult it is to place people when a pattern of work has not been
a part of their lives.

In the South, the feeling against Negro families getting
sufficient grants, or any grants at all, has played a large part
in the general atmosphere, reaching of course into the Congress.
Along with this is the difficulty of getting household help anywhere in the country, so often laid entirely to welfare, rather
than to the upward trend in our economy both in wage scales
and social hopes, especially when women both black and white
are eagerly moving from the stove to the typewriter and on up
and up.

Then there is the bitter feeling against "chislers" on relief—
which of course there are, as welfare recipients seem to be no
more honest than the rest of the population.

It has also been difficult to change our ideas about Mothers'

Allowances. I had the rewarding experience of working under Ruth Taylor and her associate Lillian Quinn in 1916 when they were organizing the Department of Child Welfare in Westchester County in New York State. This was the beginning of Widows' Pensions and Boarding Homes for dependent children, and I had charge of the territory where I lived in Rye and in surrounding towns. Finding homes for a hundred dependent children, getting them out of institutions, watching them change and develop, and coming to know the widows and their children was an exciting experience to me. The first mother to whom I delivered a check startled me somewhat. As I came happily up her steps Mrs. Carrera, the mother of 14, greeted me with, "My God, ain't you late." I hadn't known that the checks were late when I started off, but I soon found out!

Women's suffrage for New York State came in 1917 and having been a passionate adherent of women's suffrage from age ten on, I raced around urging all my widows to vote, avoiding any partisan political advice, of course, but getting them to the polls. The emphasis from the beginning, and what sold the idea of widows' pensions, was that a mother would be able to stay at home with her children and not have to go out to work. However, in the over fifty years since the plan started and which was such a step forward, we have come to feel that women should be given a choice by having other means available for caring for their children if they want to work. Day care centers for this purpose were stimulated when we needed women in industry during the Second World War. However, the idea has been slow to take hold, and it has been far from easy to get appropriations, public or private, for day care centers in New York State during the ensuing years. Some impetus was recently given to making it possible for women to work by the pronouncements that "second and third generations were growing up on welfare." Although there seems to be small evidence of this, we have generally come to the point of feeling that women with dependent children should have a chance at meaningful occupations that could lead to future independence; and I do not mean any of the plans for compulsory work that have sometimes been proposed.

Another cause for prejudice has been the proportionate change in the color of relief recipients as the years of affluence lifted more and more white families out of poverty, and left on relief a much higher proportion of black, Puerto Rican, and other minority groups who had not shared in as great a degree in the general prosperity.

However, what finally stirred the wider community to action was the continuing increase in the cost of welfare and the increase in the numbers on the rolls—all this during what were good times, economically speaking.

We in New York have been very fortunate to have had Mitchell Ginsberg as head of the Department of Welfare—now Department of Social Services—and then as administrator of Human Resources. He has not only applied creative thinking, firmness, and skill in handling people, but even more important, his direct and frank speaking on the problems of welfare have helped immeasurably to bring a better understanding of our least popular form of human protection.

When in 1969 New York State chose to save money by making cuts in welfare budgets, some pictures were published of the people being affected. One in *The New York Times* showed a blind man and his seeing eye dog, whose food had been cut out of the old man's allowance! One could wonder whether only dogs have "seeing eyes"!

VI

Settlement Studies of Unemployment

To go back to before 1927, I had been immersed in unemployment and its effect on family life since the time when we first began to feel the lack of jobs, longer lay-offs, and the complete shutdowns which had put the steady long-time workers on the street. Working people themselves did not immediately recognize what was happening to them. Often they felt it was just a "bad break." But we, whom they approached to help them find jobs, and with whom they talked over their daily out-of-work problems, began to see a new pattern around us as we checked our neighborhood problems with each other. So the National Federation of Settlements formed an Unemployment Committee in 1928, of which I became chairman. It was this committee that undertook our Unemployment Study and, as I have said, we called on the encouragement and editorial skill of Paul Kellogg, who was a member of the National Federation of Settlements' Board and had served as the chairman of its Resolutions Committee for years.

There was still so little public recognition of the growing tide of unemployment in 1928 and its effects, that we felt that we should tell the story of what we were experiencing in settlement neighborhoods in as vivid a way as possible. We chose to study, at first, only the experiences of heads of families with long work records behind them, because we were still told on all sides that it was only the shiftless who were out of work. In collecting data, I went South to New Orleans and spent time in Detroit and other cities. While in Detroit I visited Flint, a one-industry auto town where unemployment had reached 90 percent. I passed by what seemed to have been a demonstration of some kind. When I asked the police what had happened, the reply was, "It's just those Communists trying to make the unemployed dissatisfied!"*

Thus I met families in industrial neighborhoods in many other parts of the country, and heard the stories of settlement workers as they struggled with the increasing misery on their doorsteps.

Then came the market crash of 1929, and we were literally swamped by the needs around us.

My mother and father had come from Boston. In their families, Republicanism, as to politics, was taken for granted, though I must add, colored by the progressive tone of Theodore Roosevelt. I myself had voted for Hoover in 1928, because I had served with the Red Cross in France in the First World War, and had come back feeling that peace was the greatest urgency in the world. I could never blot out of my memory the suffering of the men in the base hospitals where I had served. At the time it seemed to me that Hoover, with his experience and Quaker background, and the humanitarianism with which he had been credited for "feeding starving Europe," was best equipped to deal with our relationships in Europe on which permanent peace had to be based.

So, armed with the stories of unemployment in my hands, and the misery of it in my mind, I went hopefully to Washington in the winter of 1929–30. I was introduced under the best auspices to the congressional leaders of those days, but when I asked what was to be done about unemployment, the only answer I was able to elicit was "the Administration has given orders that the unemployment bills will not come to the floor."

Those few days in Washington and the callousness of the Administration for which I myself had voted were some of the most disillusioning I have ever experienced. Finally, Colonel J. Mayhew Wainwright, who had taken me to meet the top mem-

* "When Detroit's out of gear," *The Survey*, April 1, 1930.

bers of Congress, and who was a Republican himself, was disturbed by the answers I was getting and, hoping to find an interested ear somewhere in Washington, took me to see Senator Robert Wagner.

I was to be grateful to Senator Wagner continuously as the years went on, but never more than that morning, for the preceding days had been devastating. The misery I was talking about was so real and ever present to me. I tried to make the men on Capitol Hill see, as I did, my neighbor with her baby in her arms showing me that the baby had gone from 11 pounds to 9 or hear her voice as she told me that she would steal milk before her baby starved to death. Or to see the family of young children across the street living on bread and tea for three months before we discovered their plight. And to see babies of three lying inert, not able to use their legs because of malnutrition. These real people were by that time multiplied by millions and yet the mild unemployment bills *were not to be allowed even to come up for a vote.*

But these Americans mattered to Senator Wagner, and they counted with Senator Robert LaFollette, whom Senator Wagner immediately got on the telephone. Together they planned to have me bring the settlement data as testimony for the unemployment bills for which they were planning hearings. They told me that ours was the first human material they had been able to get which showed the impact of unemployment on families.

It was in April, 1930, of that same year that I returned to testify with Clinch Calkins, who had put our stories into poignant form in a book entitled *Some Folks Won't Work**—so-called because that was what we were told so often as we tried to get unemployment relief of one kind or another.

I remember my first testimony—aside from the fact that I was scared to death—more for a personal reason than any other. My sister's second child, Kent Hunter, was born that same day. She had not been well, and, as my train drew away from where she lived, I was eaten up with anxiety. The uncomfortable fact is that "social action" seldom comes at a convenient time.

Only about ten persons, representing different organizations—

* New York: Harcourt Brace & Co., 1930.

one, the Industrial Division of the YWCA—testified at those hearings. The settlement's closeness to the situation had impelled them to lead off in what was to be a long struggle to have unemployment treated with intelligence and mercy. But by this time unemployment had become so overwhelming to social workers that two publications which stemmed from our study— *Some Folks Won't Work* and *Case Studies of Unemployment**— were said to have been quoted at every meeting of the National Conference of Social Work that year, and they were used widely during the years that followed. But the country was intolerably slow in accepting responsibility. The years from 1929 on were harrowing ones to be living in settlement neighborhoods.

While we pressed for immediate relief and work relief, many of us knew from the beginning that what we had to have was security of an over-all kind that would protect families, and business as well, from the devastating "cycles." I had sat on Governor Gifford Pinchot's Unemployment Committee while I was still in Philadelphia. Paul Douglas and Bryce Stewart, experts on unemployment insurance, brought their advice to Governor Pinchot's committee. But at that time, the business representatives on the committee were dead set against unemployment insurance and, like many other people, were sure that the "dole had ruined England." This common supposition had become such a road block, or smoke screen, in this country that I finally decided that it might be worthwhile to go to England and try to get a picture of the situation directly from British working people themselves. I was urged to do this at the May, 1932, board meeting of the National Federation of Settlements. I remember Jane Addams and Justice Louis Brandeis sent me handwritten notes urging me to go when they heard of my proposed trip.

I did go to England that summer of 1932, and it turned out to be a very reassuring and illuminating experience. When I came back, I reported on this study in four articles.†

I must say, I started off for England with considerable trepida-

---

* Philadelphia: University of Pennsylvania Press, 1931.

† "English Dole and American Charity," *Atlantic Monthly*, May, 1933; "The Little Green Card," *Survey Graphic*, May, 1933; "Charity in the Market Place," *New Outlook*, May, 1933; and "Miners Must Eat," *Atlantic Monthly*, August, 1933.

tion. Perhaps, I thought to myself, after I had visited the British
people I will never again believe in any kind of unemployment
insurance. Had the British working man been robbed of his
self-respect and his initiative? Did he no longer want to work?
That he was healthier I knew, for on that point there seemed
no disputing the figures of the Ministry of Health. But—as we
had so often been told in the United States—had the "dole"
brought moral and spiritual degradation in its wake?

These were the questions I was to probe as the English settlement workers took me to talk to their neighbors. There was
ample evidence in British reports of what the insurances meant
to the people, but I was not going to stop at reports or at what
officials, employers, and labor leaders told me. To judge the
things they said, I felt I must come to know the people themselves.

I found British working people amazingly willing to answer
questions, no matter how personal, as to how they managed
their budgets when at work or on the "Liber" as unemployment
insurance was referred to in London. I think the settlement
workers who took me around were surprised at the readiness
of their neighbors to talk.

One of my favorite experiences was with a middle-aged man
whose story was so long it took me an afternoon to sort it all
out. I learned that he lived next door to a big cemetery and,
when out of work, watched the funerals to entertain himself.
To my pleasure and my guide's surprise, he told her later that
he had enjoyed talking to the "Lidy from America" as much
as any funeral he had ever seen!

What I saw in London was to be driven home to me over
and over again by the families I visited in many other parts of
England—in Manchester, the heart of the textile district; in
Liverpool, the city of dock labor; and in the coal valleys of
South Wales. The spontaneous testimony of the British working
people I visited altogether convinced me that the minimum of
security which meant so much to them had not produced the
demoralization of family life we were told of in America and
which our own makeshift methods were producing at that moment in the United States.

But however reassured I felt about the families I had visited
in the cities not having been ruined by the dole, I still wondered

how an unemployment system worked in a mining area like the Rhondda Valley, where unemployment was so high, and so hopeless, where with the collapse of the coal industry, mines were shutting down partially or for good.

A quarter of a million people had migrated from the Welsh fields—one in ten—and more would have gone had work been plentiful elsewhere. Among the 200,000 miners who remained, the percentage of unemployment ran appallingly high. In one town that I visited in the Rhondda Valley, it was 70 percent; in many it was more than 40 percent.

But as I visited the length and breadth of the Rhondda Valley in South Wales, what I found was that unemployed people were still part of their own local villages, their choral societies, their small shops; they still owned their houses and they were also part of the greater community which is the nation. They had not dropped out of sight, nor been left to depend solely on their neighbors.

I started my visiting in the Rhondda Valley with a visit to a mothers' club, whose members were very eager to have me see their homes. One of them, Mrs. Wilsey, had been appointed my official guide by the local settlement. Tall and spare, she was more appropriately built for the job than her round little friend, Mrs. Donohue, who puffed along, very short of breath, but most determined that I should visit her. As we went, they told me what it had meant to the valley to have some mines close down altogether while others ran slack, and of the part unemployment benefit played in their lives.

When we reached Mrs. Donohue's door, I could see why she wanted me to come. Her house was her pride, and justly so. As we passed the window that looked on to the street, I could see her lovingly eyeing her plants, and when I spoke of them her hand went up involuntarily to pat the window. Behind the flowers hung a bright yellow curtain of lace, crisp and perfect.

"I've a lady from America!" she announced breathlessly, as we came into the living room. Her husband, whom Mrs. Donohue evidently wanted me to meet, came inquiringly through the door leading to the kitchen. The man had a ruddy, humorous face, topped off with upstanding, bushy white hair.

"Come and see the lady from America," said his wife once more.

"Sure now," he said, "I'd be dirtying your hands if I shake with you, for I've been messing about in our bit of a garden. It's something to keep a man busy." The search for "something to keep a man busy" was one thing the Rhondda Valley shared with the unemployed everywhere.

Mr. Donohue, it seemed, had been out of work for five years, so that his case illustrated how far the insurance system reached in time as well as in distance. He was on Transitional Benefit— the group to which approximately one-third of the unemployed in Great Britain belonged. Since the proportion is far higher for mining districts, my visit to the Rhondda Valley offered a favorable opportunity to observe its workings as an alternative to our various schemes of public unemployment relief.

It might be explained here that to be eligible for Standard Unemployment Benefit, which ran at that time for half a year, a man had to have stamps to show that he had made thirty contributions from his pay within the previous two years. His payments were matched by similar contributions from employer and government. Two-thirds of the unemployed in England were in this main standard insurance group at this time. When a man exhausted his rights under it, but still had eight stamps to show for work in the past two years (or thirty stamps at any time in his work history), he went on to Transitional Benefit. Thereafter he was subject to a Means Test, which was carried out for the insurance system by the local public assistance authorities, and which scaled down the amount if there was any other source of income in the family. If there was no other income, such as a pension or the wages of children, the amount paid was the same as under the Standard Benefit.

Men and women receiving either class of benefit had to be able and willing to accept suitable work; otherwise relief might be denied by the insurance officer, subject to appeal to a committee. Mr. Donohue was put to such a work test. He met it at the Labor Exchange with the rejoinder, "The sooner you let me put bread back on the pantry shelf, the better, for I am able and willing to work and only want the chance." At the time, the Rhondda Valley was flooded, and, taking him at his word, they mustered him into the flood work. "They thought

to kill me desire off by putting me in water up to me middle,"
he confided to me, "but I stayed the seventeen weeks until the
work was finished."

When I remarked on their ability to manage so well, Mr.
Donohue answered practically: "You couldn't go into debt, because you couldn't pay it back. We know what we have to
spend. There's the rent, and the food and the extras; so we've
to plan accordingly. We've paid the rent on the house for
twenty-three years, and we wouldn't want to be losing it, for
we've worked on the improving of it the while. It's keep on
we have to, not go back."

As we went up and down the hilly streets, my guide stopped
to talk with the people we met and to bring out bits of their
lives. In telling her own story, she gave me an intimate clue as
to what thrift means when you live on the dole. As a little
girl, when she helped with the scrubbing, her mother had always
been at her to use more "elbow grease" and save the soap. She
had been rebellious, and thought to herself, "Isn't our mother
mingy?" When she herself was first married, work in the mines
had been steady, and she saw to it that they had enough soap
to save her strength. But times had changed since then. Now
she understood her mother. On the dole one couldn't waste a
farthin'.

As if to illlustrate her point, a boy on a vinegar cart passed us.
He was singing in a high, young voice, with a soft Welsh accent,
the song that American college boys have sung so long:

> And when I die, don't bury me at all.
> Just pickle me bones in alcohol.

The housewives came to their doors with pitchers and had just
a penny's worth of vinegar poured out for them by the young
singer.

We paid calls at other solid little houses of gray stone, and
each had its story. At the Jones home the husband was out,
and the wife explained that he was "always going to keep off
thinking. You got to do things to have peace." He "topped
boots in the neighborhood," and right then he was picking up
coal from the old mine tips.

The spirit I found among the Rhondda miners and their

families I was to see so often snuffed out at home in the Virginia coal fields, where the long-unemployed families were subsisting so precariously. With a minimum of economic security, these Rhondda people seemed to live while waiting, and took advantage of the retraining centers and community activities projected on a national scale.

After I came back from England, I spent a week visiting the West Virginia coal fields with a group of Quakers. On our first afternoon we were sitting on the porch of a coal miner's shack and the amazing glory of the fall was around us while the miners' wives in their gentle voices were telling me an ugly tale, and I hated to look at the miserable, gray baby that one woman was rocking.

But they went on: "An' then last spring th' Red Cross quit givin' out groceries an' th' Quakers had to go home. There wuzn't any milk fur th' children. Most of th' men wuzn't workin' —just a day here an' a day there."

"What did you do?" I had interrupted. "Just how did you manage?"

There was a pause, and then, "It 'pears like it 'ud be easy to say, honey, but our ways 'ud be hard fur you to understand. You see it was gravy soup lot o' th' time—just gravy soup."

"What is gravy soup?"

"You puts flour in a pan an' browns it, an' then you stirs water inta it."

"Is that what you gave your baby?"

I must have sounded accusing, for the mother said apologetically, "Oh, no, honey, not when I cud help it. A neighbor up th' way has a cow, an' she wuz mighty good to me. She sent up half a pint o' milk when she had it over. Sometimes it wuz ev'ry other day, an' sometimes none fur a week. But it helped a powerful sight." And then, "I'm a-givin' him bean soup now, from beans we growed this summer."

The rest of the women joined in: "Th' ones that had gardens didn't do so bad, an' I put up seven cans of apples from some that wuz give me. Sometimes an odd job was picked up, an' some got trust from th' comp'ny stores." Each one added something in an effort to make me understand how things had been. "They wuz sorry-lookin' children in this county, but they mended

like little pigs when th' Quakers brought th' milk an' sandwiches
into th' schools. They wuzn't so cross when they got that pint
o' milk a day. There's nothin' like food to perk a child up."

Our reception was always friendly, a vein of neighborliness
seemed to run deep in the lives of these people and it was this
neighborliness that kept life going among them before outside
help came, and which had to tide them over the recurring
breaks in that help.

On another afternoon, Mrs. Bent sank into a big rocking chair
and talked. Her husband, who had started life working on a
railroad in North Carolina, had come to the mines as a young
man. "The year before, work was so slack," she said, "that he
didn't dare to 'stay out' when he felt ill. Each day's work might
be the last he would get for a long time." One night when he
came home he told his wife that he had loaded five big cars
that day, but after each shovelful it had seemed to him he
couldn't continue. She put him to bed with all the home remedies
she could muster. Then she lay down herself. The last thing she
knew he was leaning over, tucking the bedclothes around her.
When she awoke, he was dead.

"Th' county had to bury him," she said, "for when mining fell
off we had dropped the insurance we had carried for five years.
Then I had to get out of th' comp'ny house, but th' assessor
for our county—he let us in here without any rent." There were
Mrs. Bent herself, her daughter, and two grandchildren in the
family. "The assessor is a Republican," she added reflectively,
"but he's a good man, and th' whole county sez so." Next she
went to the county court in the little town nine miles away
and asked for help. They told her they had no money, and
referred her to the Red Cross. The husband had died in October;
but it was not until December that she finally received aid
from any source other than her neighbors. Then she was given
her first bag of groceries by the Red Cross. These bags she
had to carry nine miles over the mountains. Mrs. Bent is small
and shriveled, and she had had to depend on the kindness of
friends and strangers along the way to help her get her sixty
pounds of groceries home to the children.

"I went fur my bag ev'ry two weeks till June," she told me.
"Then they told me they wuz goin' to break up an' I'd better

see what th' county cud do. Th' county sent me ten dollars each month for three months; then they stopped, an' they kept tellin' me to go to th' Red Cross; but th' Red Cross wuz only givin' flour then. Th' Red Cross had give us some seed fur our garden, an' a bushel of potatoes to plant. It did us fur th' summer, but it didn't raise enough fur this winter. Th' bugs et up all th' beans here. They wuz comin' with stuff to save th' beans, but they never did. I sold all my corn to buy Orrin's shoes for school. Right now," she brightened up, "we think we're lucky, my daughter an' me. We're earnin' a dollar an' a half a week washin' an' ironin' over at th' comp'ny boardin' house. You'd know how lucky that is if you ever waited fur someone to bring you food."

All this threadbare and tangled web of life was brought very close to me on an afternoon I spent visiting families who lived in the shacks along a little creek. Ellie Emerson took particular charge of me that afternoon, and introduced me to her neighbors.

Her husband unrolled himself from an old quilt on the floor beside the stove. He had dropped there when he came back from work early in the morning—too tired to wash, and not wanting to soil the beds with the grime of the mines. He appeared wild enough after his sleep, with the coal dust deepening the shadows in his face and neck. Just twenty-seven, he looked much older and very frail.

John Emerson's work had been fairly regular until about three years before. But the winter of 1932 it averaged no more than one day a week, and last summer, to tide themselves over, they had moved temporarily to a nearby town where his wife's family had a piece of land he could work.

During the afternoon, I was shown his present pay envelope together with earlier ones. The fortnight before my visit, he had worked in water halfway to his knees. Since he was paid a little extra, he had been glad to do it.

Just at this point, Mr. Emerson's father-in-law came in to tell him that there was to be no work that night. So, since he wouldn't be going out again, he went off to get washed and dressed, and then, as his wife and I talked, settled himself to read the paper. The children, when they came in, found him reading. They both considered him seriously. Then Billie, the three-year-old baby, went out and came trundling back with his father's miner's lamp and tried to put it on him. The six-year-old boy, looking very concerned, offered to help him get off. The father laughed. "The kids is worried when I don't go to work," he said, "You see, they ain't so little but they understand. They gets enough to eat when their daddy's working, and it appears like everything's different."

England had had her coal commissions, and, like ours, their reports for the reconstruction and reorganization of the industry, which had collapsed in both countries. And, like ours, they had so far gone unheeded.

Our depression had really brought us back to the breadbasket, the grocery order, the commissary, welfare cafeterias, and the script commissaries that had multiplied over the country, all humiliating forms of warding off starvation. One community after another grasped at something that seemed to offer economies to the community but not security to the unemployed.

I was reminded of what was happening at home that same summer when I was in France and followed two very old women around a fish market in Brittany.* They were tiny, with proper white caps set above faces resembling dried apples. They handled and pinched and turned over almost every little fish in the market. They visited each fish cart, picked up the fish, inquired the price, studied it, head on one side, glanced at each other knowingly, dropped the fish and went on to the next stand.

I became so interested I couldn't leave them. They were starting to leave, to my disappointment, when an acquiescent look passed between them and I sensed that the right fish had been found. They each took two, the price murmured between them as they lugged out old leather purses from retired nooks on their persons. Then they pattered around to the back of the market where they clambered down over the rocks and cleaned the little fish. Back they came, sabots clicking on the rocks and each fish stuck through the gills on a finger. By this time I was far too interested to leave them, so at a decent distance, I hurried along behind. They had been deliberate in the market but now they scurried, for lunch was in hand. The sabots were

* Helen Hall, "Charity in the Market Place," *New Outlook*, May, 1933.

left again outside a little cottage, and, fish on fingers, they disappeared for the end of the ritual.

As I watched them, I couldn't but think of our initiative-destroying and humiliating food orders and food baskets and the comment made to me by one of the British housewives I had interviewed in London, "Do come in, miss," she said. "I'd be glad to 'elp you in any way I can, for I 'ear things is dreadful in America. I see by the pipers in some plices they're linin' 'em up for bread."

During these years there was so much nonsensical talk against the social insurances and so much misinformation spread around that you felt you had to take every opportunity to tell your story. But at meetings of those days you met the same people both for and against so often that you wondered whether you ever made any impression. It was always a comfort to have Paul Douglas, then a professor at the University of Chicago, with his keen mind and fighting spirit on your side. And you could generally count on the National Association of Manufacturers showing up at the meetings in opposition! At one meeting in Washington the representative of the NAM closed his impassioned speech against unemployment insurance to the effect that his ideal American was a man with a flag in one hand and a Bible in the other, and such a man didn't need unemployment insurance!

I don't know whether it was encouraging or not that at a round table discussion during the recession in 1954, a member of the NAM asserted that we would never have another depression because of the underpinning to our economy afforded by Unemployment Insurance, Old Age Insurance, and other of the Social Security provisions. And he assured me later that the association had *always* been for Social Security. I didn't think he looked too young to remember the early stand they had taken, but *I* certainly was not! And obviously unemployment insurance had not "ruined America"!

VII

Social Security

It was an infinite relief when in June, 1934, President Roosevelt appointed his Committee on Economic Security. At last it looked as though we would be establishing something permanent to deal with the problem of family insecurity. Frances Perkins, Secretary of Labor, was appointed chairman; Henry Morgan-thau, Jr., Secretary of the Treasury; Homer Cummings, Attorney General; Henry A. Wallace, Secretary of Agriculture; and Harry L. Hopkins, Federal Emergency Relief administrator, made up the committee.

The President also appointed a technical committee of government experts and an Advisory Council on Economic Security, on which I was asked to serve. This council was made up of citizens outside the government who were to assist the committee "in weighing the proposals developed by the staff and Technical Board and in arriving at a judgment as to their practicability."

Frank P. Graham, then president of the University of North Carolina, served as chairman, and Paul Kellogg as vice-chairman. There were twenty-three of us drawn from business and labor and the general public. We represented many viewpoints and were, I think, a healthy cross section of the national community. Our differences of opinion were very great but at that time in the Depression, the kinds of people chosen to serve were, on the whole, convinced that something had to be worked out to bring more economic security to low-income families.

The business representatives on the Advisory Council were: Marion B. Folsom, then assistant treasurer of Eastman Kodak Company, later under President Eisenhower to be Secretary of Health, Education and Welfare; Samuel Lewisohn, vice-president of Miami Copper Company; Morris E. Leeds, President of Nelds and Northrup; Gerard Swope, president of the General Electric Company; and Walter C. Teagle, president of Standard Oil Company of New Jersey.

Labor was represented by George Berry, president of the International Printing Pressmen and Assistants' Union; William Green, president of the American Federation of Labor; George M. Harrison, president of the Brotherhood of Railway and Steamship Clerks; Henry Ohl, Jr., president of the Wisconsin State Federation of Labor; and Paul Scharrenberg, secretary-treasurer of the California State Federation of Labor.

Agriculture had one spokesman on the Advisory Council— Louis J. Taber, master of the National Grange.

Representatives of the general public, in addition to the chairman and vice-chairman, included Grace Abbott, of the University of Chicago, formerly chief of the United States Children's Bureau; Mary Dewson, of the National Consumers League; Joel T. Hunter, general superintendent of the United Charities of Chicago; Elizabeth Morrissey, of Notre Dame College, Baltimore; Raymond Moley, editor of *Today* and former Assistant Secretary of State; George H. Nordlin, chairman of grand trustees, Fraternal Order of Eagles; Msgr. John A. Ryan, director of the Department of Social Action, National Catholic Welfare Conference; Belle Sherwin, former president of the National League of Women Voters; and myself.

Labor was somewhat reluctant to go along in the beginning, but William Green testified in favor of the Social Security Bill when it was finally before the Congress. While the members of the Labor group did not always attend regularly, the business group on the Advisory Committee did and were intensely interested in every step taken by the committee. They were very aware of the long-term importance to the economy of what we were doing.

Unfortunately it had already been decided to postpone planning for health insurance until a later time—and not to include it in the Social Security Bill on which we were advising.

It was felt that it would jeopardize the Social Security program. The Committee on Economic Security had included a discussion of health insurance, saying at the same time that it would be considered later, but even this caused the American Medical Association to call a meeting of its House of Delegates, in which they passed a resolution opposing government health insurance. For the record, at the same time they also passed a resolution opposing maternal and child health services to be administered by the Children's Bureau. Then began the long political fight, continuing to this day, against health insurance that has kept the American people from attaining security against sickness, the third great hazard poor people face, along with unemployment and old age. The President got only "two-thirds of the cherry," as I describe in a later chapter.

With health insurance out of the picture, the different plans for unemployment insurance were the most controversial part of the social security planning. And their discussion almost precluded any consideration by the Advisory Council on Old Age Insurance, which was the most popular part of the program and put first in the final plans introduced in Congress. The four points causing most concern were: whether to allow individual employers merit-rating for low unemployment rates; what the size of the original tax and length of benefits should be; whether unemployment insurance should be supported by employee as well as employer contributions; and most important of all, and bitterly fought over, whether it should be a national system or a federal-state system, which, unfortunately, it finally came to be. But very fortunately indeed our recommendation for a national system of old-age insurance was followed.

However, the first state unemployment insurance law had already been passed in Wisconsin in 1932 and so the Wisconsin-ites felt that it ought to be tried state by state, and it became very difficult to get any other than the Wisconsin viewpoint, that is it was hard to get any other viewpoint brought out, before the committee. Edwin E. Witte, the committee's executive director, was so strongly for the Wisconsin viewpoint, that Frank Graham and Paul Kellogg had to insist that Barbara Armstrong and Bryce Stewart, both leading authorities in this field, be allowed to discuss their opposing viewpoints with the committee.

Although I strongly disagreed, I could sympathize with them

because I had been in Wisconsin on the day this first unemployment insurance bill was passed. I had talked to Governor Philip LaFollette, and to the sponsor of the bill, and had shared in the general rejoicing that this state with its liberal tradition had been able to break the bottleneck on unemployment insurance. But a desire to have Wisconsin continue to experiment played too much of a part, it seemed to me, in the final recommendations of our committee. To some of us insurance meant pooling resources and not having either the state or the worker affected by the poor economic aspects of either his firm or his particular geographic area.

The position of some of us on the committee went a step beyond some earlier thinking that I had expressed, as a spokesman for the National Federation of Settlements, when I had testified in the early spring of that same year, 1934. This was in support of the Wagner–Lewis Bill to set up an unemployment insurance program that was similar in general approach to that which ultimately became part of the committee's program. Appearing before the House Ways and Means Committee in March, I said in part:

> On behalf of the settlements of the country I strongly urge federal initiative to bring us a unified, dependable, self-respecting system for handling unemployment. After five years of mass suffering, only one state has passed an unemployment insurance law. If we are to wait for action, state by state, and only one state acts during each depression, it will take two centuries of hard times to cover the country.
>
> We need federal initiative not only to get action but to make for unity. The piecemeal process would leave us, even if it were speeded up, with a hodgepodge of state laws, penalizing employers in states that wanted to do the right thing and uneven in the protection it would throw over the workers. Federal action as outlined in the Wagner–Lewis Bill leaves room for state initiative but lays down certain bed-rock standards which must be met nationally. Certain of the standards I should like to see raised. For example, the minimum time set for out-of-work benefits is ten weeks, as against twenty-six weeks in England—and the $7-a-week benefit does not bear a fair relation to living costs in the United States. . . .

Within the committee, some of us went even further, and urged a veritable national system of unemployment insurance. It would be hard for anyone to study today the patchwork of state unemployment insurance systems in this country and not wish we had followed the same national system that was put into effect for old age insurance. To illustrate just from the standpoint of benefits, in 1968 we had an average weekly payment of $43.73 with four states' insurance payments higher than New York's $43.67, and the rest lower, down to Mississippi's $26.79 and West Virginia's $29.78.

Some of us were so disturbed by the smallness of the benefits possible under a 3 percent payroll tax that while we signed the majority report we sent a special supplementary report to Frances Perkins urging the 5 percent, which was what the Wagner–Lewis Bill first proposed. Frank Graham, Paul Kellogg, William Green, the four other labor representatives, and I signed this report.

However, the final form of unemployment insurance was also affected by the question as to whether even the plan decided upon—a cooperative federal-state system—would be declared unconstitutional by the Supreme Court. Commenting on this problem some years later, Arthur J. Altmeyer, who from 1934 to 1935 was Assistant Secretary of Labor and also a member of the Technical Board of the President's Committee on Economic Security, writes in his book, *The Formative Years of Social Security** :

> The concern (at that time) regarding constitutitonality cannot be exaggerated. Actually between Jan. 1935 and May 1936 eight New Deal Laws were declared unconstitutional. Following the Presidential election of 1936, President Roosevelt made his dramatic proposal to increase the number of Supreme Court justices. This led to the famous "court-packing" battle which the President lost. However he apparently won the war, because in 1937 all of the Supreme Court decisions regarding the constitutionality of New Deal laws (including the Social Security Act) were favorable. One newspaper columnist, discussing this sudden reversal in the attitudes of a majority of the nine Supreme Court Justices, commented that "a switch in time saves nine."

* Madison, Wisconsin: The University of Wisconsin Press, 1968.

The Wagner–Daughton Bill containing the final plans, which attempted to take into account the views of all the committees and advisers involved, and also included changes made by the Congress itself, was passed and signed into law as the Social Security Act of 1935 by the President on August 14, 1935. Then began the two years needed to build an administrative structure. This story is told most vividly in all its detail in Arthur Altmeyer's book.

From the inception of the Social Security program to 1945, Mr. Altmeyer was to serve on the three-man Social Security Board appointed by the President, and after 1937, as its chairman, following the resignation of the late John G. Winant to become ambassador to Great Britain. The third member of the first board was Vincent M. Mills, an Arkansas lawyer.

Before Mr. Altmeyer came to Washington in the first year of the New Deal, he had served for twelve years with the Wisconsin Industrial Commission, first as chief statistician and then as secretary of the commission. I have always felt that the successful building of the system was due in no small measure to his administrative gifts, experience, and years of devotion. I have known many members of his staff and have felt a deep satisfaction in the caliber of the people he brought around him. They were able not only to do the initial building but to set a firm pattern of competence and integrity. It has been a satisfaction over the years to know at first hand how courteously and expertly my neighbors' problems have been handled—no matter what handicaps some of them may have had in communication! May it keep this way.

PART TWO

The Anatomy
of a Settlement

VIII

A General Practitioner

Paul Kellogg was the first to describe a settlement as a general practitioner and I know of no better way to describe it. It is out of an unselective and close association with all kinds of people that our programs and our opportunities to effect social change must spring. Because I believe in the settlement as a creative instrument for social change I am describing Henry Street and settlements in general in some detail.

I am not starting with a description of our buildings at Henry Street because I feel that the physical plant is by any means of paramount importance, but because our own pattern of development as it has worked out over the years, is reflected in part by the various buildings and facilities that are part of the Settlement today. We have been fortunate in having our buildings so often follow our neighborhood's changing needs for services, and I like the way Henry Street has grown. However, it is not by any means the only way a settlement or a neighborhood agency can serve its neighborhood, as history shows. Back in 1893 Lillian Wald and Mary Brewster began their work in a flat in a tenement house on the Lower East Side. Two years later Jacob Schiff gave Miss Wald 265 and then 267 Henry Street, architecturally similar buildings that had in the old days been residences. In 1934, toward the end of my first year, we were able to acquire 263 Henry Street for some of our new projects. These three buildings were all erected in 1830, the Federal Period, and are so charming that we wanted to preserve them for the neighborhood's sake as well as our own. The City Landmarks Commission took the same view and designated them as landmarks in 1965. These old buildings bring beauty and a touch of history to a neighborhood which has otherwise only the tall boxlike structures of public housing projects and middle-income cooperatives, along with the remainder of the tenements. I remember the day a neighbor from one of the worst of the old tenements settled down in one of the little parlors in our old houses after they had just been refurbished. "My," she said, "this is homey!" Hominess combined with beauty is what we aim for. Our neighbors may be subjected to so much ugliness in their daily lives that it places a special obligation on us to have the rooms in which they meet as attractive as possible. These three old buildings have remained as the settlement headquarters.

Our little theater on Grand Street, first known to New Yorkers as The Neighborhood Playhouse, was built by the Lewisohn sisters, Irene and Alice, in 1915. It was completely renovated in 1962 through a gift from Louis Abrons, who had come to the theater as a boy and has helped support it in many ways ever since, and whose son, Herbert Abrons, is now a leading member on our Board.

Our music lessons moved into an old tenement building at 8 Pitt Street in 1927 that adjoined the theater from the rear. This building had to be closed in 1963 because of the projected widening of Pitt Street. Since then we have used two apartments which were turned over to us at a nominal rent as a friendly gesture by Ralph Lippman, executive manager of Cooperative Village. (Cooperative Village consists of four cooperatives on Grand Street.) These were remodeled to suit our needs by youth crews in training from Mobilization for Youth. On Saturdays, however, the Music School and the Playhouse spill over into rooms in all the settlement buildings. Illustrative of a bit of "hominess" was the remark made by a small boy who was sitting next to me at a children's play at the Playhouse. It turned out that he took lessons in one of the other buildings. "Which place did you like best?" I asked him. "Why, the first one, of course," he answered. And when I asked why he answered,

"Because that's where the cats are!" How you love anyone who proves you right! I have always been rebellious over the scarcity of pets in the lives of the children in the slums. The low-income projects forbid, as do the middle-income cooperatives, having dogs or even cats as tenants (although the latter are often surreptitious tenants). I realize some of the difficulties involved but I still think it is wrong. Cats are beautiful and self-sufficient and those I had at Henry Street throughout the years I know added greatly to many children's pleasure, as well as having proved invaluable models in the pottery. My exchange of letters with Paul Gallico illustrates their further usefulness.

September 26, 1962

Dear Mr. Gallico:

Not long ago I came across a clipping someone had sent me of something of yours published in the *Readers Digest*. It made me feel again that I would like to thank you for all the pleasure I have had from your subtle understanding of cats.

I also wanted to tell you that cats are splendid settlement residents, a side of them I thought you might not have known about. I have always had several at Henry Street. Each of them feels of course that he is the director and has the total responsibility for the organization. One or all attend all the meetings, look the people over, and if they think it is going to be a worthwhile meeting sit down in the middle of the room for a nap. If things look dull they yawn and go out. If, however, there is a cat-hater present they go from person to person until they face him and then they sit and glare. They completely ignore the Nursery School, being much too intelligent to allow children to pull them to pieces.

Of the three I have now, one rules the kitchen, one the dining room, and a small Siamese runs my office for me. But they all take responsibility for meetings.

I thought you might be interested in cats as social workers, if you have not known them from this angle.

Thanks again for the great joy you have given me over the years.

Sincerely,
Helen Hall

15th October 1962

Dear Miss Hall:

Thank you so very much for your charming letter. It was most heartwarming and of course it explains completely why the Henry Street Settlement is not only so well run, but so famous. I might have guessed.

You were very sweet to write to me and I am most appreciative. Again with my thanks and all good wishes to you and your work in association with your feline superiors.

I am,

Yours cordially,
Paul W. Gallico

We are planning to relocate the Music School in a projected art center on Grand Street where it will adjoin our theater and give us more space for the other arts as well.

While it may be easier to clean, heat, and supervise one large building, I feel that we have been fortunate because our work is housed at six locations that are within a block and a half radius of the 265 Henry Street headquarters, and within easy reach of our neighbors. We have fitted better into the neighborhood this way.

I have always had the feeling that Pete's House grew out of a foreign policy dinner the last year of World War II, at which I sat next to Mrs. Lehman and she asked me what was happening in the neighborhood. As gang warfare was going on under my windows at the time, I described it pretty vividly and I guess with considerable feeling. Later I heard that the governor and Mrs. Lehman were planning to give a building in honor of their aviator son, Peter, who had lost his life in the war. Characteristically, they felt that if things were so bad on Henry Street, that was where they wanted to help.

Henry Street Settlement had been a part of Herbert Lehman's earlier years, since he had led a boys' club there after graduating from college, and he had been in touch with the settlement ever since. So in 1948 when his and Mrs. Lehman's generous gift enabled us to build "Pete's House" next door to our old buildings we were all very happy—staff, board, and neighbors—because we needed more space so desperately. It was a joy to work with the Lehmans for they were interested in every detail as we

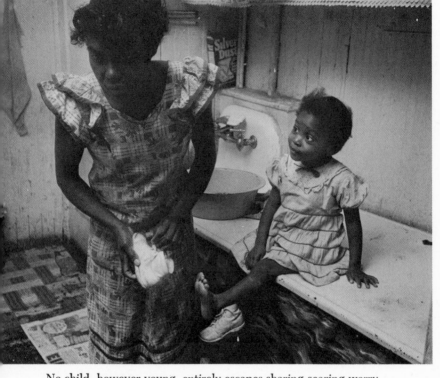

No child, however young, entirely escapes sharing searing worry
that may beset his parents (*Photo courtesy of Rae Russell*)

The playground in
back of University
House in Philadelphia
—Peg Spaulding
Noble, the Children's
Worker, and Helen
Hall

University
House,
Philadelphia

Tenements in the background of Henry Street's original Houses—
an art class makes the most of the yard
The same garden, later, with a mural done by an art class
(*Photo courtesy of Ken Wittenberg*)

Mrs. Roosevelt, Henry Freedman, Helen Hall at a meeting on unemployment of young people during the Depression—Henry Freedman was Chairman

Fiorello La Guardia at a party given by the neighbors for Helen when she went to the South Pacific with the American Red Cross in 1943

"Welcome Home" signs in the neighborhood as the soldiers began to return from World War II—they were welcomed by loving families and garbage

A problem brought to Ralph Tefferteller at the door of Pete's House

Governor Lehman visiting Pete's House. This picture of the
Governor and Helen Hall taken by a 14-year-old pupil, Louis Gaber,
in the photography class. (*Photo courtesy of Louis Gaber*)

planned on together. Equipping Pete's House was especially satisfying—to have a photography shop with the right dark rooms, a carpentry shop with the machines we had always wanted, a perfectly set up art room, and so on throughout the house in all its special rooms. At one point I started adding up and took the way-over budget amount to Governor Lehman. He said firmly that he wanted us to have just what we needed and in the quality that would last! So we went happily on making it as perfect as possible.

Fifteen years later the three old houses adjoining Pete's House, which had been done over by the settlement in 1905 for club rooms with a gym added, were torn down and replaced by the Stella and Charles Guttman Building. The treasurer of our board at that time, Paul Bonynge, Jr., had interested Charles Guttman in the settlement's needs, and brought him down to visit us. As we walked along Henry Street, Charles Guttman gave us a sense of what it had meant to him to have grown up in our neighborhood. His father had been a city marshal, but too kind-hearted to evict families who had not paid their rent, and so he had often paid it himself, which in turn was hard on his own family. Charles Guttman's concern for the children still living in our neighborhood was very evident. His disapproval of our three shabby old buildings that day was also very evident, and happily for us, led to his replacing them with a new structure in 1963. This helped us again to meet growing demands, this time especially for our increasing teen-age population.

Once more we were able to plan for a gay new building that would stand hard use as Pete's House had and we were able to use a "Friendly Jungle," a mural designed by the children in our art classes, on the front of the building.

Throughout the years, settlements and neighborhood centers, have often started in small one-family buildings, store-fronts, or their equivalent, and worked their way out of them because of the need for at least one large meeting room, and hopefully a gymnasium. At the turn of the century large centralized buildings where settlement activities could be housed under one roof became very popular. At present, store-fronts serve as an immediate answer to many of the needs of the Anti-Poverty programs.

A little tenement we bought in 1939 next door to our old "301" buildings, should be referred to as our "Emergency House," because it served to give us room for so many emergency programs until its small confines were replaced ten years later by Pete's House. Meanwhile it had served the difficult McCanns, the new tenants of Vladeck Houses, with a carpentry shop and meeting rooms as they prepared to move into Vladeck and later the Civilian Defense programs for which we had to have room.

Settlements in many cities have seized the opportunity to follow their neighbors, and at the same time, get needed space in low-income housing projects where they have taken on the responsibility for the project's community center programs. Henry Street was one of the first in New York to experiment in this way, starting with one of the basements of Vladeck Houses and adding adjoining basements as the years went on. Later, in 1954, we took on the responsibility for the community center in La Guardia Houses at 40 Montgomery Street.

Fortunately, community center space in public housing in New York has worked its way up from the basement to some free-standing buildings; if not that, at least it has slowly come above ground. In the early days of public housing the settlements in New York played a determining part in this change as they worked with both state and city officials on the need for attractive and practical recreation space.

Camps became an important part of settlement services very early and helped to set the pattern for the camping programs that became so much a part of many city-wide agencies. Perhaps settlement workers turned to camping early because they were personally so distressed by the sight and sound of a tenement district on a hot summer night. I have found it almost unbearable over the years—whole families on stoops or sidewalks half the night, trying to escape the suffocation of their flats and perhaps catch a breeze in the unstirring atmosphere. Then very late, as the street quiets down, you here the wail of a baby and a dog's sharp bark which still protests the torment of the night.

Henry Street has two camps near Peekskill, approximately fifty miles from New York City: Camp Henry at Mahopac, started in 1908 for boys; and Echo Hill Farm for girls, at Yorktown Heights, established in 1909.

Camp Henry is on a lake and we have a fine swimming pool at Echo Hill. It is good to think of the thousands of East Side children who have had their first glimpse of the country through vacations at Camp Henry and Echo Hill Farm. It is not just the three weeks in the country; it's looking forward to it and thinking about it afterward. What the camp has meant to them echoes in the lives of the campers sometimes for a lifetime.

One winter's night, three small boys were standing under a lamp post talking intently. As I passed, I asked them if they were having a committee meeting. "No," they said, "we're talkin' about camp!"

Charles Guttman told me that his week at our camp when he was a child meant so much to him that it made him eager to give us the Charles and Stella Guttman Building so many years later.

Camp Henry, our boys' camp, has been watched over and partially supported by a group of men who call themselves the "Henry Old Timers," who attended the camp as boys. Since 1937 they have added buildings and paid for many of the improvements, and contributed to the settlement program as well. Once a year they go out for a weekend and the old days come alive again. It should be said that their support and their interest have not waned as they have seen the young campers from our neighborhood change from Jewish children to Negro and Puerto Rican.

In 1961 Ruth Tefferteller suggested that we try an experiment at our girls' camp, leaving one building for girls' groups, and turning it into a Family Day Camp, so as to help the many newcomers in our area adjust to their changed environment and get to know their neighbors. It was a question of doing what at that time seemed the most important service to the neighborhood, for we felt that it would be one way to bring strength and solidarity to the family unit, as well as to bring neighbors together, and at the same time reach many more people. The whole family—father, mother, sisters, brothers, grandma, and baby—are all welcome and often they all come. Three buses have rolled toward Echo Hill Farm every day but Monday—especially with fathers on Saturdays and Sundays. Young and old get away from city crowds, have the freedom for a full day to do as they please and yet have a swimming pool, athletic field, a recreation building for rainy days, a bathhouse, cookouts, craft house, and other special facilities, with leadership insuring fun and safety.

The bus trips back and forth to camp are often spent in singing and friendly visiting. Here friendships develop, and soon neighbors who have never spoken to each other before are sharing their picnic lunches and carrying friendships, made at camp, back to the city.

IX

Residents and Visitors

To the founders of the settlement movement, beginning with Toynbee Hall in London, residence was a part of the basic idea. For almost the first fifty years of the American settlement movement, its founders and their fellow workers lived in the low-income neighborhoods where they worked. In later years, as new generations have taken over, this pattern has gradually changed. Many of the directors of settlements today live in other neighborhoods, sometimes as far off as the suburbs.

Many factors have entered into these changes. It is often said that it was because the early pioneers were in large part unmarried men and women and there were no children to consider that they could live in settlements. It is not as simple as that. Gaylord White at Union Settlement in New York Ciy, Mrs. Mary Simkhovitch at Greenwich House in New York City, Albert Kennedy at South End House in Boston, Charles Cooper in Pittsburgh, Graham Taylor at Chicago Commons, and later Clyde Murray at Union Settlement in New York all brought up children in the settlements they directed. I would like to point out again that Bertram Beck today is living at Henry Street with his family.

I would also like to say that I do sympathize with the added problems that growing children present in the resident situation. However, with their usual flexibility, the settlements have adjusted to all sorts of different living arrangements as time went on. But with few exceptions, of which Henry Street has been one, they have been drawing away from residence in the sense of a central dining room, with rooms for a staff and resident group. We at Henry Street have also felt some trend away from congregate living, although the residence is fully occupied at the present writing. Since its inception, there have been members of VISTA —Volunteers in Service to America—living in residence. But opportunities for service and for interesting experiences have greatly increased both at home and abroad. Perhaps freer behavior patterns between the sexes have brought about some of the changes. Even very young girls today take apartments alone or in pairs or groups, in old tenements or elsewhere. While this has been going on for some years, the age is getting steadily younger, even though the neighborhoods in which many of them live are getting much more dangerous.

Recently, however, there seems to have been a return to the idea of neighborhood residence. There has been the dramatization of the slums and again the desire of many young people to live in the area and share its problems. This is seen in the VISTA appeal. There is also the growing self-consciousness and pride of minority groups, with the concurrent reaction against helpers who come from the "outside." This presses workers to be identified with the area both geographically and psychologically.

There have been a wide variety of interesting and distinguished people among our residents—students of social work, mature people interested in social problems, students of all kinds interested in a neighborhood such as ours, foreign students, and social workers from all over the world. All have given some time and many have contributed valuable work and ideas.

I need hardly say that having Paul Kellogg as a resident at Henry Street enriched the settlement beyond measure. I used to think it was the best thing I did for Henry Street! He wrote for us, he entertained guests, he spoke for us, the neighbors knew and loved him, and above all, his creative mind generously took on all our problems and helped in their solving and he made the headworker very happy!

My dear friend, Lillie Peck, a long-time director of the National Federation of Settlements, was one of the most helpful residents in my day. She had been Albert J. Kennedy's assistant at the National Federation of Settlements, and when he gave up this post to direct the University Settlement in New York, Lillie Peck took over as director while living at Henry Street. She died in 1956, and because what I said at the memorial to her in Philadelphia expresses what she meant not only to me, but to the settlement field, I quote it here:

It has been lonely at Henry Street since Lillie Peck's death. It is very lonely, too, in our country place at Cornwall, where Lillie stayed so often with Paul Kellogg and me.

This spring, as I stepped out to see the beautiful Holland bulbs, and the masses of ever-multiplying daffodils that Lillie had planted over the years, I thought how like her! The kind of comfort and cosiness and loveliness she always brought with her, wherever she went. She made no show about any of it. She just brought small paper bags with her and went around putting indispensable little things in place, and then with as little fuss, went out into the garden where she tucked away bulbs and seeds and all sorts of special things that have given us joy.

It is symbolic of the way she dealt with the settlement movement. She traveled from settlement to settlement, here and abroad. The eternal gardener, planting, cultivating, encouraging. Bringing the best any of us had to offer to enrich or stimulate, as she went along. Listening to our troubles, and sometimes our furies, but never passing them on. She forever gave us her attention, happily and creatively, never looking at her watch or seeming to wait for her turn, only growing restive when something unkind was said. She forgave us our faults and she hoped for the same quality of generosity from us toward each other.

This concentration on people around her strengthened her intuitive gift of placing people where they would be at their best. Like bulbs, she planted people where they flowered, and I think it was this gift that gave her the most personal satisfaction. All the larger things she had accomplished, and it is an amazing record, she always seemed to feel someone else had done. It was impossible for her, being Lillie, to wholly accept her own accomplishments.

Lillie knew our neighbors, as well as our work, and as a resident she especially undertook to initiate our constant flow of foreign visitors, as well as our new residents. Her gentle but no less firm awareness of quality, as she went in and out of the

Henry Street buildings, brought reinforcement to us all, for her judgment was so sure and so informed. We have all of us counted on her, Board and staff, residents and neighbors. However, it was not only as a partner that I counted on Lillie, but as a very dear friend.

After I came back from serving on the Foreign Policy Commission to Cuba in 1934, the sister of the President of Cuba came to spend a winter with us while she studied social work. I always think with sadness of the hopefulness of Cuba's leaders that summer as they explained their plans for giving Cuba's poor a "New Deal." I also think of their fears that our government might encourage Batista, who was already in the offing, and of the American minister's comment to me to the effect that Batista wasn't a bad fellow, and that he went horseback riding with him every morning! When the missile crisis came, I wondered whether we hadn't ourselves to blame.

When the Nazi persecutions began to cast their shadow over the world, many refugees came our way as residents. Among them was a member of the Prussian Diet, the editor of a women's journal, finished musicians, physicians, social workers of distinction—some, refugees because of their religion, others, because they were liberals or socialists. Some stayed with us a few days, some a few weeks, others many months, and a few joined the staff. Henry Street once more, we hope, proved a friendly and helpful way station to uprooted people. Whatever may have been our success, there is no question that in spite of their own harassment and need for readjustment, they brought enrichment to the life of the settlement.

We place a high value on our dining room as a catalyst of no mean kind in a neighborhood. It serves many purposes, one of the most important being the opportunity to extend hospitality to guests of all kinds. People meet over breakfast, lunch, or dinner and innumerable small conferences take place around our dining room table. Our dining room is also a useful meeting place for members of our own staff who do not live in the settlement. Board members and many of our fund-raising groups use lunches and dinners as a stepping-stone to further interest in the settlement. During its first two strenuous years, LENA's (Lower Eastside Neighborhoods Association) executive committee met at breakfast here to beat the clock and their own taxing schedules. The Consumer–Farmer Milk Cooperative Board meets once a month for dinner before their board meeting. When Dr. Howard Brown came to direct Gouverneur Clinic, doctors, nurses, and other personnel from the clinic and their guests met often at lunch. A group of Job Corps boys and girls from Mobilization for Youth have met for lunch once a month. For several years our junior high school girls serving in the nursery school came for luncheon each semester, meeting their principals formally, and their teachers said they talked more about this than anything else! There are so many ways in which our dining room has served us that it is hard to think of our work without it. While perhaps no one thing is sufficiently important to keep a residence going, the sum total of its services has made it a serious contribution to the work as a whole.

We have been very fortunate in having three women, Sally Loftus, Nora O'Malley, and Peggy Staunton in charge of our kitchen and dining room at Henry Street for well over thirty years. Their degree of devotion, as well as competence, is extremely rare. They have done the marketing as well as the cooking and serving. They take a dinner for fifty in their stride, and their good temper and Irish humor rule out any tension in our daily living as well as in our constant entertaining. They have been a part of our team and we have planned and worked together.

There are two aspects of the Henry Street resident program: the central dining room with bedrooms and apartments in our own buildings, and apartments in the neighborhood. We have felt so strongly the value of having our staff members and colleagues at least *living* in the neighborhood that we have gradually acquired apartments in the area in nearby cooperatives that we rent to Henry Street staff members.

Neighborhood apartments are not new in settlement work. Hull House had apartments, with and without meals in the central dining room. Union Settlement built an apartment house with the idea of attracting resident workers. When the Depression hit them, they were glad to rent without requiring any service to the settlement. Christodora House was somewhat of the same vintage in New York, with an entire building of rooms and apartments of which the settlement quarters were merely a part. This was in the period when the "income-producing unit" idea hit churches as well as social agencies. The Depression also made the Christodora plan anything but income-producing, and the building was eventually sold to the city. And the settlement moved into a low-income housing development.

There runs through all the history of the settlements an effort to get people associated with them to live as well as work in the neighborhood. Perhaps in the years to come, according to some present-day thinking, this may be considered too large an investment of one's self and one's family but at the present time our experience with apartments seems to be successful.

I am sure that living in the neighborhood as a voting member of the community can add an extra dimension to the job of understanding urban problems and politics, and leads to better appreciation of the many other nuances that characterize a slum. What happens from 12 midnight to 8 A.M. can teach us a good deal, as can weekends. Weekends, no matter how carefully we plan, can be exhausting, with countless emergencies of an unbelievable variety: arrests, robberies, broken plumbing, and unannounced out-of-town guests. I don't offer weekends on the job as the most attractive part of settlement residence!

It should be said, too, that living near one's job has certain practical advantages, especially for staff members who handle evening work, which is such a large part of the settlement job. Meetings for adult neighbors have to be adjusted to children, supper dishes, night work, and the myriad of family emergencies. They often start late in the evening and go on well beyond what is thought of as closing hour.

At the same time that there is a great deal of talk about having "indigenous" people on the staff, there has been this trend among social workers to live away from the neighborhoods in which they work. Yet of all forms of social work, group work and community organization are the least amenable to regimentation of hours and are best served by the social worker who can adapt somewhat to the life style of the neighborhood.

The continuous stream of visitors that come to Henry Street are an integral part of our work and have been so from the beginning. They come singly and in organized groups, and call for staff attention throughout the week. However, we never quite face the amount of work and planning it takes to do a good job of showing and interpreting. And this is one time when we wish we were in one big building instead of six locations!

What the visitor sees in our own buildings takes on more significance against the backdrop of the tenements. I often wished, before Vladeck Houses was built, that I could get visitors, who were looking at our gymnasium showers, for instance, to go across the street into one of the tenements and see the toilets in the halls and the washtubs in the kitchen that had also to serve as bathtubs. Today's visit across the street to Vladeck Houses would not carry the same social message, but the tenements down the street still would, and much of the Lower East Side still would, and other great portions of the city still would.

As with many social agencies, visitors come from all over the world and from all over the United States; but because of the visibility of much of their work, it seems to me that settlements have an extra share of visitors. We are a part of sociology courses and nursing courses. Visitors are sent by the Department of Health, Education and Welfare; the Department of Labor; the Department of State; and the United Nations. Whatever the source or reason, we feel that we must do as good a job as possible to make what they are seeing useful. They come for an afternoon, an evening, for dinner, for lunch, and for a few days or weeks, to study the work more intensively.

Because the settlement is open evenings and weekends the visiting may spread over seven days a week, even though we plan otherwise. When discussing visitors one day at lunch I happened to say that Christmas was the only day we hadn't been asked to show the settlement. I left to answer the telephone and a hopeful voice explained, long-distance, that he was going to be in New York over the holidays and could he come down on Christmas Day to see Henry Street!

X

The Board

Partnership has always seemed to me to be one of the best words in the English language. It connotes so many possibilities in human relationships, and I have thought of it as of necessity applying to the board, staff, and neighbors of a settlement.

I inherited an interested and interesting board when I came to Henry Street. Al Smith was serving on it at the time and I was grateful for that as it was the only thing that my largely Irish-Catholic neighbors in Philadelphia could see as a possible reason for my leaving them! At that time Al Smith was their idol. They had felt that I would be living among the dingy tenements they had seen when we had visited for a basketball game the year before. "The Slums" they called it, and to make Henry Street seem even less worthy we had beaten them at basketball. Before I left they made me promise that I would arrange to have them meet Al Smith. They would hire buses and come to Henry Street for the occasion. However, sadly enough, before the date was set Al Smith joined the very conservative Liberty League and I got word from University House not to mind, they didn't want to come.

The board built after the corporate separation of the settlement from the nursing service, in 1944, became an unusually active group, made up of people drawn from many different professions and backgrounds—as to my mind it should be.

Winslow Carlton, president of the board for many years, played a large part in building this group. He is a natural board builder! He knows how important it is and spares no pains in its accomplishment. Many other institutions besides Henry Street have benefited from this gift of his. Fortunately for us, from the beginning he took on Henry Street as a major concern and gave us his skill, understanding, and time so generously that he personified the word "partnership."

While the board of a voluntary agency must be able to raise money in New York, where the Greater New York Fund raises such a small proportion of the budgets of the voluntary agencies, there are many other ways in which they should be able to serve as well, and this does not mean to deemphasize the responsibility for raising the budget. Another reason for choosing a board member with infinite care is that a board seldom wants to be in a position of terminating membership, no matter how obvious the reasons may become.

Boards are so often built without enough thought, that the fact does not seem to be faced that they carry the ultimate responsibility for the institution they are serving. They choose the director, and the kind of partnership that ensues is bound to determine not only the growth and development of the agency, but perhaps even its life. I feel that the executive should also play a responsible part in this process.

There have been so many board members who have contributed in many different ways to Henry Street's growth that I will only attempt to write of a few of them to illustrate what I mean when I say that a board should be made up of people able to bring a wide variety of experience and knowledge to bear on the work. There were many others, and my gratitude and apologies for my selectivity go to them when I say that without the kind of board we have had it would not be Henry Street.

First, however, I could not speak of a settlement board without paying tribute to the late Benjamin West Frazier, president of the board of University House in Philadelphia, who exemplified this particular kind of creative partnership over the many years of his generous service to University House and its neighborhood. Let me say here, also, that it is wise to have strong representation on your board in "Chest" cities, too, if you are to get a fair share of the "Chest" pie! This is not just automatic, and, very importantly, new programs have generally had to be started with special funds raised outside the "Chest." Certainly this was my experience in Philadelphia when we opened a branch house in another neighborhood.

Newbold Morris, the first president of our Henry Street board after our reorganization, was City Council President under La Guardia, and then Parks Commissioner. He brought his knowledge of New York to us and his especially warm friendliness to our neighbors. I remember his making a speech at some occasion from a platform in front of one of our buildings and when he finished I saw some of the mothers surround him, shaking their fingers at him. Later he told me that they were asking him to go back and say something good about President Roosevelt, which he promptly did. Newbold did not know that his last illness would be fatal and as he was no longer Parks Commissioner he had planned to make Henry Street his chief interest when he got out of the hospital.

The first Vice-President of Bankers Trust, B. A. Tompkins, took on the very complicated financial business of our reorganization and separation from the nursing service and handled the settlement's portfolio for over twenty years.

Benjamin Schoenfein, another banker, and one of our best fund-raisers, had grown up in the neighborhood and brought an understanding of what a settlement could mean to a child, and had a great gift for interpreting this to possible contributors.

Lawyers seem to me to be very generous in their services to social causes; and Nicholas Kelley, representing one of the oldest legal firms in New York, had lived at Hull House as a young man and was the son of Florence Kelley, the first executive and the real builder of the National Consumers League. He handled those fine things called bequests for us! This source of support has some of the elements of a fairy godmother, coming sometimes from such unexpected sources, and, of course, sometimes the other way 'round!

Fairfield Dana, a lawyer, and president of the board at this writing, brings not only legal talent and devotion, but great clarity of thought and understanding to our problems.

Mrs. Winslow Carlton for years has turned her unusual executive skills to our fund-raising, after Mrs. Joseph Lillienthal's many years of service in this part of our work. Mrs. Carlton was the originator of our Fiftieth Anniversary Armory Show, bringing together again many of the works of art exhibited in the First Armory Show in 1913, where its "moderns" caused such a furor in art circles. This proved to be the most glamorous and financially rewarding of all Henry Street's efforts in this difficult direction. A long line of stalwart ladies have contributed toward the onerous job of fund-raising. Mrs. Arnold Askin for many years has made a thrift shop operation produce; Mrs. Robert Potter and Mrs. Edward Murrow are experts in theater benefits, and in the many other forms of involving the public in our support.

I have sometimes noticed a tendency on the part of some social workers to feel that they should be above the battle when it comes to fund-raising. This, it seems to me, is wishful thinking and avoids the job of interpreting their work and the problems they are trying to meet. While the board of a social agency is ultimately responsible, the director of any voluntary agency must be at least a partner in the onerous job of getting the wherewithal to support the work that they, above all people, must believe in deeply. The support, which may come through public funds, doesn't fall off trees, either. Just filling out the forms and questionnaires required to get public money is an exercise in perspicacity and endurance, aside from the real job of interesting the beleagured public servant in even your most creative plans. You really have to feel that it is enormously worthwhile and exciting if you are to get anyone else to believe in it. There is no good in being objective about it. If you don't feel intensely about what you want to do, don't try to raise money for it!

These days a good deal of an agency's money comes to them for "special projects." By the time we get the grant the projects are apt to be a combination of what the people who conceive them want them to be, and the pattern they may have to fit into in order to get help from federal, city, or private foundation funds. Sometimes the combination is a reinforcement and improvement on the original plan, and sometimes a distortion. The time element, too, often plays too determining a part in the success of a project. That you must prove something in the time set by the pattern of the donors is not always best for the social workings of the project. And when you finish those "one, two, three years," where do you go? I have often wished that more foundations would decide to give not only to new projects but to put aside a good percentage of their funds for the support of the basic on-going budgets of the kind of agencies in which they are interested, using the rest for the experiments of limited duration.

Felix Warburg was president of our board when I came to Henry Street, and the Warburg family have continued their interest to the present time. Mrs. Frederick Warburg is now a very active member of our board. Mrs. Edward M. M. Warburg, the wife of another son of Felix Warburg, has helped in many generous ways, but never as much as when she suggested that her son, Stephen Currier and his wife Audrey, come to see Henry Street. Ralph Tefferteller and I took them around, and even on that first trip we realized their response and sensitivity to people. Stephen came on our board when we were having an especially hard time with our budget, and immediately helped in the planning of our fund-raising, as well as in giving generously. I found him incredibly understanding in the years we worked together. It was not only a comfort to talk to him about Henry Street's problems, but it was good to look forward with him as he planned to help in his many other causes. It is seldom that as much power for good falls into the hands of such gifted and generous young people as Stephen and Audrey Currier. The plane that took them to their deaths robbed us all so immeasurably that I have never quite believed it was true.

Arthur Harlow, who died while president of our board, was executive head of Group Health Insurance, and, with Winslow Carlton, who was its founder, we could always count on expert advice in the health field. In addition, Arthur Harlow had a very special quality of youth and of understanding which I counted on for many years. These qualities he brought to bear on all our undertakings and I always felt he could see problems before I got through explaining.

James Felt's help from his real estate firm got us land costs which proved a determining factor in getting Vladeck Houses built, long before he was chairman of the City Planning Commission or was on our board. Hyman Schroeder's wisdom stretches over everything we do, but he could also give us advice and help too in this his special field.

Mrs. Leon Keyserling, a distinguished economist in her own right, first visited Henry Street when she was teaching at Sarah Lawrence. Her father, Louis Dublin, had been an old friend of Miss Wald's. I was so taken with her charm and intelligence that I did my best to pry her loose from Sarah Lawrence and get her to work for us at Henry Street. I did not succeed, but she did do volunteer teaching in our Workers Education project for two years, and I still remember a fine bill for national health insurance that her neighborhood group produced at that time! Fortunately for me, the years have brought us together often and I think of Leon and Mary Keyserling as my Washington family. It has been stimulating and fun to share the turn of events with two such brilliant and concerned people.

Governor and Mrs. Lehman have taken an active part in the Henry Street story, starting with Herbert Lehman's early association to their building of Pete's House, and their long service on our board, on which Mrs. Lehman has continued to serve since Herbert Lehman's death. Their wisdom and experience, as well as their generosity, have played an important part in our development. Their being associated with Henry Street served a double purpose in that the neighborhood knew and respected Governor Lehman for his long service as Governor of New York. I remember also their admiration for his courage in attacking Senator Joseph McCarthy from the floor of the Senate at a time when few people dared to lift their voices against him.

Jacob Markowitz, now a State Supreme Court judge, William Calise and Samuel Schneeweiss, now chairman of our Executive Committee, are lawyers and all grew up in the neighborhood. They have been able to bring a special kind of firsthand knowledge of the community that has been invaluable. Bill Calise and Jack Markowitz played an important part in Democratic politics for many years, and I could count on a behind-the-scenes account of what was happening which added greatly to my own awareness of the forces at play in the neighborhood.

One of the many ways we got the neighborhood viewpoint was through a very active Adult Council made up of elected representatives from all the adult clubs. They brought their thinking to bear not only on Henry Street programs but on the social causes they thought we should all press for, and they represented Henry Street at hearings and city wide meetings. Mrs. Betty Trager, the president of our Adult Council for a number of years, exerted a great deal of very spirited leadership, as did many different women through their work in the clubs throughout the years. As the neighborhood changed they did their best to draw the new neighbors into the settlement. Mrs. Betty Trager, Mrs. Matty Silber, and Mrs. Lillie Schierer, for instance, started a club aimed at accomplishing this, called the "Community Club," which drew in members from among Puerto Rican, Negro, and Jewish women. They stressed special causes along with social activities. During this changing period after the war, we were fortunate in having a very competent staff member at the head of our adult club work, Ora Dorsey, who was black and handled both the older clubs and our new members with equal skill. However, it was a difficult time for this work, for so much of the old leadership was moving out of the neighborhood and the new neighbors were just getting their footing in a strange setting. At the present time a somewhat comparable group to our Adult Council is being formed at Henry Street of which two elected members are to serve as members of the main board.

There has been a great deal said, and some things done, in relation to having the beneficiaries of an agency serve on the policy-making board. "Maximum feasible participation" (a term describing this, stemming from the Office of Economic Opportunity), is a valid objective in this connection. The term is vague enough to be interpreted in various ways, some of them emphasizing "maximum" and others "feasible." However, in spite of mistakes and impracticality, efforts to put this concept into action have brought a wider neighborhood participation in decision-making that has often proved healthy. However, "feasible" has to be stressed when a voluntary agency is responsible for raising its budget.

While the "community action" programs were supported through the Office of Economic Opportunity by public funds, knowing something about fund-raising was not an essential for board membership; however some knowledge as to how to spend it, and how to choose staff, were needed as some of the anti-poverty corporations in New York have painfully illustrated. While it should be part of it, firsthand experience in living in poverty alone is not necessarily preparation enough to accomplish the complicated job of building neighborhood services. The task needs a combination of skills and experience, otherwise, in order to conform to some current thinking, we belittle the importance of the job to be done.

As far as the settlements and other community agencies are concerned, it should be as a partnership that neighbors, board members, club members, parent groups, teen-agers, and our own staff members help build the programs to fit the needs we are attempting to meet. The intimate association that should be inherent in the settlement setup can be the best base I know of for understanding. And this close-up experience can mean a great deal to our board members. They can, and do, use this insight effectively in the wider community. This might well be considered one of the most valuable of the settlement's contributions to the wider community.

XI

The Staff

The staff in a settlement are not only drawn from social work but from a wide range of skilled people whom we hope will be able to bring different kinds of enrichment to the poverty of our environment. Above all, those responsible for the program should be sensitive to the forward reach of the people of all ages around them and make sure that it is being met more than halfway.

Fortunately, in 1946, the year after the war, Ralph and Ruth Tefferteller came to work for us at Henry Street, and for the next twenty-one years played a major role in the settlement's development. Ralph Tefferteller had just been demobilized after nearly five years' service in the Army. He came as associate director, and his wife, Ruth, took on the children's work, and later was program director, as well as a kind of general assistant to both Ralph and me.

Ralph Tefferteller had grown up on his father's large farm in Tennessee near the TVA, and after college he had graduated from Union Theological Seminary in New York City. Ruth had come from Albany and had been trained for teaching. They had met, years before their marriage, as volunteers at Madison House, a settlement on the Lower East Side, while Ralph was a seminary student and Ruth a teen-ager. "Teffie," as Ralph was known to his friends, had helped organize textile workers in the South when on the staff of the Amalgamated Union before joining the Army.

Both he and Ruth had such a way with children and young people that it was not long before they were Mr. and Mrs. "T" all over the neighborhood. It was always a heartwarming experience to walk around the neighborhood with either of them and watch the faces of the children light up as they caught sight of them. Teffie brought a delightful skill in folk-dancing from his background in Tennessee, and Ruth's gifts in leading singing added to the gaiety of Henry Street's programs immeasurably.

Ruth Tefferteller directed our girls' camp for many years, and during these years it was called the "singing camp." As well as an extraordinarily creative mind, she had a joyous quality that held children enthralled and to which their parents responded as well. Whatever she did was touched with warmth and fun. Without giving up her responsibility for our camp, she took two winters off to get a degree at the Columbia University School of Social Work. Of all their varied gifts for working with people, I always felt the greatest was their warm, immediate response to each individual. As the years went on, we had a steady stream of young and old coming back from other parts of the city, from the Army, from institutions of one kind or another, even from prison looking for a welcome they knew they could count on. I used to feel that the word "neighbor" was meant to describe them.

You start whatever work you do where people are, but you must be sure that you are always on your way to excellence. Take children and teen-agers who come to your open doors with only the afternoon or evening in their hands. On the other side of the door must be activities geared to catch the interest of the infinite variety of young living in the neighborhood. Some just naturally know what they want when they hear about clubs, basketball, game rooms, boxing, music, dancing, dances, photography, pottery, and lots of so-forths. But there are those who try things and drop them, and the staff has to be very alert to these children and to their next interest. And then, there are those who run up and down stairs, in and out of the front door, in and out of club rooms, in and out of the games room, who might be called the recreation "drop-outs," those restless youngsters members of the staff know well and have to struggle hardest to catch and hold.

Luckily there are always success stories galore, and the following is just one of a recent try to catch the interest of this particular kind of restless child. It turned out to be called "Pete's House Productions," and it both educated and integrated at the same time. An especially restless group of teen-agers was discussing with Ruth Tefferteller how dreary summers were in the neighborhood, when the leader of a girl gang said, "Can't we have an acting club?" and then added brightly, "We might do Shakespeare!" These young people had never even seen live theater or been in a play and would not have dreamed of going to our theater to study seriously. Up to that time it had been impossible to sustain their interest in anything; so Mrs. "T" rejoiced at the suggestion, especially as she believed strongly in the power of the theater to develop individuals at any age.

Out of this grew a trial summer from which the idea of Pete's House Productions was born. We were able to borrow Joe Balfior from our Playhouse, where he had headed the Drama School for six years and been especially successful with teen-agers. So our Playhouse was brought into this informal effort at Pete's House. They chose the name because the rehearsals took place at Pete's House where they had always met.

Because of Joe Balfior's skill and patience it did not matter that no one showed up for the first rehearsal; he went after them! But that was not necessary for long. The project took hold, and the summer was so successful in keeping this particular group of black, white, and Puerto Rican youngsters together in a sustained activity that we decided to try it during the next winter, and it has continued as an important program at the settlement.

Pete's House Productions is a long story: Its success and glamour stimulated many younger girls and boys in the program at Pete's House to work hard to learn to dance and to sing so that they could join the group. An uptown committee helped raise special money for the work and brought exciting people down to see the shows and meet the cast. The whole project became "Arts for Living."

The value of such work as Pete's House Productions can be measured in so many ways: Young people behind in their school work began to take an interest in learning after their successful efforts in the shows. Young actors who could not be relied upon for rehearsals, finally came on time! "Loners" began to take pride in being part of a group. All good preparation for the working days ahead.

A twelve-year-old girl had been "sentenced" by a Children's Court judge to join a music program at Henry Street, and Pete's House Productions took her in! A young man appearing in the dream ballet of *Oklahoma*, stopped the show during a benefit attended by an audience of "uptowners" but he could not hear the applause because he was a deaf mute. A fifteen-year-old girl, recovering from a mental breakdown, finally found the strength for a hard role in a major show.

But we haven't yet tried Shakespeare! And in spite of our belief in the use of social themes and personal experiences in dramatics, it seemed wiser to start this group off at that particular moment with gay musicals that had been earlier Broadway hits in which the music and dancing would give them almost sure-fire success and lots of fun along with it.

XII

Personal Service

Helping with personal problems is so all-pervasive throughout a settlement that it cannot be separated from the regular day-by-day work of the whole staff. Each staff member is bound to be involved in, and to follow through, on some of the individual problems of those with whom they work—going to court with a teen-ager in trouble; arranging for an emergency loan to a club member; helping the drug addict trying to get into a hospital. These and many more such problems will often be taken care of by the workers whose relationship with the individual ties them to the problem. However, we have always had on our staff people experienced in what we term "personal service," and to whom the rest of the staff as well as the neighbors may turn for expert help.

We use the term "personal service" to differentiate it from long-term casework which we refer, when it is possible, to casework agencies, except when the problem has been one for our Mental Hygiene Clinic, which has been leaned upon by the staff in the handling of many different kinds of problems other than psychiatry.

It is not with our club members alone that we are concerned but with troubled people who come in off the street because the sign is out, access is easy, and perhaps our name is known. The main point, and our switchboard operators and receptionists are always on the alert, is that no person is turned away without an effort toward solving his or her problem, or by getting them to someone who can. We try to keep Henry Street from being a part of the unending rejection that dogs the footsteps of the poor. We call our Sunday switchboard operator the "Mother Superior" because her sense of responsibility is so all-encompassing! This is help that should be available to everyone living in our kind of neighborhood, for the first step in help may be the preventive one.

For many years Mrs. Marie Gebiner, who had come to us in the Civil Works Administration days carried the major part of our Personal Service with competence and devotion. "Gebbie," as she was known to all of us, was like the famous inscription on the U.S. Post Office—neither snow, nor rain, nor the gloom of night could keep her from her appointed rounds. It was typical that when she got word that her daughter was very ill in Washington she waited until a big adult party for which she was responsible was over at midnight, and then took her frail self off in the midst of a blizzard. I must add that she got thoroughly scolded when she got back for not letting us know.

When the Puerto Ricans first began to come into the neighborhood in numbers, we looked for Spanish-speaking staff; and they were hard to find in those early days. Two young men I had met in Puerto Rico who worked with the Community Services there, lived and worked with us for a winter. Later, José Villegas headed up our special project at La Guardia Houses where the proportion of Puerto Rican families was very high.

Mrs. Luz Bustamente came to us in 1954. She had started a school for social work in Bolivia and brought Spanish liveliness and warmth along with an indefatigable zest for solving problems. One of her specialities was doing away with welfare red tape for the hundreds of our most forlorn non-English-speaking neighbors. Another was getting the Puerto Rican children to our camps. The children were eager from their beginning in the neighborhood, but the mothers were afraid to have them go. They didn't know what it was all about. So, Mrs. Bustamente undertook to make it clear even if it took several visits to the family and a great deal of Spanish conversation. It was always a triumphant moment when she and the Puerto Rican mothers waved the buses off with their children, properly equipped with camp clothes by way of the "welfare" or our own emergency stores. It took a number of summers but today it is the mothers themselves who come to get their children on the camp lists. Mrs. Bustamente's methods were not always classical, in spite of her background, but comforting, ingenious, and successful.

In mentioning some of the typical functions of the settlement and a few of the people who have had responsibility for them, last, but anything but least from the standpoint of the director and the board, is Leona Gold, our assistant treasurer. She has the rare capacity of being friendly and patient with people, and brilliant with figures. Any of us just have to murmur "I wonder if we could afford that?" and Leona has the answer sitting in front of us! And when it is no, she can make the answer reasonable and even palatable.

For seven years we had a woman resident who was a lawyer and a full-time volunteer. We missed the luxury of this when Victoria Foster had to retire. So many problems our neighbors face are, at least partially, legal in character. We often call on those members of the board who are lawyers to volunteer to tackle neighbors' problems along with all the other legal work they do for the settlement.

It was our awareness of the continual need for legal services in the lives of the poor, other than those that could be met by the Legal Aid Society, which made us include legal service in our first plans for Mobilization for Youth. And this as it was developed turned out to be one of the most valuable contributions coming out of Mobilization.

In club-leading, as in the other aspects of our work, many of our neighbors have given valuable service. They have served both as paid staff and as volunteers. With the exception of Maria Kron, our whole staff in the Home Planning Workshops and the Good Companions program (for the neighbors over 60) has been drawn from the community. This has always been a part of settlement practice. Local workers on the staff are often referred to these days as "indigenous" or "para-professional" and a greater emphasis has been placed on training, and giving them responsible roles. This is an important development, for as our services to poor neighborhoods begin to come a little nearer to meeting the need—only a little nearer, as yet—through such organizations as Mobilization for Youth, and all the various manifestations of Anti-Poverty programs, or their successors we must draw on man-and-woman-power that professional social work cannot supply.

A number of interesting training experiments are now going on. It is not always easy to work out training programs because the workers start with such varied experiences and different educational backgrounds, but this can, at the same time, be one of the things that makes the neighborhood workers so valuable. Training on the job will probably continue to be one of the most practical ways of developing skills among untrained neighborhood workers, as field work became, long ago, in the training for professional social work.

XIII

Young Neighbors

A while ago, Bert Beck and I stood looking at what was left of the tenement next door to Henry Street's three lovely old houses where I had lived so long. It still made me angry to look at this piece of folly, for the tenement was one of a number pulled down to make way for a highway for trucks to come off South Street and pass by two low-income housing projects, an elementary school, and two middle-income developments! Many years before, James Felt and I had tried to persuade the city engineers to stop this plan. We even had a local expert in the field develop practical plans for other routes. The answer at the time was that this had been "on the map for twenty years," and I was assured that they would not touch our Playhouse. I couldn't seem to make them understand that I already knew this and that it was the children in the projects and the schools, having to cross that broad street, that were our concern. Anyway, to make a long, aggravating story short, we failed, and the trucks won! The widening does leave our own Henry Street buildings with more light and air, and even a little park, but it reminds me too much of a small boy who was killed and others injured at our nearby crossings and all our mother's protests at the time.

And those tenement steps reminded me very sharply, too, of the children and their families I had known and worried with throughout the years. The ground-floor window that was still left had framed an old woman's face whom I had always waved to as I went by, but who was completely silent until one day during war-rationing she had beckoned to me from the stoop to ask me if she had to go back to public school to get her sugar; and if so, would I get it for her!

It was a miserable, old-law tenement with the toilets still in the halls. One of these toilets had been used by a clean-cut, good-. looking teen-age boy who had gathered together the "works" needed for mainlining heroin and was letting other boys in the neighborhood use them at so much per. He wasn't even an addict, just making money! The toilet happened to be next to the bedroom of another boy's room. He could hear the business going on so plainly through the thin partition, that he realized where the "works" were hidden. He had studied photography in our class at Pete's House so he went in and photographed the equipment of syringe, needles, and bottle cap for mixing the heroin, and took his photographs to Ralph Tefferteller, who took the situation over from there on.

A big Italian family lived in one of the lower floor flats when I first came, and the father beat his children so unmercifully that we had to get the police to stop him. In spite of this, when he moved away he wanted us to buy his big, flourishing fig tree growing in the tenement back yard—which we did, and he moved it into our yard for us. But in spite of his endless instructions, it missed his skillful fingers—so gentle with plants, so cruel with children.

Two of the families we knew best had little girls who ran in and out of our lobby as a part of their own homes, and our receptionist, Agnes Marshall, was their unofficial leader and adviser, as she has been to so many children. But Janis, aged seven, a Negro, and Blanca, aged six, a Puerto Rican, were close to us all, as well as to Mrs. Marshall. Janis' special love was our camp, and she seemed to exist from year to year to get there. One Christmas season when I took a little group into St. Patrick's Cathedral on our way to the Christmas tree at Rockefeller Center, and as the children stood gazing I whispered, "Isn't it beautiful?" "Oh, *beautiful*," said Janis. "It's just like our church at Echo Hill." Her love for camp had even clothed in glory the little Protestant church where we took her on Sundays. She came back from Harlem years later to be married in St. Augustine's, the little Episcopal chapel across from us on Henry Street.

Blanca represents the most heart-breaking memory of that tenement. She was a gay, beguiling little girl in a family of four boys (who are a story in themselves), all of whom adored her, as we did. One Sunday her mother took the children to Coney Island to spend the day. They were on the crowded beach when Blanca ran off for a few minutes, never to come back. The family and the police searched all the rest of the day but could not find her. The ugly story finally came out after Blanca's little body in its red bathing suit was found floating in the ocean. A man had gotten her into his nearby old car, attacked her, and thrown her little body into the sea. The shock was so great that the family seemed to disintegrate from that time on, and work as we did, we were not able to stop two of the teen-age boys from constant drinking.

A beautiful little Puerto Rican girl of ten and her younger brother who lived in this tenement spent much of their time in our pottery next door. It became home to both children, and we were family. To our dismay, their mother spirited them away in the middle of the night, without allowing them even a good-bye, and we were never able to find them again. "She's gone with a man," was all any of the neighbors could say.

Another little four-year-old disappeared from our sight in the same way. She and her mother, who had married a gypsy and had left him, lived in the basement. When I visited them at Christmas time a big tree was practically all there was in the little room. After much effort we succeeded in getting her mother to allow Marty to come to our nursery school. She wouldn't bring her, but because Marty loved it so, she was called for each day. When she wasn't in nursery school she stood at our entrance waiting to greet us as we came and went, holding tightly to a big pocketbook of which she was very proud. One day she and her mother vanished—maybe with the gypsies; but we could never find out where Marty had gone.

One of the most senseless tragedies in this tenement occurred when the supposedly obligatory electric light in the dark hall had gone out. Tomaso was running downstairs fast, as children do, and fell over something left on the stairs which he couldn't see, breaking his neck and dying almost instantly. We still have a little bas relief in our pottery made by Tomaso. It was made in answer to some mean things being said one afternoon about Puerto Ricans. The teacher was out of the room for a moment, and as she came back she heard enough to bring the meaness home to the boys so understandingly that they tried all the rest of the afternoon in awkward little ways to reach out to Tomaso. His answer was to make the little bas relief with his cabin "home," his father "going to work," and a big sun shining down on them, which he showed the boys and told them it was "my home in Puerto Rico."

I didn't need the tenements in New York to show me that poverty and all its concomitants bore down hardest on children. The children in the little houses in Philadelphia had already taught me that.

Drinking was the overriding, never-ending problem in my Philadelphia neighborhood in those days, with all its tie-up with police and politicians and organized crime. I lived through Prohibition and its aftermath there. I could look out my window at night and see the women, shawls over their heads, trying to lure or force their sons or husbands away from the drinking gangs on our corners. During the Depression days, one woman put it: "Even if we don't have anything to eat in the house, he can always get his whiskey." When things got too violent at home, little girls would come running over to get our help. "Me father's beating me mother. Come quick!" was a plea we heard as a child stood breathless on our doorstep.

But it was not only the children who came for help, as the story of Mrs. Finneran illustrates.

"You'll just have to come over and help me. He just threw the breadboard at me and I'm afraid to go back." Mrs. Finneran sank down helplessly in the office. Her straight black hair was pulled back tight from her face in a little knot on the back of her neck, and her black eyes were pools of worry and distress. "He made Tommy go for more drink for him last night and you know how bad that is for a twelve-year old boy. He brought it upstairs to his father and his father just lay there in bed and drank. I said, 'Tommy, you have no right to get it for your father,' and Tommy answered me back, 'Well, a man's got to have some pleasure.'

You see the father's got Tommy ruined already. He's mulish like
the father anyway, and he hears the ugly things he calls me and
of course that makes him saucy with me. You know it ain't the
throwing things at me that I mind, it's his ugly words. They beat
on my ears so I think I'm going crazy." Mrs. Finneran illustrated
this with a nervous gesture of her hands to her ears and her
eyes were for a moment haunted by the things she remembered.

"Well, I got to get back because I can't leave Mary over there
by herself. She's only eleven even if she does seem to take care
of us all. I don't believe Lilly and Edna are going to be the same
as Mary; they aren't so serious, but of course they are kind of
little to be serious. Lilly's only six and Edna only four."

As we walked along toward the Finneran house, I wondered
vaguely if Mr. Finneran had another breadboard handy, but
knowing the general incompleteness of the house furnishings, I
presumed he had used up all the ammunition of this variety. Mrs.
Finneran went ahead and up the narrow stairs, announcing as she
went, "Well, I've brought Miss Hall." Mr. Finneran, a huge, dark
man, met us at the top of the stairs with razor in hand. I was glad
to be able to associate the razor quickly with the lather on his
face, and to hear a very polite and pleasant voice say, "Come
right up, Miss Hall. Of course the house don't look fit to receive
you for she is too bad a housekeeper, but you are always
welcome."

"You see," he began amiably, as he wiped off a chair for me
with a sweeping gesture, "you see, I was brought up to better
things." Mrs. Finneran's ire rose at this, and I quickly intervened,
before the situation got beyond the chance of an amicable settlement. Mrs. Finneran had warned me that her husband had a way
with him and that she was at some pains to convince anyone of
her need of protection after Mr. Finneran had talked to them.

As Mr. Finneran's graciousness increased with his ease, I began
to see what Mrs. Finneran meant, and perhaps the only reason
I was not impressed was the memory of little Mary's sober sen-
tences at one time to me on the subject of her father. That, and
Mrs. Finneran's hunted look.

And when I thought of Tommy and the things he learned from
his father, my heart grew hard toward the gentleman who was
assuring me that I above all people would understand a man who
wanted a well-kept home.

It was not fathers alone whom children had to worry about,
it was mothers, too, as young John Martin and Mrs. Doolin and

her children show us. Fortunately they were in the minority in the neighborhood, for as frightening and disrupting as the father's drunkenness was, when the mother drank it really took the props out from under the children.

There was a terrible crash, and then another, and then another. And I ran upstairs thinking to myself, "It's John Martin again. We just can't stand it any longer."

Sure enough it was. This time, among other things, he had been putting hockey sticks into the piano. John was a tall, lanky boy of seventeen, unkempt and dirty, but with that undefinable something that made other boys follow him into devilment. This evening the hockey sticks took the shape of the last straw, and I decided that John was doing no good to himself or to the house by remaining in it. But first I decided to have one last try. Painting his past behavior in no uncertain terms, I asked what he would do in my place. "Well," he said, "it would be all right if I had a nice quiet place to read, but there's just too much going on around here for me." This seemed to be a bit unjust, as he had generally been the center of the vortex, but I replied by asking him what he would like to read. "*Popular Mechanics*," he said promptly. "Very well," I said, "you can come back to-morrow night and read."

Popular Mechanics was purchased for John and I pressed it upon him with some firmness when he came, not expecting any results after the first five minutes. He fooled me though, by spending the entire evening bent double in the corner of one of the rooms. At the end of the evening he returned the book, saying that that was the way he liked to spend an evening. The next evening there were more books, and so we went on, as a completely new relationship sprang up between John and our house.

A short while after the reading had been instituted he asked me to come and help him with his mother. As I came in, he began at once: "I wish there was something you could do about it. I have hid her eyeglasses so she can't see to go out, but I can't keep her from getting that stuff." The mother, who was a very pious and proper-looking old woman, was sitting up begging querulously to be allowed to go out and get herself a little something to make her feel better. It was obvious she had had enough to make her feel something, and that she was getting beyond John's control. While we were planning with him, he said bitterly, "There was never a time in my life I can remember that my mother or father ain't been like this."

As erratic and unprepossessing as John was, he always managed to work. One day while on a job he fell out of a third-story
window, breaking his hip. All things considered, we felt books
were the thing to take him when we went to the hospital, but we
found that the thing he liked best was flowers!

Finally John married and after struggling in vain to combine
wife and mother, he gave it up, and a married daughter undertook the burden.

He lived in another part of the city, but quite often he came
back to see "how the old place goes" and to see one whom I am
proud to say he describes as "the best woman I ever bumped
against." When I heard him say it, I blessed *Popular Mechanics*
and the unlikely but successful last try to get along with John.

Before coming to get our help the children had hidden their
mother's shoes to keep her from going out to get another drink.
Our doctor and I tried to persuade Mrs. Doolin to go to sleep and
not worry the children by going out again. She did get up that
night and all the next day she locked herself and three little
children and an older daughter in the house and wouldn't answer
our knocks. Finally the oldest girl came over again for help. This
time we took a bottle of milk, thinking what a pallid substitute
it would seem to Mrs. Doolin, but knowing that she must have
something strengthening at the end of a week's drunk. We heated
the milk, persuading and talking the while, the oldest daughter—
who was sixteen—helping us while tears were running down her
cheeks, the other children patting their mother. "Please take it.
It will do you good," they said. They all adored her and looked
upon the drinking lapses as something sad and inevitable, and
not in any way her fault, and nothing she was to be blamed for.

She was a thin, little gray-haired wisp whose husband had
deserted her years before, and who had brought the children to
a day nursery at seven each morning and herself to the mill by
seven-thirty, and who cleaned offices on Saturday afternoons to
make a little extra money. Their house was clean and cozy in
spite of everything, and she was never mean to them.

That night we finally got her upstairs to bed and rubbed her
head until she went to sleep. The three youngest children were
sitting up in the bed next to their mother, their little faces
anxious and white in the flickering light of one gas jet. Margaret,
the oldest, tiptoeing and breathless, was anxious as to whether we
would be able to get their mother to sleep. They felt that if she

could just get a night's rest without another drink and after good warm milk she wouldn't drink when she woke up in the morning. This time it was true.

After she came out of this last bout, we went downtown shopping with her, the settlement lending her money for a new stove. The excitement of a new stove and more fixing up in her kitchen occupied her mind over the first bad period. After about two years of success, Mrs. Doolin came over to see me and was told I was busy. "That don't make no difference," she said, "you just tell her it is Mrs. Doolin." As she explained to me, "Those young people tried to keep me away from you, but I knew you wouldn't like that, so I just come along up. There's been one thing I been wanting to tell you a long time, and that is that I don't even like the taste of the stuff now. I thought it would make you kind of comfortable to know it." It certainly did.

The thing that stands out in these children's lives is how helpless children are in city slums, or maybe in country slums, not only in tenements but equally in small houses. Anywhere that poverty degrades a neighborhood and surrounds its children with misery, we are mortgaging our future as a country. It is not only cruel but stupid.

XIV

Health or Lack of It

Since health, or I should say the lack of it, is the heaviest burden the poor must bear, with the exception of unemployment, Henry Street has been continuously involved with different aspects of health care. Lillian Wald's achievement in starting the Visiting Nurse Service was the settlement's most important contribution in the health field. Next, perhaps, of broadest significance, was the school nurse. Miss Wald raised the money for the first school nurse, and the experiment was so successful that the New York City Board of Education took over the plan at the end of the first year.

We have continued to experiment, believing that our responsibilities in the health field have had three dimensions: what we could offer in actual services at Henry Street; what we could do in the neighborhood, such as our fight to get a decent city hospital in the place of Gouverneur; and how we could affect the national picture. The two latter I have handled in separate chapters. What we attempted at any given time was stimulated by what we saw around us and when it came to sickness and the misery it caused, we didn't have to look far.

The services we offer in most fields we hope will point the way to helping solve what may appear to be a serious and continuing problem. For ten years, for example, in the late thirties and early forties, the settlement, in a demonstration project, gave a health examination to each member of the children's program, and a nurse and social workers followed through with the families in carrying out the recommendations of our doctors. One study of this work showed that out of 1,040 children we had examined, there were only fifteen who did not need treatment of some kind, from tonsils, to eyes, to heart murmur. During this period, health examinations in the schools began to improve enough so that when we took our final results to the school health authorities they decided that we no longer needed to continue our work in this area.

I was a little skeptical then, and I still feel strongly that public schools are not making the most of their great opportunity to insure as far as possible, by early detection and treatment, the health of every child who comes through their doors. It is one of the great preventive opportunities in the city but we handle it so meagerly.

We have tried to put our attention, which also means our dollars, where it will do the most good at a particular time, so as the school health authorities were so hopeful at that time, we did not continue this work. Instead we turned our attention to what could be done about bringing some of the benefits of psychiatry to the poor. Twenty-five years ago psychiatry was not reaching down into neighborhoods such as ours, much as our neighbors needed it. Emotional instability is hard to handle, rich or poor, but almost impossible when compounded by the pressures of extreme poverty. Over the years our accumulated evidence and two studies made within two years of each other, had shown us that the number of disturbed children in our groups was increasing steadily.

I have always felt that a little eight-year-old girl named Janet helped start our Mental Hygiene Clinic. The child became so violent and unmanageable in our club program that we knew we must find some help for her quickly. The best we could do at that time was to get an appointment for her six months ahead at a psychiatric clinic in a hospital far uptown. It was at this point that we raised enough money to employ a psychiatric caseworker and a part-time psychiatrist.

I had been fortunate in having Mrs. Evelyn Hamilton's volunteer help in starting our nursery school at University House in Philadelphia. She had run our school there for its first year and continued to supervise it. She also gave generous financial support for this work, and later at Henry Street when she came to New York. She had been trained as a nursery school teacher and as a psychiatric caseworker as well, so we became the beneficiary, first of her help in getting our nursery school going at Henry Street, and later in the organization of our mental health work. Evelyn Hamilton supervised the nursery school at Henry Street for a number of years, and during this time had given advice to the mothers of the nursery school children when they needed special help. So we had an experienced and skilled person to help us as we worked out our plans to build further psychiatric care into our program.

We did not start out with the idea of establishing a mental hygiene clinic. Basically we wanted to find more ways in which the concepts of psychiatry could effectively reach the poor. In the process we did develop a neighborhood psychiatric clinic. When we started in 1941, Henry Street carried the full support for this work, but for many years the City Community Mental Health Board matched our expenditures. Our clinic is in the Community Center which we sponsor at La Guardia Houses. It is from this vantage point that we have continued to look for new ways in which psychiatry can best serve a neighborhood such as ours. There have been many innovations over the years. When Rachel Levine took over the directorship from Annelise Thieman in 1961, her first move was to do away with the waiting list. A waiting list in psychiatry really goes against nature, for one of the most characteristic things about an emotional crisis is the immediacy of its need. This also is the time of greatest client motivation. We saw people at once and determined with them what help was needed to cope with their problems.

In a clinic such as ours, one of the main problems is to find ways to reach the parents of our most difficult and troubled children. To many of them a weekly appointment at "3 o'clock on Tuesday" is an insurmountable obstacle.

We found this particularly true of the families who were part of a thee-year demonstration in cooperation with the Board of Education in which we cooperated with local public schools. We took eight seven-year-old boys whom the schools could not manage in the classroom, and yet who did not seem disturbed enough to be institutionalized. We provided a classroom in our clinic along with psychiatric care, and the school provided a teacher. The result of this experiment showed enough improvement in six of the eight children to warrant sending them back to school; only one had to be institutionalized, and one returned to Puerto Rico. However, it was felt that one of the determining factors in our success was the method of treatment in the home that Miss Levine devised with this group and continued to develop as a method of treatment with other families when it was indicated. Many parents are overburdened, uneducated, some non-English speaking, and frightened. When the caseworker comes to the home the burden of making herself or himself welcome falls on the skilled person instead of on the mother when she has to come to the caseworker's office. It is not always easy even for social workers to make themselves welcome to a whole family at once, but some of the results have been amazingly successful, especially in getting help through to families who have been thought unreachable.

The pattern, borrowed from psychiatry, had too often been of closing a case when the "mother was uncooperative." Over the years, before "reaching-out" came back into social work, we had seen children in the neighborhood whose cases had been marked "closed" left alone to handle the most difficult parents and the worst situations.

I need hardly say that no method works all the time, but if anything can make us more successful with our most vulnerable children, then it is worth seeking new ways of treatment. We have only to remind ourselves that worry, exasperation, and fatigue generally make for short tempers which so often result in cruelty to the child within reach of a strap.

Henry, a Puerto Rican child, aged seven and a half when he came to our clinic class, was typical of the eight children who were too difficult for the school to keep and so were at that time condemned to wander the streets. He was one of five children in a home without a father. Henry's mother, who spoke little English and was unfamiliar with American ways, was completely overwhelmed by the burdens of raising her family without a man's help. Although she was on "welfare," she did not know how to get all the assistance that was available for her there. She beat her children cruelly and neglected them. One boy, age ten, was in a state mental hospital; another son, age nine, was awaiting admission to Bellevue's psychiatric ward; the oldest boy, eighteen, had been arrested on two occasions; the youngest, five, did not speak. Henry himself was not mentally retarded but could not read at all. He was moody and completely unable to cope with the discipline of a regular classroom. The special class in the clinic turned out to be a haven for Henry. Here he kept all his valued possessions that he feared would be destroyed at home. It did take him months, but in time he began to trust his teacher and his therapist, and then he started to learn. At the same time, the clinic worked with Henry's mother, showing her by doing it with her how she could better organize her home and get the assistance that was due her from "welfare." The worker also demonstrates how the children's need for attention can be satisfied without recourse to violence.

After three years Henry was ready to go back to public school where, as extraordinary as it seemed, knowing his beginning, he was able to adjust to the pressures of a normal classroom. Of course we continued to work with the family, so he could count on help from his friends at the clinic.

This three-year experiment was expensive, but very inexpensive if you measure it against the cost of maintaining a child in a mental institution, possibly for life, where these children might well have gone if this experiment had not taken them off the streets. It changed their families' attitudes toward them, and gradually worked the change that made it possible for them to return to school, holding their own and not disrupting their class. I, myself, had watched and listened to the wild screaming that sometimes took place at a moment's notice, and then seen the gradual orderly learning that very slowly began to take place in the classroom in the clinic. Fortunately the schools, as their part of the experiment, contributed a teacher Nellie Jones, of unusual capacity and understanding, who worked closely with our social workers and psychiatrists.

Even though this school demonstration program was eminently successful, and this is probably the hardest thing to bear in all our work, deeply disturbed children who are too young for

New York City's "600" schools, are, at present writing, still being suspended from school every year, with no place to go but to the streets, or to an institution unless the school was able to provide some of its limited home instruction. Again it is money versus social disruption and misery, and our failure to make our experiences tell in the way they should.

In our Henry Street clinic, treatment of children of all ages and of adults has not only centered around the home, but around participation in other settlement programs. We treat more of the under-eighteen's than we do adults—in 1967, 446 of the 733 patients served were the younger ones—and that is good. The earlier in life the better if adjustment is to be achieved.

To describe how our clinic methods evolved, Rachel Levine published three articles entitled: "Treatment in the Home," "A Short Story on the Long Waiting List," and "Stand-Patism Versus Change in Psychiatric Clinic Practise," which have proved valuable in the field, judging by the many requests we have had for these pamphlets. "Treatment in the Home" was translated into Spanish, and was the first article in a new publication, *Selecciones del Social Work*, published by Editorial Humanitas, Buenos Aires, Argentina.

In an annual report Miss Levine writes:

> The never-ending search to bring psychiatric help to our families in ways other than the orthodox resulted in the establishment of the key principle . . . help must be useful to the person needing it. To accomplish this as a working principle, the clinic not only developed a range and variety of methods of giving service from brief, intermittent, crisis intervention, short-term to long-term therapy, working with the individual, or with patients in a group, or with the family as a unit, to be provided in the home as well as in the clinic, but also utilized, as part of the treatment plan, the other settlement programs such as the performing arts, the music school, arts and crafts, home planning workshops, nursery school, summer camp and others.

XV

The Playhouse

While a theater such as ours seldom grows out of a settlement's work, some kind of stage soon works its way into whatever building, small or large, a settlement or community center comes to use. For dramatics and its fellow arts of music and dance are an essential part of any creative program.

Miss Wald had been fortunate in having three young girls come to work with her as she expanded her work. Alice and Irene Lewisohn and Rita Wallach Morganthau, who came as volunteers in 1904, were very young, very spirited, and gifted in the arts, and Miss Wald encouraged them in their enthusiasms as they took a salient part in developing the arts in Henry Street's program.

They started in the usual neighborhood way with the children who knocked on the settlement's doors with only a child's natural hunger for adventure and opportunities beyond the tenements and the street. A settlement or any community work should grow in answer to that knock.

As the Lewisohn sisters began their informal teaching of dance and drama to the children's groups, they found such response that they themselves grew in enthusiasm and creativity so that it is not such a long story to the building of our lovely Little Playhouse in 1915.

The story of the next twelve years has been told in Alice

Lewisohn Crowley's book, *The Neighborhood Playhouse*,* published in 1959. Suffice to say that the neighborhood Playhouse as the Lewisohns developed it became one of the most important of the little theaters in the United States. Their distinguished and original productions brought uptown audiences down to our neighborhood to appreciate and savor the very special quality of theater that was being produced there. In 1927, after twelve years of contributions to experimental theater, Irene Lewisohn and Rita Morganthau decided to start a school of dance and drama uptown, which would crystalize what they had learned through their work at the Playhouse. This became the Neighborhood Playhouse School of the Theater.

By the time I came to Henry Street, the Playhouse was again a part of the settlement's programming. A group of players who had studied there and formed a dramatic group, somewhat as an unprofessional repertory company, were producing excellent plays, and there were drama and dance classes for both children and adults. However, the Playhouse program was not, it seemed to me, as close to the neighborhood or as experimental as it perhaps could be.

There were a number of changes in directors in those years. A group of three very creative eager young people, Chouteau Dyer, Betty Lord, and Marshall Brooks, started some interesting work along the lines of the Living Newspaper, initiated by the controversial Federal Theater Project of the WPA. This is an ideal medium for teaching in our kind of setting, as it involves the discussion of topics of immediate social concern to the neighborhood, along with dramatization and writing to make effective the ideas evolved and decided upon by the group. A large number of teen-agers were the first to be involved in producing our Living Newspaper type of show.

In May of 1939, the three young directors tackled a very sore subject: the kind of medical services our neighbors were getting or not getting. The play was called *Medicine Show*, and was composed and performed by members of the settlement with great emotional urge and gusto. In one scene, a woman played the part of herself trying to get the accident ward of Gouverneur

* Theater Arts Books, New York.

Hospital to take a bone out of her throat. The audience almost choked with her and certainly agreed with her about the accident ward. The play itself was used widely elsewhere, as propaganda of a diverting kind.

I have to say that this kind of drama needs very knowledgable direction, for the many ideas and scenes written by members often have to be drawn together into a well-knit whole.

When, to my great disappointment, our three young directors had to leave us in 1940, we were fortunate in having the late Helen Schoeni accept the leadership at the Playhouse. In 1941, she undertook another Living Newspaper called *Dutchman's Farm*, based on our studies of that name. Focused on our need for housing, it told the history of housing on the Lower East Side, starting with the Indians and ending up with Vladeck Houses, which had just opened. The performance was so all-encompassing that it seemed to have everyone in the settlement involved in its production.

A tense moment came in rehearsing *Dutchman's Farm*, when one of the scenes written by a group of women about their own experience as testifiers in Washington was finally pronounced technically too difficult to put on. The dramatic director looked to me to discuss its omission with the mothers. I tackled the job unsuspectingly, to be met by a far from happy silence. Dashed, I started again on the difficulties in scene shifting when one of the older women interrupted me, "What do you want to do, Miss Hall, make a fool of me before my children? In the kitchen for three weeks my children rehearse me in my part and now I don't act?" her voice rising to outraged question. That scene and her four lines stayed in!

Helen Schoeni asked Paul Kellogg for editorial advice, and he even wrote some of the lyrics for us. It ended on a triumphant note, with some of Vladeck's new tenants in the dance chorus that was its grand finale.

Consumer problems were portrayed in the next Living Newspaper in April of 1942, and was called *Dollars and Sense*. If there can be anything gay and funny about consumer problems, this play was it! It also served a much wider audience than our own.

One of our theater's most delightful contributions to the neighborhood has been its "Saturdays at Three," introduced by Esther Lane, who followed Helen Schoeni and directed the Playhouse during the later war years. It is, to me, a cruel fact that most of the children in neighborhoods such as ours grow up without ever seeing a "live" play—cheap neighborhood movies are the most that they can afford, or that they even know about. Over its twenty-five years, this Saturday matinee show—open only to adults who have children with them—has been an important part of the Playhouse program. Grownups often borrow children at the door so they can get in, and a goodly number of fathers bring their children. Betty Young took on this responsibility and was largely responsible for the richness and fun of the programs—sometimes a play, perhaps one by children, sometimes puppets, special films, live animal shows, magicians, clowns, Murray Louis dance shows, etc. Making sure that neighborhood children get in was always a problem, since busloads of children from other parts of the city, brought by teachers and various agencies, would have taken most of the seats. This was part of the children's program at Pete's House and the Guttman Building as groups planned their Saturdays.

In September of 1948, our Music School and Playhouse were licensed by the State Board of Regents, so that veterans could enroll with us for full-time study as a part of our student body. Grace Spofford, the director of our Music School, became director of this combination of the theater and music school. It was during this year that Alwin Nikolais came to direct our Dance School. Miss Spofford has always been proud that she was the one who started Alwin Nikolais off with us, and well she might be! For the last twenty years, we have had the joy of watching the creative growth in the work of our Playhouse under his leadership. Two other people, Murray Louis and Betty Young, have shared with Alwin Nikolais in what has become a serious and important artistic contribution to both dance and theater.

Murray Louis was born on the Lower East Side, around the corner from the Playhouse. He studied dance in San Francisco when he was discharged there from the Navy after World War II. He later studied at Colorado College, where Alwin Nikolais was teaching with Hanya Holm. This was what brought him to the Henry Street Settlement Playhouse, where he not only studied but taught and headed up our children's dance and drama classes throughout the years. Two leading critics have called Murray Louis the greatest modern dancer of today, and we have been proud of the many distinctions that have come to him since he came to Henry Street. One of the latest was his tour in India, under the auspices of the State Department, with his own dance company drawn from students and teachers at the Henry Street Playhouse. When I think of Murray Louis, I think of the joy it is to see him dance, and of what he has brought to his profession, but even more, I am grateful for his genius in the teaching of children—the hundreds who have been lucky enough to draw inspiration from his spirited and creative alliance with them. He has not only taught our children himself, but also the teachers who teach them, so that his special viewpoint and technique have permeated all this work over the years.

This is the way that Alwin Nikolais has built our Dance School. He has not just produced dance companies of distinction, but the members of the dance companies are also our teachers, so that the methods, the viewpoint, and the quality go from the oldest to the youngest student—and what is inherent in the school is that all the students matter as much as human beings as they do as dancers.

Because many of our neighbors would not be able to protect themselves from poor teaching, everything we teach should be taught well and creatively, but we have an added responsibility to pick artists of whatever skill who care about people and their whole development. While Alwin Nikolais has played such a determining part in the development of the art of dance and body movement and its accompanying music, he has never swerved from this viewpoint, nor have Murray Louis and Betty Young.

The tours and concerts and lectures in this country, and abroad, have been training ground for the students involved. In 1962, the Nikolais Dance Company went to the "Spoletto Festival of Two Worlds" in Italy. In the fall of 1968, the company went on a ten-week tour in Europe, ending up at the Paris Festival, where Alwin Nikolais was awarded "The Grand Prize of the City of Paris." This is all very reassuring for the students of our school, who are working their own way to achievement.

The real story of the Playhouse and all its activities is of the graduates and how it has contributed to their interest in beauty, self-expression, and development as people. I know that the quest for creativity runs through the whole school, and that teaching people of any age to express their particular selves in whatever they strive to do, and encouraging them to work on their own is healthy, no matter what their capabilities or potential. They gain enrichment for life, even if it does not lead to a career.

Betty Young, co-director of the Playhouse with Alwin Nikolais, lived very near the settlement as a child, and as she grew up was a member of a settlement club. Her first introduction to the Playhouse was when her club gave a play there! She found this experience so fascinating, that her chief interest centered at the theater from that time on. While she was at City College, she volunteered as stage manager for Esther Lane, who was then director. She has a Masters in Dramatic Arts, having spent two years at Chapel Hill in North Carolina, and from 1946 to 1954 she worked in summer stock. But in spite of many temptations to go elsewhere, Henry Street always held first place; so in 1949, she became stage manager for us, and two years later, co-director of the Playhouse. While Nik and Murray are both good administrators, Betty Young, along with her knowledge of the theater, brought a hardheaded understanding of how to run a school and keep within a budget that was a comfort to us all. Perhaps a degree she got long ago in accounting, along with the dramatic arts, gave her a special touch of practicality. And her tireless devotion has been spiced by a very special quality of wry humor, which has helped tide everyone over the inevitable tensions inherent in theater deadlines and such.

XVI

The Music School

Because of the impulse to make music when people gather together, it seems almost inevitable that teaching music of some kind should grow, as it so often has, out of a settlement program. We were no exception. The already-going music lessons moved out of the clubrooms in 1927 to a tenement building on Pitt Street, which was attached to the back of the Playhouse. There, more children and grownups could be taught and more instruments learned. If you add a separate building and dynamic music school directors, as we did, with pupils clamoring to come, you have a music school! Then, if it is to serve families with low incomes, there must be scholarships as well as low fees, and this means a deficit! But, it also means a precious contribution to human development, and so Henry Street Music School came gradually to the point of serving nearly eight hundred pupils yearly, with a faculty of over ninety!

We have been fortunate in our two directors for the last thirty-four years. Grace Spofford came to us from having been dean of Curtis Institute in Philadelphia, and for nineteen years brought what that implies in excellence to the building of our Music School. Miss Spofford lived at Henry Street during that time, and her knowledge of the neighborhood helped in building a school the people needed, as well as one of quality.

Robert Egan followed Miss Spofford as director in 1954. He

had worked at the Music School and lived at the settlement five years before. Then he had returned to his native Cleveland, where he had taught both in the public schools and in the Music School Settlement of Cleveland, one of the most distinguished in the country. Robert Egan, too, had a taste for excellence and unbounding energy and enthusiasm. Like Miss Spofford, he has been able to attract teachers of high caliber, who also in the time they give us have made a generous contribution to our budget, as well as our work. And again above all, there has been a spirit of caring for the students as people, as well as students, throughout the school. Bob Egan and his wife lived at Henry Street until their family of five boys outgrew our apartments.

One of the many who have lent distinction to the school and brought joy to the children has been a young Negro pianist, Frank White, who served as administrative assistant to Bob Egan for ten years. Frank White trained at the University of Kansas and Western Reserve, and has a doctorate from the University of Texas. Along with his administrative work, he taught and was also in charge of our Opera Workshop.

Not only do the children from our informal programs come to the schools, but in turn, and this is important, the schools have upgraded and permeated the quality of the less formal programs for old or young, carried on anywhere in the settlement. The Music School has supplied music for meetings and parties of all kinds—soloists, pianists, violinists, the Jazz Band. This has been so often, that scholarships have been given to the students at the Music School who have helped most in this work. Frank White was especially interested in arranging this, and generous about accompanying the many young people who performed at the meetings. It got so, that when Frank came, he got a special hand of appreciation from all the clubs' members.

As I have said, in 1963, the Music School had to move out of their old tenement, as it was to be torn down for the Seward Park Extension, a middle-income cooperative. Ralph Lippmann, a very good neighbor indeed, arranged for us to have two ground floor apartments in Hillman Houses.

During the year that these apartments offered by Ralph Lippmann were being made ready, our nearest public school lent us the space we needed after school hours. Robert Egan had worked with the principal of the school, and handled all the delicate business of using public school property.

The over-all impact of any institution comes from its day-by-day performance, but its special events also lend it quality. In 1937, Aaron Copeland, the noted American composer, wrote the *Second Hurricane* for Henry Street's Music School, and arranged for Lehman Engels to conduct it.

In 1938, a performing group was organized by Robert Scholz as the Mozart Chamber Orchestra, and later became a professional group, known as the American Chamber Orchestra. Since then, the Music School has continued with two orchestras, the Pitt Street Orchestra for young people, and one for advanced students. The orchestras have been a delightful mixture of all ages and kinds—twins, policemen, black, white, grandparents, as well as parents.

From our first planning of LENA (Lower Eastside Neighborhoods Association) in 1955, we decided that it would be healthy to have the Lower East Side stand for something in the public eye besides gang warfare. Betty Young and Bob Egan attended many of the planning meetings and contributed ideas as to how we could do this. The result of their planning and early pressures on all the rest of us was what has become known as LENA's "Evenings by the River," a concert series in the East River Park Amphitheater, which seats 2,500 people and is free to all comers. Betty Young ran the concerts the first summer and Bob Egan ran them thereafter. The series have presented from three to eighteen concerts each summer, depending upon available funds. The concerts have been carried over radio station WNYC. The principal funds for these concerts have been raised by Mrs. Lillian Weinfeld, a lifelong Lower Eastsider, and the wife of Judge Edward Weinfeld, who was from the beginning the chairman of LENA's Cultural Arts Division.

A very rewarding piece of work from Bob Egan's standpoint has been lending a hand to the establishment of a music school in Harlem by Dorothy Maynor, the famous Negro soprano. In 1939, she had come to our Christmas party, soon after her spectacular Town Hall debut. She once told us that the impression that the children made on her remained with her. Many years later she founded a school in Harlem for children to study the arts in all forms—music, dance, drama, and painting. The St. James Community Center School of the Arts was opened in 1963 at 141st Street and St. Nicholas Avenue, under her leadership, and is now known as the Harlem School of the Arts. At the time of this writing, it has an enrollment exceeding three hundred students and is growing very fast.

One of the most delightful things our Music School has undertaken recently is the institution of the Suzuki technique of teaching violin to very young children. One of our violin teachers, Louise Behrend, visited Japan and met Shinichi Suzuki. She became so much interested in his methods that she volunteered to start a program at Henry Street, at the same time contributing the tiny violins. She began with the children in our nursery school, assisted by a VISTA volunteer, Dorothy Schalk. The next year, we took on teaching Suzuki in our local public school's kindergarten. Mr. Egan invited Mr. Suzuki to spend a week at Henry Street, not only working with our little violinists, but to give lectures, ending with a meeting at our Playhouse, attended by teachers from other parts of the country.

We raised money for the Music School separately for the first few years. The proceeds from a performance of *Parsifal* went to the Music School budget. It finally seemed more practical to combine all our fund-raising, but we have had a Music School Committee, headed by Richard Korn, which has been particularly concerned with getting financial help. When we were particularly pressed, a neighborhood group composed largely of mothers and fathers of the children who had used the school formed a group, chaired by Bill Calise, calling themselves ARCCO (Art Center Community), to help toward raising scholarships to be given to the Negro and Puerto Rican youngsters of the community through the schools. They started off with a very successful art show in our gym.

I could not mention the Music School Committee without speaking of the late Mrs. Lionel Perera, who stood by us for so many years in our struggle to build support for our Music School. She was a fine violinist herself, and bringing music nearer to others meant a great deal to her. Many years ago, at a low point in the Music School's life, (and there were quite a few of them, speaking financially) the then chairman of the Music School Committee, who had made big promises to us, resigned in the middle of the year, withdrawing her promise of a contribution. I knew this was a particularly bad moment and that our main board would take it hard. So I went to see Mrs. Perera and asked her whether she wouldn't please take on the chairmanship, at least for the rest of the year. "Yes, my dear," she said at once, "I think it's important for our committee to have a chairman right now." At this moment her husband, who was a well-known banker, came in and she told him about our conversation. "Well, you can't do it, my dear," said he. "You are doing too much already." With which statement he went on upstairs. Mrs. Perera turned to me and said cheerfully, "Of course I couldn't do it if Lionel doesn't want me to, but I will be acting chairman, and it will be just the same." And it was just the same and she continued as "acting chairman" for a long time.

The life story of the Henry Street Music School has been told in a 377-page doctoral thesis by Robert Egan. It is a valuable as well as an interesting account of the building of a community music school. Its quality and direction are very typical of its well-loved as well as gifted "doctoral" author.

XVII

The Art Department

In the process of bringing the arts into a very athletically oriented program at University House in Philadelphia, I undertook to teach some extremely tough little girls to make pottery bowls. My reward came when one of the children brought me a picture of a beautiful Grecian vase which she had culled from a magazine, saying, "That's what we're making, isn't it?" That her small bowl could lead her eyes and relate her spirit to something so beautiful, is reason enough to put opportunities to create in children's hands. It is not so much what they make, but what happens to them in the making. We hope not only to make bowls or paint pictures, but to reach the inner spirit of the child at the same time.

Our Art Department at Henry Street is one of our prime examples of the arts reaching into other aspects of the settlement. Our pottery classes themselves take in all ages, and many of our students have become skilled potters and have gone on to create and teach. Teen-agers and children also have an art room in Pete's House where they can get together for all sorts of creative adventures or just make posters for a dance that may lead no further—but can and often does. Then the painting and pottery and handicrafts the Good Companions—our older folk—do in the Home Planning Workshops is often a delightful surprise to everyone, including themselves. Their work is dignified by exhibitions and sales several times a year.

We have a small salesroom in the pottery where there is a special exhibition at Christmas, and one in the spring in our back garden. A small room off our lobby at 265 Henry Street displays every month a fresh exhibition of the work of neighborhood artists. This little display has extra virtue to me, as it also serves as the room where neighbors, in trouble of some kind, wait to see our Personal Service worker. All too often, the places where worried people wait to be helped are cruelly dreary.

Over the years, work of so many varying kinds has grown out of the Art Department that it would take a book in itself to do justice to its output and the many gifted teachers and students. I wish Bess Schuyler, who now heads the Art Department, wanted to get a doctorate (not that she needs one), so that she might write her dissertation on the history of Henry Street's Art Department as Robert Egan did his on the Music School.

To go back, our arts flourished enormously in WPA days, which brought us many teachers. One of the projects at that time that I enjoyed greatly was initiated by a teacher who took children to old tenements being torn down to collect soapstone from the wash tubs. It was ideal for carving bas-relief, and the children carved animals of all kinds. I mention the bas-reliefs particularly because they are still decorating our back-yard garden and other places in the settlement, and I have on our terrace in the country, a soapstone bird, an elephant, and a giraffe, which I cherish immensely.

We have always tried to use our buildings as something practical to learn by. The mural on a cement-block back fence in this same back yard was decorated by a Mexican teacher and his young class. The cement blocks, taking the place of a decaying wooden fence, had been a gift from the Turner Construction Company and had been erected by our young people with their help. But when it was finished, it looked so like a prison that we had to decorate it. When the mural was finished, the names of the boys were at the top of the fence, and a small boy cut the ribbon at the ceremony over which Newbold Morris, who was then Parks Commissioner and the president of our board, officiated.

Teaching through use of the buildings was a specialty of Douglas Lockwood's in the WPA days, when he was head of the Art Department, but not until Lilli Ann Killen Rosenberg came to Henry Street to head up this department in 1950 did it come into its own as a real way of life for the children working with her. As she was a sculptor, potter, and painter with a Cranbrook Academy of Art and Cooper Union background, she had the knowable skills; but much more than that, along with her very unusual creativity, she had an extraordinary belief in what children can accomplish. She approached each child and each new project with a buoyancy and confidence that all ages found contagious, but which is irresistible to children.

Our Community Center at La Guardia Houses is another example of having children experience satisfaction in making the buildings that they and other children will be using more beautiful. In this instance, many of the tiles were made by children whose families eventually moved into La Guardia Houses.

The story of the decoration of La Guardia's Community Center, which Henry Street had agreed to run, is an interesting one. Community space in public housing had been deadly dull as to uniformity and color up to this point. The Housing Authority was persuaded to let us choose our own colors and to use our own plans to make the center as lively and interesting as we possibly could. Lilli Ann and Bess Schuyler and the children in our art classes took it in hand. To begin with, the colors chosen for each room were inspiriting and gay. As you come in, charming tiles done by Bess Schuyler show all the buildings of Henry Street and serve as a kind of welcome to the rest of the settlement as well as a decoration. There are large pillars in the clubrooms that hold up the building, and these useful but ugly objects were decorated by tiles made by the children and teen-agers in the pottery. They not only took the curse off the pillars, but are delightful in themselves. The halls, too, are decorated by tiles. A recumbent lion greets you as you go down the stairs that lead to the Mental Health Clinic!

The one large room in the center was a difficult one to make attractive, so we decided to have a mural competition to decorate one long wall. The Rothschild Foundation gave us a grant for this purpose, and a member of our board, Jay Kay Lazrus, headed up a committee for the competition. Three distinguished judges agreed to serve: Ben Shahn, Alfred H. Bar, Jr., and Roy Neuberger. Our only stipulations were that we wanted the mural to represent the building of the Lower East Side from the Indians to the very latest comers, and that the mural be of imperishable material, not canvas, as the space was low enough to be touched by children's hands. A mosaic by Elemer Polony was chosen, and we were very gratified at the beauty of the mosaic but also by the fact that he was not only a gifted artist, but cooperative when we visited his studio while the work was in progress and urged him to put more stress on the importance of the Negroes and Puerto Ricans, our latest neighbors, in the mural.

Besides enjoying the charm of our new La Guardia Houses Community Center, we were even more pleased when it led directly to a plan to beautify other centers by the Housing Authority. An Art Advisory Council was made up of leading people from the museum and art education fields, and was headed by Ira Robbins, of the Housing Authority, and the late Charles Cook, director of University Settlement. Ira had been interested in all our plans from the beginning, and had always encouraged beautification throughout the buildings of the Housing Authority. He obtained a Rockefeller Foundation grant and Henry Street shared Lilli Ann Rosenberg with the Housing Authority so that she could become their art consultant.

As a kind of postscript to the decorating of La Guardia Community Center, a Sculpture Garden, or small playground, in front of the entrance to the center was started by Lilli Ann in 1965, and children, along with practically everyone who passes by, have been working on it ever since. It acquires more animals, more birds, and more colors each summer!

While the decorating of La Guardia Center had far-reaching effects in other community centers in New York, our next big project far outstripped it in interest and in its impact outside the settlement. That was the tile mural decorating the front of the Charles and Stella Guttman Building, which was to become well known through the film *Mural On Our Street*.

I will let Lilli Ann Rosenberg tell the story as she has described it in her recently published book, *Children Make Murals and Sculpture.** But first, I want to pay a tribute to Benjamin Mosko-

---

* Reinhold Book Corporation, 1968.

The Library at Pete's House—Jane Hall Hunter, Volunteer, in charge
(*Photo courtesy of Ken Wittenberg*)

The entrance to the Home Planning Workshops and The Good Companions at Vladeck Houses, showing Benny Berg, who has been our official greeter for many years, coming up the ramp

Mrs. Ida Liebowitz in the Home Planning Workshop with her grandchildren admiring her work (*Photo courtesy of Ken Wittenberg*)

Gaiety in The Good Companions with Milton Frankel leading
(*Photo courtesy of William E. Barksdale*)

Marie D. Leslie and Milton Frankel preparing spirituals for the
Good Companions

Mrs. Betsabe Rivas in The Good Companion's pottery workshop
(*Photo courtesy of Ken Wittenberg*)

A party in our residents' dining room given by The Good Companions for a VISTA Volunteer, Mrs. Herlihy—Ruth Tefferteller leading the singing and Mr. Tobias, chairman (*Photo Courtesy of Ken Wittenberg*)

From grandparents to babies: The audience at an "Evening by the River" Concert sponsored by LENA and

some of our guests who helped make it possible: Newbold Morris, Helen Hall, Mayor Wagner, Mrs. Eleanor Roosevelt, Mrs. Edward Weinfeld, chairman of the Community Arts Council of LENA (*Photo courtesy of Doug Quackenbush*)

Mayor Wagner and Winslow Carlton at launching of plans for
Mobilization at Pete's House, February 2, 1959

witz, the architect of both Pete's House and the Guttman Building. He had helped us in many ways over the years that had
elapsed between the two buildings, and had grown used to our
vagaries! So after his first sense of concern over the idea of
having children decorate the front of the Guttman Building, he
took it on and helped us in making it a practical as well as
an artistic success. Mr. Moskowitz had at first not reckoned with
Lilli Ann's capacity for leadership and the children's innate
talents. Recalling every step of the ambitious project, she was
to write later:

When the opportunity came for the creation of a mural on the
front of the new Charles and Stella Guttman Building of the
Settlement, the Art Department and the youngsters in the program were ready.

In a project of this complexity, there are always too many
voices saying, "It can't be done." But it *can* be done. The major
ingredient for its success must be a firm belief in the work of the
children which is beautiful and deserves a place of importance.

In order to synchronize the work on the mural with the construction schedule for the new building, our work had to be
completed within 11 weeks. The 49 "artists" were chosen, not by
their talent in art, but by a simple process of elimination based
on their available time, ability to sustain interest, and to work
cooperatively in a group with their peers and various age groups.
The theme for the mural developed from discussions with the
children indicating their desire for more trees and animals on
Henry Street. One child commented, "Let's make it a friendly
jungle . . . where nobody hates anybody and animals don't fight
each other." The magic quality which emerges as people work
hard together is not surprising as is evidenced in the film which
was made during the project, where you hear a child's voice
saying ". . . and I drew and drew until my fingers hurt . . . and
when I got home I told my mother I was tired, but then I wanted
to go back and draw some more."

When the Good Companions Club members heard about the
mural, three of them eagerly volunteered to work with us. They
concentrated their efforts on a few sections. . . . These portions
are indistinguishable from the children's work, as the extremely
divergent age groups have the same capacity of expressing themselves freely and simply.

. . . The tiles were then fired once in the huge kilns at the factory and were ready to be permanently installed by the builders.

Each of us on the staff, all the "folk artists," and the entire neighborhood feels, "IT'S MINE!" This is the wonder of working together in the arts.

The film, called *Mural On Our Street*, which was shot picturing the progressive steps in the creation of the Guttman Building mural proved to be a great success. Made by Kirk Smallman, with special assistance from Dede Halleck, it has won several awards and international recognition. The narration is a combination of taped comments made by various youngsters and adults involved with the mural, and the interesting musical background is provided by Henry Street's Steel Drum Band. *Mural On Our Street* was shown for many months as a "short" in commercial movie theaters in New York and is now available through Public Film Libraries.*

One of my favorite comments came from a small boy as he patted a butterfly on a tile. "That is my butterfly," he said to a friend. And at another time, one of the young artists, who had moved away, brought two of his new friends from Brooklyn to see "his Kangaroo." All the artists have their names on the front of the building and this gives them an added sense of ownership.

Because of the wide circulation of *Mural On Our Street*, we had constant visitors who wanted to see it—a number of them planning new buildings. So we hope that children may make other "Friendly Jungles" or their like on other streets in other cities.

* Contemporary Films, Inc., 267 West 25th St., New York, N.Y.

XVIII

Our Credit Union,
A People's Bank,
Young People's Cooperatives,
and Buying Clubs

Our Credit Union has been an integral part of the settlement since 1937, and is a "natural" for neighborhood participation. A credit union might be called a people's bank, for it is the membership dues and the members' savings that comprise its capital.

We sometimes boast about our Credit Union's record of loans, of nearly $6 million in its first twenty-seven years, and its negligible loss during this period. This is unusual for a neighborhood credit union, that is, one functioning without payroll deductions, unlike credit unions made up of employee groups. But what we should really boast about is the way in which it got started, and of the thoughtful, painstaking work put into its planning by its young neighborhood committee, Franklin Harbach and other members of the Henry Street staff, including a visiting nurse, Asta Weddin. Franklin Harbach had an unusual amount of downright practicality, which a credit union needs. There is an increasing realization at the present time of the value of credit unions to low-income families, but there is not, as yet, an equal realization of the time and pains involved in getting one going and keeping it going.

Henry Street's Credit Union started in 1937 with a group of boys and girls, one of whom, in the course of two years, had paid $500 interest on $25 borrowed from a loan shark. The group came to us not only for help for the victim but also to find a better way to get loans. A Henry Street resident, Felix Greene, then with the British Broadcasting Corporation, who had had experience with the Cooperative movement in England, met with the young people all winter. In the process the boys learned about the credit union movement, sold shares, put on a Living Newspaper in our theater, and generally made the neighborhood aware of what was happening. Discussion was so widespread that a former loan shark, who was running a local pool parlor at that time, came over to the theater during a rehearsal to see where his customers were. He was so disgusted at the way the loan shark was being portrayed that he offered to do it himself, and did!

But—and this is important—the settlement staff never made a decision about a loan, but saw to it that it was always the young people on the Credit Union Board who, themselves, took the responsibility. The decision, however, was generally accompanied by before-and-after-meeting discussions.

In the early days I sat in on a Credit Union Loan Committee meeting chaired by a gentle-voiced girl of about nineteen years. A vociferous middle-aged woman came in for a loan. It was discussed at great length by the Loan Committee and, in the light of the women's irresponsibility with a former loan, her request was turned down. When she came back into the room and the chairman, Jennie Raemer, explained this to her, she was very angry and told Jennie that "she was old enough to be her mother and knew a great deal more than she did." Jennie replied very politely but firmly, "Yes, Mrs. S., you do know a great deal more than I do about everything but credit unions, and I know more about credit unions than you do."

When La Guardia Houses opened in 1954 and Henry Street took on responsibility for the Community Center, we planned to move the Credit Union into the center to reach the new neighbors more easily. But one of the Housing Authority members of that day, a banker, was very much against credit unions and refused his approval, although both Winslow Carlton and I tried hard to point out its usefulness. This policy was changed under the next chairman of the Authority, William Reid, who was president of the Municipal Credit Union and the New York State Credit Union League, but our Credit Union could not benefit by it, for the space had been adapted to other purposes.

A credit union can be very valuable in helping families over the hump of trouble. It can be an important way to learn to save and to manage slim earnings. For instance, as we had pointed out to the Authority member, at one time the greatest number of evictions from public housing were for nonpayment of rent. Working people are so often paid by the week, and project rents are paid by the month. For the beset mother, or poor manager, the pressure on the dollar, kept in the bureau drawer or pocketbook, is too much to resist when emergencies come up such as shoes for school or medicine for a sick child. With the money in a credit union, there is much more hope that it will be there when the rent is due.

Some of the boys who started the Credit Union in the mid-thirties became successful businessmen and moved away from our neighborhood, but some still come back from all over the city to serve on the Credit Union Board. They have tried in many ways to draw in the newcomers in the neighborhood, and at one time Henry Street engaged an experienced consumer adviser to work with them to speed it up.

Many people helped make our Credit Union a spirited affair. Jack Landau, who became the President of the Credit Union Board in the World War II years, has continued ever since and has given the special kind of devotion without which no organization succeeds. Samuel Schneeweiss, who now serves as chairman of the Executive Committee of the Henry Street Board, helped organize the Credit Union and has served on the Credit Union's Board ever since, as have Mike Katz, Leon Gross, Molly and Louis Pollack, Nat Rafterman, Joe Goldberg and "Chesty" Gelber. Our success, of course, has been due in large measure to the kind of long term accepting of responsibility by neighborhood people.

The story of what the Credit Union loans have been used for would be a very moving history of our neighborhood.

Our Credit Union led to an interest in cooperatives. With warm encouragement from Franklin Harbach, they became the chief focus of the program for the upper teens for a long time.

Their first co-op project was children's sneakers. Some of the boys and girls had noticed that few of the children playing on the gym floor had sneakers, and their stockings were full of holes. They talked about this, and out of their concern grew a Sneaker Cooperative. They bought sneakers wholesale and the children paid for them nickle by nickle, wearing them on the gym floor but not taking them home till paid for!

The success of this joint venture gave the young cooperators so much satisfaction that they branched out into further adventures: one was a bicycle coop for hostel trips, and we became part of the hostel movement of that day; one was an egg coop, and they candled eggs like mad and sold them to the adult clubs. The search for a cooperative cabin in the country took some of the older members out on many weekends; although the search didn't come to fruition, there was a lot of fun involved. The oldest and most highbrow of the groups started a "Latest Book" co-op. Their leaders conferred with the local public librarian and the local book store. They were surprised and pleased at the help they got from both these sources.

An over-all board composed of members from all these small coops met often to discuss their successes and failures, and to consider expansion into new fields. This was about as meaningful a young people's program as I have seen. It continued with zest for several years, until the days of the Russian–German Pact. This ended the "United Front" and, as political directions seeped down from on high, we began to lose many of our best workers in all the co-ops, who had been United Fronting with us for so long. We had realized the ideological differences among the members but until this period there had been small effort to subvert the various co-ops' avowed purposes of whatever kind. As this changed, a resolution to condemn Great Britain and France for the "Imperialist War" became a must to the communists in any group. The results of the pact reached down in the Co-op Board. They had been a small but helpful part of the group but now they were bound to get that resolution passed. While the cooperative principle is to exclude politics, and the noncommunist members tried to insist on this, it became impossible to get any business done as each meeting was taken up by heated political discussion. The resolution was never passed, but many of the young people lost interest in what became a political discussion group rather than a cooperative adventure.

Along with the Credit Union and Cooperatives, Buying Clubs, are a likely activity for consumer-interest groups. All sorts of them have been a part of Henry Street's work over the years, with varying success—eggs, butter, meat, groceries of different kinds. These clubs or groups often have been very fruitful in interesting and educating housekeepers, but they have seldom been of long duration in the complicated field of food. But as I look back on some of the excitement surrounding these ventures and the leadership they brought forth, I feel the buying clubs can be a very worthwhile tool in the long consumer education process.

XIX

*From Community Studies
to Community Action*

Social action is so inherent a part of what we do in a settlement that it is hard to separate it from our day-by-day work. Much of our neighbors' social action has grown out of what was referred to as "sociable action" by a young man who was fed up with what he considered his group's overemphasis on repairing the social system. What he tried to tell me was that he wanted a little more fun between protests! He was expressing, somewhat, the settlement's philosophy in down-to-earth terms. Ordinarily we do not organize groups for protest alone but for an association of which social concern and action may form an important part, along with friendships and sociability of all sorts. If a tired and worried woman has laughed with her neighbors, we don't consider her evening wasted. This differs from some experiences in community action, which seems to rely so much on hostility and anger to make people willing to get together and act.

Lasting social relationships can be the best springboard for continuous action lasting over the years, as the espousing of one cause after another leads to growth and self-confidence. However, this is not the only way of expressing neighborhood concern. Organization for a special cause at a particular moment, which may not lead to the forming of a permanent group, can also be very important to the neighborhood as well as to the cause. But we do try to make sure that the groups understand the issues and are not just expressing the feelings of the leader. Among the many ways to effect social action, and often the most successful, is a partnership. Sometimes neighbors, settlement workers, board members, and experts of one kind or another can offer different kinds of testimony that may be telling and needed at a special time or place—at public hearings, meetings with officials, or wherever it will do the most good.

We started our Community Studies Department in 1933 partly to equip us for social action by a systematic gathering of facts close-up so that we could speak with some authority when urging change. Many of our studies were summarized in the Helen Hall papers in 1957. When Mobilization for Youth was started, involving so much research, we hoped that for the time being a great deal of this work would be taking place under its auspices. But at the same time, I felt that community studies in one form or another should always be a part of Henry Street's work. When you work in a neighborhood you get what is happening through the pores—if you keep them open. But to have our daily work serve its full purpose, observations must be tested by continuous sampling to make sure that they are in truth facts and not merely impressions.

There are few rules to guide the gathering of such findings except that they be timely, and pertinent. They do not as a rule have to be costly and too time-consuming. Timeliness often depends upon circumstance. Sometimes a fact-finding project does not get finished until it is too late to serve its particular purpose. Sometimes it's ahead of its time, or ahead of the moment when attention will be paid to it. However, for the most part, facts that we take the pains to use sooner or later will serve the community in good stead.

I had a satisfying experience once when, stopping into the gallery of the House of Representatives in Washington in the early days of the Depression, I heard from the floor of the House the story of one of our unemployed settlement neighbors quoted by a congressman to illustrate the mounting need for some form of unemployment relief. The congressman was quoting from the study of unemployment made by the National Federation of Settlements in 1928.

There are, of course, diverse reasons for making such work continuous since there are many different objectives in the gathering of social data. Sometimes the facts may illustrate a need for nationwide action to meet basic social problems, such as unemployment, old age, housing, or health care. Another time, they may throw light on purely local problems, such as the lack of street lights at a dangerous crossing. But if the studies are continuous, they are bound to keep the agency in touch with changing neighborhood conditions, which, in turn, should stimulate constant revision of our programs. What we undertake in research stems from our first-hand contacts with club members, with children in nursery school, with individuals in a mental health clinic, in our workshops, and is also stimulated by the day-by-day contact with people as they come to us for help in trouble.

While facts can serve as a useful tool for social change, their gathering can also serve as a creative instrument in reaching our neighbors. The actual work involved in collecting material can be stimulating and enlightening to members, staff, board, and volunteers. It is so easy to go along with established patterns and old friends, visiting the families who are already coming to the settlement. Reaching out in house-to-house visiting is of value in itself. It keeps us more surely abreast of living conditions behind the walls of old tenements and new housing, and, at the same time, is bound to bring us into friendly relationships with fresh arrivals. It often takes time for newcomers to work their way into a neighborhood, and they may need a lot of individual encouragement to feel at home. For many years we had a resident who was an inveterate caller. In order to get people out she distributed tickets to our plays and concerts with the promise of meeting the family at the theater where she was always in the lobby with a warm welcome to make good her promise. It was a gimmick that worked. If we just wait for people to come to us, we may find ourselves serving predominately the extroverts in the neighborhood who perhaps do not need us as much as those more inhibited by temperament or circumstance. A passive approach in neighborliness often neglects the most inadequate and disadvantaged, just as it often does in casework.

When on information bent, we try not only to get information but to engage the interest of the mother or father, or whatever member of the family is directly involved, in the object of the study. But first of all we get people to talk about themselves. That is, of course, the social worker's trump card, and our neighbors respond to it in much the same way that anyone else does.

We at Henry Street have used many volunteers in our studies, and it is one of the most meaningful jobs that we can give them. The work must be supervised carefully and first visits made with an experienced worker. Some people are just not natural visitors and should not be inflicted on a family or made to suffer themselves. Many of our neighbors themselves have, of course, made fine visitors.

One of the most important results of our early eleven-block study, incorporated into *A Dutchman's Farm*, was the discovery that the land costs had gone down. As we saw the delapidation of that area, the very low rents, and the over 40 percent of vacancies in the old tenements, we began to question whether land could still be so high as to prohibit the building of subsidized low-cost housing there. "Land costs on the Lower East Side are too high for public housing," was the answer given me when I asked the City Housing Authority of that day for a review of the situation. In order to satisfy ourselves, Mrs. Samuel Rosenman, a member of our board, interested James Felt, at that time the generous and concerned head of a real estate firm, in determining whether high land costs had held through all the years of increasing delapidation, decreasing population, and depression. As we anticipated, values had actually dropped to a level at which federal subsidy could rightly be used. I took the results of our inquiries to Mayor La Guardia, and he assured me that if a further canvass of the rest of the property brought out the same results, the Housing Authority would build there. So with combined urgency from many forces on the Lower East Side, Vladeck Houses, a public housing project covering eight blocks, stands today in the heart of our eleven-block study.

The building of Vladeck Houses caused great rejoicing among our neighbors, many of whom had helped bring the necessity for action to the attention of the general public and, particularly, to their own representatives in Congress. With members of other New York settlements they had called meetings, walked in parades, gone to Washington at Senator Robert Wagner's invitation, and carried their case to the White House. Tenement dwellers, organized by the United Neighborhood Houses of New York, had been among the very few "consumers" of bad housing who had a direct share in helping to better conditions. I stopped to talk to two women sitting on a bench in front of our settlement buildings watching the demolition of the old houses across the street to make way for Vladeck. The falling bricks raised a sizable dust storm that hot summer's day, but that did not matter to them. "I'm glad for every brick that falls," said one, and the other rejoined, "Yes, I've lived in that place there for over twenty years and being a single woman I won't get in the new one, but I'm glad for every housing parade I walked in and every meeting I went to."

That was in 1938. The New York City Housing Authority had been created in 1934 and the Federal Housing Act, the Wagner–Stengall Bill, was passed in 1937—long before the first "ghetto" eruptions of the mid-sixties, but it has been a continuous struggle since the thirties to get new housing built for those families who cannot pay the market price for decent housing. The results achieved in the years since then are disgracefully meager when compared to the need. We have moved ahead in the social insurances: unemployment and old age, inadequate as we still feel the latter to be. But housing and health care have moved so slowly that one feels ashamed of everybody concerned, especially ourselves, along with the real estate lobby, the American Medical Association, and all their allies.

For a number of years a very active neighborhood group met at Henry Street, the Lower East Side Public Housing Conference, a group cooperating with the National Public Housing Conference headed by Mrs. Mary Simkhovitch, founder of Greenwich House in New York. The early leaders of our group told me they would like to have very well-informed speakers address their meetings so that when they went to Albany or Washington or anywhere else to work for housing they would be knowledgeable enough to be listened to. They often worked long into the night to prepare themselves for a meeting the next day. Today, one of that group, Harry Levy, does legal work for the New York City Housing Authority. Another, Mrs. Sheba Ziprin, was a public housing manager for many years.

Work for improvement in housing could not confine itself to crusading for new public housing. A small breakthrough came in 1934, after members of the New York settlements made a pilgrimage to Albany to stop another moritorium of the 1929 multiple dwelling law which required landlords to fire-retard halls and put a toilet in every apartment. The Henry Street Visiting Nurse Service had prepared a study for me of some of the conditions under which they cared for the sick, and I read their horrendous report in Albany that day to be greeted with boos and shouts of "lies!" by the delegation of landlords seated behind me. We not only had the landlords against us but also many of the banks. For during the Depression the banks had come to hold so many mortgages on old tenements that they had used their influence to have a moratorium put on the effective date of this law, and they were there at the hearing. But luckily so were settlement mothers, in a delegation from all over the city to testify. The moratorium was beaten that year— not so small a thing when you consider the danger of fire in the halls and the health menace of hall toilets. I talked to Henry Bruere in Albany that day. He was president of the Bowery Savings Bank at that time, as well as president of the United Neighborhood Houses, and a member of the Henry Street Board, and I recall his satisfaction, in spite of his own bank's and other banks' mortgage problems, with the settlements' delegation and the lively testimony our neighbors brought to bear on the situation. I had an example of the *value* of this law, not long ago, when a fire started in the lower hall of a tenement near the settlement on Henry Street. The fire traveled up the stairwell so fast that the reinforced doors of the flats were almost burned through, but, because of the fire-retarding, every family had time to get down the also-mandatory fire escapes. As I looked at that hallway and the almost melted metal doors, I couldn't but think of our Albany trip so long ago, but I also thought of the fact that that old building was still standing in 1967!

I remember making a speech in my early days, representing the Philadelphia settlements at a national conference, in which

I gave statistics regarding the many miles of unsewered streets and the many toilets in backyards that were still in that city. But it took climbing the tenement stairs on the Lower East Side of New York to make the improvement of housing conditions an obsession with me.

These filthy, frightening halls opening into sunless, rat-infested apartments where the tidiest housekeeper generally lost the battle of the bugs, and also lost the battle to keep hall toilets decent, have never failed to make me ashamed and angry.

In this chapter I am using examples drawn largely from the community studies used in our work for better housing, as I have used other examples of other causes in other chapters, but I want to point out here that consumers of bad housing or bad anything else can, if they raise their voices, do more to change social conditions than any other group. There is another element, too, in all this and that is the satisfaction people get from having had a hand in changing things for the better or in even trying to! This was an extra dimension in all our crusades.

But no social worker or housing expert, however convincing their figures, could convey as well as our neighbors what it meant to bring children up in dark, windowless rooms, to find a rat in the baby's crib, to use filthy hall toilets. As a member of a Washington delegation of mothers said to me, "We made those senators cry before we got through!" I had to admit that no testimony of mine had ever met with similar success.

I have always remembered the words of a member of one of our oldest mothers' clubs as we stood looking down the street at an old building. "You see that tenement by the church on Scammel Street? Well, I went there as a bride and every morning for twenty years I put my mattresses on the window sill because of the bugs. No matter what I used or how I scrubbed the walls, I couldn't get rid of them. That was forty years ago, and there's that house still, and it certainly isn't any better now. I guess women are still working there like I did. I'm better off now, but I'd do anything to get rid of such things for other women." Mrs. Sadie Cohen had done everything she could and nothing was too hard. I recall a long parade we walked in together about which nothing comes back to me but a sense of satisfaction that I had overcome my natural distaste for public demonstrations, coupled with the fact that her arches and mine gave out at about the same time. But we hobbled along together to the end—our consciences taking over when our feet gave out. That was years ago and my friend is dead, but that tenement, although slated for demolition, stood for many years more in its moldy filth and symbolized to me what the Congress has turned its back on every time federal housing funds are cut.

Another episode in the long, and it now seems losing, fight for better housing involved a visit to the President by three representatives of the League of Mothers' Clubs of the United Neighborhood Houses. Its president from the Educational Alliance, and two vice-presidents, one from Union Settlement and one from Henry Street, took a book of six-hundred photographs of mothers living in old-law tenements, with their names and addresses, as a petition to the President. The pictures had been taken by members of the photography classes at Hudson Guild and Henry Street, and the whole episode involved the participation of many people in the process of planning, selection, and preparation. One day I came upon the boys who were pasting the photos in a big book for presentation to President Roosevelt and discovered that they were cutting the pictures round and thereby eliminating the women's hands. No matter how hard pressed or of what age, their hair had generally been arranged with a touch of style that tended to mitigate the story of hardship that their faces revealed. But the work-shaped hands told their story without compromise; so we persuaded the boys in the name of art to make oblong pictures, and the evidence stayed in. The mothers had paid a nickle apiece to cover the cost of their pictures and were deeply interested in the project—it was the next thing to going to see the President themselves.

The expedition was later reported to me by the young woman who went from Henry Street. The interview with the President was summed up triumphantly with, "We knew the President was so interested. If those secretaries hadn't kept interrupting, we'd have been there all afternoon."

Can We Renovate the Slums? was a local study we made in 1939 that had city-wide application in the housing field. It involved one of the first of the many movements to repair old tenements in New York, with the city lending money to this end. There was much talk for and against. To see whether it was a wise move and really served both the neighborhood and its people, we undertook to find out what had happened in fifty-five renovated tenements in our vicinity. The study showed that only where there was a minimum of renovation were the same low-income families able to pay the increased rent. But where a decent job was done, only families with much higher incomes were able to move in. As far as I know, this was the only detailed study at that time of what actually was happening to the people in renovated tenements, and I think could fairly be said to have played its part in helping to keep New York City from doing an extravagant patchwork job at that particular time.

Earlier, when the old "coal in the bathtub" story was being revived, we made a quick inquiry into *What Some Slum Dwellers Want in Housing*, calling on 219 families in one square block. In the early discussions of slum clearance, some opponent was sure to bring up the "coal in the bathtub" story as an argument that slum dwellers wouldn't know how to use proper facilities if they had them. I always wondered how the story started because, in those days, there weren't any bathtubs in which to put coal even if they wanted to! However, this inquiry of ours played its part in laying that silly old myth. Our neighbors were in no doubt at all about what they considered essential, and a bathroom headed the list. Why it should have been news that slum dwellers shared the American predilection for modern plumbing, I don't know, but it was, and the newspapers made much of it at a time when it could count. To our own surprise, clippings came back to us from all over the country headlining this startling news as put forth in our study!

A study called *Rooms of Their Own*, issued in 1939, was thought of as local in nature although it happened to have rather wide use at the time. We know how much talk, argument, and headlines can be based on mere surmise. An example of this kind of community furor caused us to embark on a study of twenty-eight cellar clubs in our neighborhood. "Dens of Iniquity," the police called them, and we set out to see. Members of the clubs had been coming to get advice on many subjects from our staff. Some of the groups had started from boys' clubs at the settlement so had had a long association with us. As they grew older, what they wanted was a room of their own to which they could come at any time with no adult supervision. It is impossible for agencies such as ours to answer this particular need when our rooms are used continuously by children, teen-agers, and grownups—each group having its own period for use. The cellar clubs occupied store-fronts or basements.

The boys came to us for advice on how they could protect themselves from unfavorable publicity and frequent police raids. One of the ways we pointed out was to be pretty sure the allegations were not true. In line with this advice, self-chosen representatives of the cellar clubs met at Henry Street Settlement on Sunday afternoons to work out a "code of behavior." It was a simple and direct little document known as a "model code," and dealt with the basic problems of girl-guests, closing hours, bad language, gambling, and "gentlemanly behavior." The latter seems sort of out of date at the present writing! As the public clamor over the cellar clubs mounted, we realized that we were being counted upon heavily to interpret and to defend. Consequently, we felt we would be standing on firmer ground and would be of more use to the boys themselves if we took an intensive, unselective, first-hand look, club-to-club, so to speak. This had never been done as far as we could find out; so we put considerable time and effort into its accomplishment. It involved continuous late evening visiting on the part of Emeric Kurtagh, then our educational director, and his assistant, George Stoney.

We did not find that a "cellar club problem" existed on the Lower East Side in the way it had been pictured. We found only one club whose conduct revealed seriously questionable elements. In the others we felt convinced that the social life of these boys and young men was improved through the use of their club facilities, since the alternative would be hanging around street corners. However, we did find that the existence of the clubs and their lack of supervision created a number of lesser problems with landlords and neighbors, which had to be met. With our aid, a Federation of East Side Clubs was formed, aimed at establishing self-regulation. The federation adopted the "model code" which had been developed by their representatives, published a newspaper, conducted sports tournaments, dances, theater parties, launched a series of educational symposia, and even ran "charity affairs." Through the efforts of the federation, the clubs' relations with neighbors, landlords, and the police improved considerably. Our own work with the members of the cellar clubs grew at an accelerated pace while we were gathering materials for *Rooms of Their Own*, and illustrates again how in fact-gathering we stand to deepen our relationships.

Our neighborhood research reached out in many directions. One spring we made a house-to-house canvass in nearby blocks to determine just how the children who did not get to our summer camps were faring. Another time, an early study of soup kitchens in our neighborhood served in the move that was then beginning for better care of homeless men. School lists of new arrivals were often used as a basis for friendly calling and introduction into the settlement. The noncitizens discovered through another study led to establishment of more and smaller citizenship classes. A new piece of work with old people grew out of a study made primarily with an eye to new Puerto Rican neighbors but which disclosed that many more old people than we had realized were hidden away in the same blocks that seemed so alive with Puerto Rican children. A young people's group going to Washington to talk about jobs went armed with stories and figures collected through our community studies.

No piece of work in the settlement—in art, music, mental health, nursery school, or what-have-you—should be in an airtight compartment, and, to insure this, staff members themselves, however expert in their special fields, should not be airtight in their thinking. It is not always easy but it is a part of the administrative function to keep the settlement operating this way.

I have been writing largely of some of the work done by Henry Street through our Community Studies Department. There is, however, the other important business of cooperating with many other agencies for social action. The National Federation of Settlements and the United Neighborhood Houses, of course, have been our most frequent and fruitful partners, but there have been many others.

To illustrate what we might refer to as the invisible struggle that has almost always had to go on behind new housing projects and which is not evident to the uninitiated as they see neat new projects, a young man from the Office of Economic Opportunity in Washington came to see me, and, as he looked out of my office windows on the mixture of cooperatives and low-income housing projects, he said rather scornfully, "Sterile, isn't it?" Well, it didn't look sterile to me! What I saw across the street, in my mind's eye, were the filthy tenements we had fought so hard to get rid of a few years before, and the studies we had made of conditions there. I saw five-day eviction notices in the hands of tenants who poured across the street to ask us what to do. I saw the busloads of tenants we had escorted to court to get action on violations the landlord had ignored. I remembered how, when we bore down hard enough on the Departments of Health, and Housing and Buildings to get out a warrant, the landlord would always disappear into New Jersey where it couldn't be served on him. I remembered the result of the long legal struggle and the trips to court and the reduction of the rent to $1 a month, and how, at this point, the tenants and Henry Street found themselves running four of the worst old tenement buildings in New York. How, to begin with, we called all the families together in our gymnasium and, with the aid of our resident lawyer and a Yiddish and Spanish interpreter, we explained that they could now run the buildings, as the landlord had disappeared. So, if the tenants from each building would gather in the four corners of the gymnasium and select their representatives, they could choose a committee to take over the responsibility.

The tenants were made up largely of old Jewish people and young Puerto Rican families with very little English between them, but it was a heartening sight to see what had seemed like a mass of helpless, bewildered people turn into a self-governing group, as in each corner of the gymnasium they appointed two members from their tenement to represent them on a Tenants' Committee. It is always good to see democracy come to life before your eyes as it did that night, as the representatives the tenants had selected took their places at the head table and proceeded with plans for collecting rents, hiring a janitor, and arranging to put the money, when collected, into our Credit Union and to get the worst of the repairs done.

For the next two years, the Tenants' Committee functioned successfully until the Housing Authority took over those buildings. It is a long story, full of leaking roofs, burst pipes, and almost no recalcitrant rentpayers. That committee turned out to be a credit to themselves and a satisfaction to us.

Then, of course, came the heartbreaking job of relocation, in which we helped as much as we could, as the Housing Authority moved to clear the land. There are few situations harder to face than that of a family with roots in our neighborhood and in their hands a notice of an apartment in the Bronx.

One thing which I actually did see from my office window that morning, and had seen every morning, were two large trees—"Trees of Heaven" as the ailanthus is so rightly called. When the tenements had finally come down, after the Housing Authority had acquired the land, two very big trees were revealed that had been growing in two backyards. A big tree is so precious in New York and bulldozers so ruthless that I telephoned Ira Robbins, then vice-chairman of the Housing Authority, and asked if they couldn't be saved. He sent an architect down at once to see if it were possible. The architect said it was, as far as the plans went, if the Housing Authority, from "top to bottom," was determined to protect them. This I passed on to Ira Robbins, who was just leaving for Europe. He humorously told me that he was leaving the order to the affect that, if it was a question between the trees or the houses, the houses would have to go! But he added I had better keep an eye on them anyway, which of course I did!

One morning, early, I looked out and saw a pile of old wood, ready for burning, which seemed dangerously near the trees. I hadn't finished dressing so I asked our maintenance man to go across quickly and talk to the construction superintendent. He returned well satisfied, saying that the superintendent had told him that "those trees were world-famous, planted by George Washington or Thomas Jefferson or someone like that, and he had orders from the 'top' to save them!" They were saved and they look beautiful, and I saw them from my office windows at 265 Henry Street that morning—and they did not look sterile to me!

But to end on a less hopeful note, the almost total lack of

building in the low-income and middle-income field is probably one of the most shocking lacks in our society today. Taking into account the increase in population, we are going backward in housing our people.

XX

The Aged Are People

As the proportion of old people has increased in the population, and particularly in the Henry Street neighborhood, we have tried constantly to develop the kind of services that would best fill their needs. My real education in this subject has come through the older members of the two settlement neighborhoods in which I have lived. The elements of a post-graduate course are always there waiting for us in our daily encounters.

I have been made aware of the gathering depression that can settle in with the years—but also of the buoyancy that can only be defeated by the last breath. Some have shown me that romance is no respector of age, many others, that the creative impulse can burn strong to the very end, some, that familiar surroundings give a security worth fighting for. But they have all taught me that the aged are people, only with the human need to be needed greatly intensified. Some years ago one of the saddest of my daily encounters was with a small, white mongrel dog who was aired each day by my next-door neighbor. He had belonged to an old man who had hung himself in the tenement right across the street from us. The neighbor who aired the little dog in telling me of the old man said, "He lived to himself—he spoke to no one—he didn't have no friends; so," she added, "I have took his little dog for him—it was no more than right."

The march of the small dog past our house symbolized to me the lonely old folks hidden away in our big cities whom no one reaches. In this case I felt especially sad because, with all our visiting we had not discovered and perhaps halted this retreat from a world that was giving too little to endure.

Fortunately, not many old people take life so hard, and some charge ahead and give the oncoming years a run for their money. Mrs. Dolan, one of my most zestful neighbors in Philadelphia, who brought this home to me early in our association, would stand for hours cackling in our front hall as she tantalized the boys about their girl friends. Then she would end her visit with, "Well, I guess I'll take a little race up to the store and get me victuals."

In those days we distributed flowers to old people, which were brought into Philadephia from outlying gardens. Small girls bunched the flowers and then scurried as delighted messengers all over the neighborhood. One of them came back very crestfallen one day with a rather tired-looking bunch of flowers, saying, "Mrs. Dolan says to tell Miss Hall that if she can't do better than that, don't send!" For a moment we were set back on our heels, for it goes hard to have one's good works rejected, but then we all laughed, for Mrs. Dolan was not taking life on any but her own terms. We cashed in on her inveteracy by having her help us build a grandmothers' club made up of women over seventy.

One of the most cheering things to learn, and to the young the most surprising, is about that matter of romance. Katie and Jimmy Hainey were my first effective teachers on this point. They had married, aged seventy and eighty, from an old folks home and had set up housekeeping in our neighborhood. You might have thought Jimmy would have been satisfied along those lines at this point, but no, he was inclined to tarry at the Widow Farrell's stoop on his way home from any errand. Katie, as she told it, would put a "comfortable wooden crate" outside their stoop and then march down the three doors to where Jimmy loitered and say, "Jimmy, see that box? Well, that is *your* box, and it's on *your* stoop, and it's where *you* sit!" Finally, when Jimmy left his earthly stoop and we went in to pay our last respects, Katie sat in proper mourning beside

Jimmy's coffin. But what never dies was still alive behind the immediate moment, and after a proper discussion of what Jimmy's death meant to her, she ended with the reflective comment, "I'm going to cut my hair now; Jimmy never would let me."

It is good to remember that the greatest of all human experiences knows no rigid age boundaries, and seems to be able to touch life with adventure to the very end.

A Barbara Fritchie-like incident highlighted for me what familiar surroundings can mean to the old, and the hardihood that can be summoned to fight for them. I can see to this day a small, white head leaning out of a top-story window of a little Philadelphia house, hurling invectives on the heads of friends and neighbors beneath. They were trying to move her out because the house was to be torn down, and they had brought me up as reinforcement to persuade her, but my embattled old friend saw me coming up the block and she left me in no doubt as to what she thought of my joining such a lot of trash under her window, and I beat an ignominious retreat. The old lady held them off for several days to the great embarrassment of her family.

These folks and many like them have highlighted the problems as the years went on, and the inescapable statistics have pushed us toward finding new ways not only for making the last years endurable, but useful and often creative. In 1953, Henry Street received a grant that allowed us to start a special piece of work that we had been planning for a long time. We had an ideal place, we felt, in a very large room that adjoined our Home-Planning Workshops in the basement of Vladeck Houses. Many older people had worked in the shops and had helped develop two of the programs, so they were familiar with the surroundings. Now they had a room of their own, but were not isolated since all ages came to the shops.

We believed that it was important to keep old people in the stream of life as long as possible. We have found, for instance, that many old people react against housing that is just for their age group.

When our program for men and women over sixty finally started, the first thing, of course, was to pick a name and elect a president. I was grateful that the name turned out to be the

"Good Companions." This had a lively connotation and did not suggest the sentimental nonsense that this was a "golden age" at a time when most of them were lonely, living on miserably little money, and their feet ached! While I don't feel that it is a "golden age," I do feel that the Good Companions have turned out to be an everlasting credit to the human race—when they had some place to go and something exciting to do they entered into the situation with such enthusiasm and gusto.

Our first plan was to be open all day in the pattern of some of the first old-age centers. However, it didn't take long for a committee to tell me that they did not care about being open in the mornings but preferred the evenings. The mornings were for shopping, cleaning, and sleeping; but the afternoons and evenings were for fun, and if there was no fun, very lonely. So Mrs. Josephine Smith, who was their first leader and very proud of the start they had made, had to reorganize the time schedule to suit their needs.

Mrs. Maria Kron has been the head of the work with the Good Companions for the last thirteen years, and the president of that group introduced her at one of their parties with, "And now I introduce our darling leader, Mrs. Maria Kron, *vid* all modern improvements." I agree heartily with their president. Her leadership has given the Good Companions a sense of both fun and purpose. She has such warmth and exuberance, along with wisdom, that she creates a climate of gaiety wherever she is—and the Good Companions agree with me.

The group of over four hundred was at first almost entirely Jewish, but as the neighborhood changed and the years produced grandparents in the Puerto Rican and Negro families, we worked hard to draw them in. Introducing new members into an already established group requires a great deal of skilled and determined leadership involving above all the planning and help of the group itself. Many discussions preceded the welcoming of new neighbors into this situation, which gradually became the job of the Good Companions themselves.

A Puerto Rican neighbor, Carmen Rodriguez, who has both drive and natural skills, joined our staff and visited and encouraged the older Puerto Ricans to join the Good Companions. She ingeniously brought them in by way of the arts. The classes in pottery and painting in the Home-Planning Workshops particularly interested them. Their talent in handicrafts helped to establish their identity, and then, as members of the Good Companions admired their work, they were drawn into the club itself, and a great mixture of Spanish and Jewish customs began to emerge. Even a Spanish dish made by Kosher rules was concocted—pretty awful to taste but served in triumph! And a Christmas party given by Puerto Rican members of the Good Companions served food from a Kosher delicatessen.

In one of the pictures in this book, you see a Negro neighbor teaching a spiritual to Milton Frankel, Mrs. Kron's assistant. This woman sings beautifully and has established a rapport with the leader which helps him in other ways. Mr. Frankel knows a great many spirituals himself and he felt that if he could learn more of them and teach them to the whole group it would be one way of making the Negro neighbors, who were also beginning to attend, feel at home. Milton Frankel had started as a neighborhood volunteer to lead dancing and singing, and shown such unusual gifts that, fortunately for us, he left his bakery business for full-time responsibility with our Good Companions. Aside from his other gifts, he could make a zombie sing and dance!

Folk dancing, singing, pottery, painting, serving tea, giving parties; trips to Washington for Medicare, Social Security benefits, or other social purposes; making up a play and acting in it, and intense politicking in their own presidential elections—all these give a lift to the hours. These might be just words until you hear the dance music, the clapping, and the laughter, and see the folk dancers as they swing each other around and teach each other steps and songs. I worried at first about heart attacks in the midst of all the exuberance but I soon gave that up as we have never had one.

When I took visitors around Henry Street, I tried to end up with the Good Companions if I was tired because they take on visitors with such zest. The visitors are off your hands and get a quick education, generally including a little hot tea.

One of the most interesting activities that has grown out of the Good Companions group is a volunteer service project called "The Elderly Helping the Elderly." This volunteer work, first begun as a small "sunsine committee," which Mrs. Kron developed into an important part of the program, was expanded, thanks to a subsidy from Washington. Mrs. Juliet Brudney, of the staff of the United Neighborhood Houses, had gone down to investigate the possibilities of government support for special settlement projects. In the course of her investigations she told the U.S. Public Health Service about our Elderly Helping the Elderly project, and they became interested in enlarging the work and establishing well-defined training methods. They felt it was worth developing because it could be applicable in so many places. When they gave us a grant, we invited three neighboring settlements—Lillian Wald Settlement, Grand Street, and Educational Alliance—to take part as we felt it would be good to have the methods tried out by groups other than our own.

Our volunteers are asked by hospitals and other local agencies to call on people in the neighborhood who need special help; perhaps someone just getting out of a hospital who may be too weak to go down and do their own shopping or even cook their first meal. A neighbor coming out of Bellevue Hospital after an operation needed X-ray follow-up but was too weak to go for the treatments by herself. One of our elderly volunteers took her every morning for three weeks and waited several hours to bring her home. I knew all about it because the volunteer told me about it himself when I came to visit. His satisfaction showed through his story with every word.

The "Friendly Volunteers" perform a surprising variety of services. One of the Good Companions has been kept out of a state mental hospital for the past eight years. She has periodic breakdowns, and as her friends in the Good Companions see her becoming disturbed they rush her to the hospital where the treatments bring her around again and she functions normally for many months. At one time the doctors at Bellevue were determined to send her away but they hadn't taken into account the "Friendly Volunteers," who put on a scene at the hospital that was not too "friendly" to any such diagnosis and back she came to her own apartment, which had been kept clean and safely looked after. There are double benefits in such a relationship. The volunteers feel needed and make friends with the person they have helped, and their stature increases in their own eyes.

Some of our projects were carried on in close cooperation with the local Gouverneur Clinic, and services other than individual help to people in special need have grown out of this cooperation. The establishment of a coffee lounge at Gouverneur Clinic was a very useful by-product. On one red-letter occasion, a luncheon party was given at the settlement by the Good Companions who ran the coffee lounge for a well-loved member of VISTA (Volunteers in Service to America), spry and delightful at eighty, who had helped them manage the lounge. We have a picture taken in our dining room with Max Tobias, the president of the Good Companions, also chairman of the work in the coffee lounge, presiding; and Ruth Tefferteller leading the singing.

Max Tobias illustrates what such a group can mean in the lives of its members. He had had a little painting business, and over the years did much of our painting at Henry Street. He also led a men's club from the unemployment years on, and was the leader of many of the protest groups of the early days. He had escaped from Russia at age fifteen, having crossed the country dressed as a girl.

In the old days, Max Tobias headed a men's club at the settlement which was named after Governor Lehman and dedicated to carry out his social ideals. Herbert Lehman was loved throughout the whole Lower East Side but the members of Henry Street considered he belonged especially to them. For a long time, the Lehman Club felt greatly thwarted by a member who created many embarrassing scenes which they felt kept them from developing along the fine lines they envisaged for themselves. They talked it over with me many times; always, I felt, with the hope that I would rid them in some miraculous way of Mr. Stern, since they couldn't bear to put him out themselves. One day a committee from the Lehman Club arrived in triumph. They had worked their way out of the situation. The whole club, they said, "had resigned off Stern, and left him with the club."

After Max Tobias' long years of hard work as a painter, as club president, and as a fiery protester whose spirit made up for his English, it was hard indeed to see him standing disconsolately on the corner, his wife dead, his business gone because of his age and his arthritic hands, and his spirit seemingly gone with his usefulness. We all worried about our old friend, and finally Ralph Tefferteller managed to inveigle him into joining the Good Companions. It took time, but gradually, after he joined, his sense of importance came back. For the past two years, Max has been president of the Good Companions and can give as fiery a speech as ever. And now he has married again!

At Henry Street we are always painfully aware of the cruel meagerness of Social Security benefits to those who depend solely upon it, and do whatever we can to bring it home to those lawmakers most responsible. In 1967 when an increase in Social Security was being considered, we made a survey among 205 of our Good Companions that showed that their Social Security averaged only $66.05 a month with an average rent of $33.50. This left an average of approximately a dollar a day for food, doctors, medicine, dentists, clothes, carfare, and the multitude of other needs that arise. In spite of these figures and the privation they point to, only eighteen people out of this group had applied for welfare.

Mrs. Kron has a story that has been quoted many times and that illustrates this point so perfectly. A nice-looking older man, who appeared to take the fancy of several of the ladies, joined the Good Companions. Finally one of them seemed to be the favorite, and Mrs. Kron asked her how things were going between her and Mr. Wise. "Well," she answered, "it's this way. He is a good man, he is a clean man, but he is on 'welfare' and I am on welfare and I want a man on Social Security."

Before I leave this subject of age I would like to point out that the old-age program that starts when you are young is perhaps the most satisfying of all. A group of women still known as the "H. H. [Helen Hall] Girls" met with me at University House in Philadelphia when we were all young. Their association with each other has continued through all the years, and has meant a great deal to them, as it has to me, and they still come to visit me in New York or I go to Philadelphia for an annual get-together.

At Henry Street, we have had a group of women who have been together for over sixty years. There are few original members left now but they first met with Miss Wald around a samovar with shawls on their heads, and a new country to learn.

I feel they have been the lucky ones among our aged because they have grown old in such close comradeship, and each one has shared in more than a hundred other lives. I am sure the years have dealt more kindly with them because of that recurring Wednesday evening when the Lillian Wald club meets. As the years go on, a tried comradeship gives some stability to each separate member. That they belong to such a longstanding body adds a little to each one's stature and to each one's security.

At the end of a big party in which all ages have joined in, I have often felt that more of our money *must* go into work for the aged because of the way the older folks say good night—it is enough to break your heart. The young and middle-aged, as they go off, shake hands in a friendly, casual way; but with the older people it is different. Their hands and eyes reach out for a moment of *real* recognition—an affirmation that you know they are different from anyone else. The demand is so marked and poignant that it takes all one's resources to meet it half adequately, for with each one you must bring to bear all the special things they feel you have in common. I remember one eager wrinkle-faced questioner: "You remember me? You spoke at my graduation." I was taken aback for a moment as I looked at her, and then I remembered the English classes! So after the goodbyes are over, work for old people seems to be the most important thing we can do.

Then the next morning comes and you may see the babies trudging into nursery school. You may see a pale, small girl playing happily with other children when a few months before she sat unspeaking, like a frightened animal, crushed against the farthest wall; or you may see the four-year-old Suzuki nursery schoolers with their tiny violins. So perhaps in the morning you say to yourself, "*Our* old age program is going to start right here in the nursery school. This is the time we must begin." But you know you can't let it go at that, that all of it should be done at the same time and that no age waits for the exigencies of another.

And we know that we can help make any age a more golden one by putting opportunities within reach from the beginning to the end of life, and that is what civilization should be about.

XXI

Cooperation
with the Public Schools

A close relationship with other agencies—churches, hospitals, political clubs, and above all the schools, is an essential part of neighborhood work. We have a long-standing commitment to the upgrading of educational services for children. I served on the local school board for a great many years. I must say they were not as important as they are today, and were largely political appointments, but it still brought me in close touch with the superintendents of our district and many others in the school system with whom I often worked closely.

This is not to suggest that there were no difficulties or differences of opinion over the years between us and the schools, particularly when I first came to Henry Street and before I went on the school board, but it is to say that many useful things came out of our cooperation.

I remember in my very early days a nearby principal who told me that he would never allow a parents' association in his school, and as he was incredibly rude to parents, I went to see him about some parents who wanted to form an association. He also told me that he would never let a child in his school go to the Child Guidance Bureau of the Board of Education, no matter what his condition was. I decided the Board of Education had better do something about this far from benevolent dictator. When I took the matter up at headquarters, the first response was, "He is to retire soon and where will we put him anyway—out in the suburbs?" "Nowhere," seemed the right answer to me, but in the suburbs was better than in my neighborhood where parents couldn't protect themselves from him as well as they might in a better-to-do neighborhood, and I said so. Finally I began to sense that there was another element in the situation. This principal stood in strong with the local Tammany Club across the street from the school, and I judged the Board of Education didn't want to tangle with the club.

I happened to know that my influence with the Ahearn Club was not very great. In fact, I had been told that they planned "to get rid of that woman." I passed the club each week on my way to the Monday Night Forum at our Playhouse and on warm nights they were sitting outside, cigars and all. I used to wonder how they were planning to get rid of me! I should explain that this was before Jack Markowitz and Bill Calise risked their political futures by breaking away from the Ahearn Club and starting a Reform Democratic Club which backed Robert Wagner in his first term for mayor against Vincent Impellitteri, the Tammany choice.

I'll have to admit that I did not succeed in dislodging the principal before the date that normally retired him, but I should add that this has not been typical, nor is the next episode, of my association with the schools.

James Marshall, then president of the Board of Education, and I joined in a fight against these same antagonists. It was over the opening of a school near us, and he had called a meeting to discuss it with the neighborhood. The neighbors came but so did arranged interrupters, somewhat in the pattern of the present time only without the obscenities! Perhaps it was not even as violent but it seemed pretty violent to us that night as we tried to make ourselves heard over the shouts planted in each corner of the room and also the planned noises coming in through open windows on the street. I don't know how I heard it through the din, but when I got up on a desk to speak, I heard the glass on the top break. However, James Marshall was not only socially minded but determined, and the school was finally opened—but certainly not that night!

I found Florence Becker, who was assistant superintendent in our district, very helpful in all my dealings with her. When Mobilization for Youth was being planned, a group sent by the National Institute for Mental Health visited the Lower East Side to see whether the community was really in sympathy with the plan. Hers was one of the most favorable and careful appraisals of our Mobilization plans that the visiting group heard that day. At another time she took me by hand to get permission at 110 Livingston Street for our experiment that involved junior high school girls working for credit in our nursery school, which was technically illegal without approval from the top.

Association with the schools works both ways. Very often we can be the means of school personnel being drawn into the community. As important as we hope we can be in the lives of the children, we know that the schools can be more so, and for the children's sake the lines of communication should be kept open between us and we should do everything within our power to keep them so. I do not mean to imply that this will always be possible at times of acute disagreement, as it sometimes turned out to be during the teachers' strike in 1968, only that it is of great importance to the children and parents with whom we work. This association may be improved under the decentralized school boards, or in some areas it may prove more difficult.

Conferences on the problems of individual children, initiated by Henry Street or by a principal or teacher, have been almost a daily occurrence when the relationships were good. Seminars of all kinds with teachers, on the subject of handling difficult children, were planned by our Mental Hygiene Clinic and given warm encouragement by the assistant superintendent. This same assistant superintendent, Dr. Victor Berger, helped so much when we were getting LENA going that the neighborhood awarded him a special honor at a LENA dinner.

We have also had a number of mutual experiments with the schools lasting over a period of years. The following seems to me one of the most significant because I believe so strongly in pre-school education anywhere. But particularly in neighborhoods such as Henry Street's. I had started a nursery school in Philadelphia at University House, and for over thirty years we raised the money for a nursery school at Henry Street. We tried different approaches, with parents playing a big part as assistants, with psychiatric advice for problem children, with children coming three times a week instead of five (which was felt to be a good plan for the three-year-olds), and at one time the graduate mothers of the nursery school formed a club to let the whole neighborhood know by meetings and discussion what they had learned through the nursery school.

The last and by far the most significant plan served a second purpose, that of using junior high school girls as assistants as part of their formal school work. The one thing we are reasonably sure of in the girls' future is that, if they are biologically able, they will have children; yet in the usual routine of the Board of Education, young girls have come out of school with no understanding of how to handle little children. It seems incredibly shortsighted for us not to be sharing what we know with the girls who will be bearing the responsibility for the next generation, many of them under deprivations that will be aggravated by ignorance.

From the very beginning, the mothers of the children in our nursery school had asked us why they had not learned in public school what they were learning about children in our nursery school. So, finally, in searching to find ways of preparing girls for child-rearing, we worked out a cooperative arrangement with one of our local junior high school principals. He agreed with us that the program was valuable and promised to send ninth-grade girls to our nursery school as aides one morning or one afternoon each week as part of their school curriculum. The school, the settlement, and the aides found the plan so stimulating and educationally valuable that we then sought an opportunity to enlarge it. This opportunity presented itself when we were fortunate enough to obtain a special grant from a foundation to enlarge our nursery school so that we could experiment further by adding another junior high school tripling the number of girls, as well as putting more emphasis on improving the curriculum patterns we had already worked out with the schools. This also meant increasing the number of preschool children to over a hundred which meant we had to have more space. The Housing Authority made this possible by making over a large room at La Guardia Houses especially for nursery school use.

Many conferences always took place between the nursery school director and the guidance counselors in each school while selecting the girls, scheduling their time at the nursery school, and setting goals for the year. It was explained to the girls that they were to be regarded as student-teachers, and that they would actually take part in guiding the activities of the children. Group meetings were held twice a month. During these meetings the girls were given the reasons for the methods they were taught as well as answers to other questions on how to handle specific problems with the children. Very often in the course of these discussions some of the girls' own problems came to light and they were helped to find answers.

For some girls the experience stimulated them toward a career. They expressed a desire to go into teaching, nursing, or even child psychology. However, the most important reason for the experience was to help them gain a better understanding of the problems of motherhood so that their own children might reap the benefits. The cooperating schools seemed as eager as we were that training programs such as this would be a regular part of every junior high school.

One year we decided to follow fifty-five of our nursery-school graduates on to kindergarten to see how they adjusted in comparison to those who had not had a chance to go to nursery school. The consensus of all the teachers was that the children who had participated in our program the previous year were more "adequately prepared and well adjusted," and that for the most part, these children turned out to be the leaders in their own kindergarten classes. It was also pointed out that the level of maturity manifested in the children's work was higher than in those children who had never participated in nursery school. I realize that there have been studies recently which seem to show that Head Start graduates did not show continued improvement. I cannot but wonder whether the experience in the Head Start class was as good as it should have been for we had such a different experience. A significant comment came from one teacher who felt that the parents also had been better prepared for the public school situation. Parents were described as being more relaxed at conferences, and their children had better attendance. Of course in any plan we were using in the nursery school the parents had always played an important part.

In 1965 the moment came for which we had been hoping for so long: our local school was able, through the Head Start Program, with Anti-Poverty funds, to take over our nursery school. To be sure the program was only for four-year-olds, but considering the temper of the times we felt hopeful that it would not take thirty more years to get the three-year-olds in! Unfortunately, while we were in the public school system at last, the Head Start emphasis on the mothers of the children and on "indigenous" workers was so great that it seems to have squeezed out our junior high school girls for the time being at least. We were very much concerned when this happened but we are hoping that the groundwork has been laid well enough so that our aide program will be resumed.

I do not want to minimize the difficulty involved in changing the New York City school system, as the present decentralization chaos has certainly illustrated, but I do want to stress the importance of a neighborhood agency taking advantage of every possibility for cooperation with the schools for the sake of the children. When we are free to go in and out on matters that go wrong between children and teachers, or between parents and teachers, we can be performing an extremely valuable service for our neighbors, and we can often do much more than this, but this alone is worth doing.

This project with junior high school girls has survived its temporary eclipse. The two junior high schools with which we cooperated are planning a renewal of the work in cooperation with Hamilton Madison House and Henry Street. The Citizens Committee for Children is hoping to introduce the idea to school boards in New York City, and the National Commission on the Resources for Youth, under Mary Kohler's leadership, is planning to use it as a model to be implemented across the country.

To add to this encouraging postscript: The three-year-olds are now accepted in Head Start.

XXII

The National Federation
of Settlements and
the United Neighborhood Houses

The National Federation of Settlements has always seemed to me
to be an integral part of each individual settlement, extending
and strengthening what we are able to accomplish. In the same
way it is possible for the local city federations to make the settlements as a whole more effective in each city. I felt this from
the beginning and worked closely with the Philadelphia Association of Settlements as well as the National Federation of Settlements as soon as I came to University House.

Aside from what the National Federation of Settlements meant
to me in my work, I am especially grateful because it brought
me in direct touch with the pioneers in the settlement movement,
with whom I worked on the board of the Federation from 1926
on. They were without doubt the most gifted and delightful
group of individuals I have ever known. Individuals most certainly, but humorous, tolerant, good-tempered, and wise, and
back of them was a record of achievement both city-wide and
national. They had espoused and influenced: Women's Suffrage,
Prohibition, Peace, Disarmament, Civil Liberties, Abolishment
of Capital Punishment, and Health Insurance—which they had
come out for in 1917. Jane Addams had given courageous leadership at Hull House in Chicago, to the Labor movement and
peace movement, and had worked in Theodore Roosevelt's Progressive party. The establishment of the Children's Bureau

stemmed from Lillian Wald's and Florence Kelley's work at Henry Street in New York, and the bill establishing the Children's Bureau was introduced by a congressman from the board of South End House in Boston.

The first meeting of the National Federation of Settlements had been held in Boston in June of 1911, with Jane Addams as president. Typically enough she led a discussion on "A Human Standard of Living," and John Elliott headed a discussion of "A More Thorough-going and More Democratic Organization of Neighborhood Life." Both titles sound pretty up to date!

Board meetings started early in the morning and went on until late at night. As I look back on it, there were long discussions over everything. Jane Addams listened intently, adding her comments both wise and humorous. Mary Simkovitch, from Greenwich House in New York, was gay and witty. John Elliott, from Hudson Guild in New York, had a rare wit, too. Albert Kennedy, of South End House in Boston, always encouraged the arts; and Charles Cooper, from Kingsley House in Pittsburgh, was strong for social action. Paul Kellogg was determined to know what was happening in neighborhoods across the country; Lillian Wald had a practical fighting spirit for whatever cause she was espousing, as did Graham Taylor, from Chicago Commons. He was followed by his daughter, Lea Taylor, who always brought a healthy downrightness to any discussion.

It was a spirited and valuable kind of education for someone who was starting in the settlement field. I know I never missed a conference or a board meeting if I could possibly help it because I found the exchange of experience so valuable. I wanted to know what was happening in the other neighborhoods, too, and to bring judgments other than my own to bear on what were the most serious national problems. This has been, to my mind, the most important contribution that the National Federation of Settlements has made to its members. I do not mean to imply that it stops there—just that this has meant the most to me.

Perhaps because I was chairman of their Social Action Committee for twenty years, I especially appreciated not only a channel for bringing together our common experiences but the readiness on the part of the members of the federation to take action. The settlements are homogeneous in their conviction that they must act to change basic social ills. This in spite of their differences in local programs, and their varying approaches in different neighborhoods. On issues affecting the living standards of their neighbors, they have stood together, been willing to speak out and speak out early. A study of resolutions over the years shows this very vividly.

I visited many settlements over the country to gather data for our unemployment study. Later in 1936 to 1940 when I was president of the Federation, I visited many more. I have always found these visits extraordinarily interesting, and I felt that many of the settlement leaders, both early and later additions to the movement, were first-class strategists in their own communities. In my visits, I came to see at first hand what was happening in the different cities, which reinforced my feeling that these general practitioners had something special to contribute to the field of social work.

The National Federation has had only five executives and this, I think, has played a part in its stability. Starting in 1911, Robert A. Woods and later Albert Kennedy were the first executives. Their early books on the settlements, scholarship and Albert Kennedy's knowledge of community planning played an important part in the development of the National Federation of Settlements, and in the whole settlement movement. Albert Kennedy, who took on full responsibility in 1922, was a perfectionist, and had a wholesome scorn of anything shoddy in settlement performance.

Lillie Peck followed Albert Kennedy in 1934, serving until 1947; John McDowell then headed the federation for eleven years, leaving to go to Boston as dean of the School for Social Work at Boston University. Margaret Berry was made director in 1958. She had had first-hand experience as the director of Soho House in Pittsburgh. Margaret combines a high order of intelligence with a firm backbone! I mention the latter only because she is so gentle, small, and charming that one might not realize her strength.

Under Margaret Berry's leadership, the staff of the National Federation has been indefatigable in visiting member houses and seeing that advice got to where it was wanted most. Very importantly, their budget has greatly increased over the years.

I have never thought that the settlements or that the National Federation of Settlements got a fair slice of the Community Chest pie. Perhaps the settlements' insistence on social action may have had something to do with their coming out on the short end. Fund-raising and social reform are uneasy bedfellows. Fern Colburn who, to my infinite satisfaction, was put on the federation staff in charge of social action in 1950, has greatly broadened and strengthened the National Federation in this field.

In New York, United Neighborhood Houses has had the advantage of Helen Harris' executive leadership since 1947 and this was combined with Stanley Isaacs' chairmanship until his death in 1962. Helen Harris brought not only her unusual executive ability, but a willingness to fight for what she believed was right, all of which has served the city's settlements well.

My long friendship with Helen Harris began when she worked with me as director of dramatics for a few months during my first year at University House. That winter she tackled the job of introducing drama into University House in place of minstrel shows! Helen made a bargain with me. She would get the boys off the basketball floor if I would be the leading lady to lend the occasion importance, she said. She picked a show of Richard Harding Davis' with burglars in it. Helen is a hard one to refuse and I knew I had a long way to go to get the arts into University House, so that is how we started off. We had a dental clinic at University House, and one of the boys had a front tooth out which made him look just like a burglar. I remember he was trying to get the dentist to put it in before the show, while I was trying to get him to keep it out!

I was very lucky in my struggle to introduce drama because the next year another very persuasive friend, Fonrose Wainwright, took on the job where Helen Harris had left off, and the Irish gift for drama finally blossomed in real earnest as Fonrose wrote plays that they found unable to resist. She even took the dramatic troupe for a number of summers to her home in Vermont where they played in surrounding villages to the great satisfaction of farmer viewers and the city performers.

At that time Helen Harris was hesitating between the careers of social work and drama, but luckily for the settlements she chose the former and went to Pittsburg to work with Charles Cooper at Kingsley House in developing their work in what at that time was a not-too-easy city to develop social programs.

She then went to Union Settlement in New York and directed that settlement until she left in 1938 to run New York City's National Youth Administration, taking over from Mark Mc-Closkey. This was considered one of the best youth administration operations in the country, and I have often wished the Anti-Poverty programs of today had been willing to learn more from some of the NYA's job-training programs. She then did another citywide job with La Guardia's strong backing in setting up and developing the Day Care Centers that had grown out of the war years. This was before she joined UNRR (United Nations Relief and Rehabilitation Administration) in 1946, returning to head up the United Neighborhood Houses.

Helen Harris continued in the tradition of fighting for social legislation which had been the most important part of the work of the United Neighborhood Houses since its inception in 1900. While the record has always included a broad spectrum of causes, that of housing has headed the list as of the most continuous concern.

Another citywide organization in New York that has given me great satisfaction is the Citizens Committee for Children. I feel as though every city should build itself a similar membership of concerned lay people and experts working together on the problems of children. Mrs. David Levy headed up the planning of this organization 25 years ago. At her death, her sister, Mrs. Max Ascoli, became the moving spirit on the board. The Executive Head, Trude Lash, with a brilliant staff, has made the Citizens Committee for Children a formidable tool for the protection of children in New York City. Importantly, members of these committees visit the agencies they are criticizing and so bring first-hand evidence to bear in their reports and testimony.

The Citizens Committee works through committees of their members with staff, bringing to bear their special skills on the problems the committee has undertaken.

The Citizens Committee has been able to supply ammunition in the way of figures and many striking reports which have helped them change conditions for children, not only through their own work, but they have been able to supply other agencies with material whish has involved them in widespread action. This has helped make the Citizens Committee for Children's influence statewide as well as nationwide.

I want to mention a national agency which I feel has had great social impact in the country. Sitting on the Public Policy Committee of the Advertising Council for many years I have found it both a great satisfaction and very stimulating to see the skills of the greatest advertisers in the country brought to bear on selling and interpreting national social causes.

The Advertising Council started twenty-eight years ago during World War II when they worked with the government to help sell War Bonds, attract nurses to the Armed Services, and helped the war effort in many other ways. When the war was over it was decided to continue this kind of volunteer service for other social causes in the country, and they appointed a Public Policy Committee to advise on all requests for campaigns and on their relative importance and public interest. The twenty-four people on the Committee are drawn from education, business, labor, social service, foreign affairs, and journalism. The campaigns they undertake cover a wide range of interests, and some are of short duration and others run for many years. To give an idea of the variety I will start with the well-loved "Smokey the Bear," who was created many years ago to give life to their "Prevent Forest Fires" campaign. Some others have been or are: Aid to Higher Education, Crime Prevention, Rehabilitation of the Handicapped, Traffic Safety, a campaign to interest young people in the Peace Corps, the Red Cross, United Fund campaigns and at the present time, the campaigns are directed toward minority group problems, drug addiction and the crises in the cities.

The Advertising Council is nonprofit and private and supported by advertising and business. As they put it: "In the past 28 years the nation's communications media have contributed more than $5 billion worth of their services and facilities to persuading individual citizens to take actions which would improve their own lot, or their community's or the welfare of their fellow citizens."

PART THREE

The War Years
1940 - 1945

XXIII

The Shadow of War

La Guardia kept his word about building Vladeck Houses; and it was fortunate that the final decision to build the project came in 1938, before the war stopped the building of homes which included public housing.

I mention in some detail programs designed to meet the needs of tenants moving into Vladeck Houses and later into La Guardia Houses, for even though their building has slowed down so cruelly, low-income housing projects of various kinds have become a pattern of life, and can become a more successful one if more effort is made to help the newcomers not only as they move into the projects, but continuously. It is an area where social work has a fine chance to be truly constructive, for a decent home helps, but does not always solve the families' other problems which seldom evaporate entirely when a family moves into new housing.

As an illustration of one small but successful project that met a continuing need in the housing projects: at one time, Recreation Rooms and Settlement, which runs the Community Center in Breukelen* Houses, was told that fourteen families were to be evicted for poor housekeeping. It really had to be horrendous to get to that point. But it isn't always "moral turpitude" that makes a bad housekeeper, cleanliness and godliness may or

* Old spelling of Brooklyn.

may not go together, many things can enter in. So the manager of Breukelen Houses and the settlement planned a series of meetings with those families, under the leadership of a gifted and practical Home Economist from the Jewish Family Service. The one stipulation was that the whole family—father, mother and children—were to come. As their homes were at stake, they all did. Whole families turned to and washed walls, mothers faced up to the mother's bad back or other ills, mothers faced up to their own bad managing, children helped as they never had before. All but one of the families were able to change their way of living enough to make good. This was one bit of imaginative social work that can help make for successful living in our low-income projects and this kind of service which should always be available.

In 1939 Henry Street was lucky in being able to acquire 305 Henry Street, a small tenement next to our complex of three old buildings at 297-301-303 Henry Street opposite the Vladeck Houses site. This gave us more space to experiment with programs designed to help the tenants coming into Vladeck Houses. This was before Pete's House was built and we were horribly pressed for space for new work. So many things were started in this little building in its nine years of service that it should have been called the "Emergency House."

Douglas Lockwood, the head of our Art Department at that time, and his Work Group of teenagers, took on the job of doing over the old tenement to fit our changing needs. His imagination and enthusiasm carried him and everyone near him into projects of all kinds and proportions. Give him a piece of old iron and we had a project. A whole dilapidated building was a dream come true for Doug and his boys, and not only a building but a backyard adjoining the backyard belonging to a "cellar club." As Doug and his crew started getting rid of the awful mess, the Cellar Club boys watched with some skepticism, then interest, and then became involved in cleaning up their own back yard. Soon the fence between us came down, replaced by low wire, and, before we finished, there was a garden in common. And one club member, who turned out to be a skilled woodworker, got interested, volunteered at first, then finally became a member of our staff.

The first floor was taken up with our first model apartment, set up for incoming tenants, with furniture made by some of the future tenants themselves, in our little carpentry shop in the basement. Because of the success of this apartment, when Vladeck Houses was finally completed, the Housing Authority set aside an apartment in the project, and asked us to furnish it for them to use as a model. This we were glad to do as we felt it important not only to help set the pattern for model apartments in the public housing projects but to be as close as possible to the way public housing was serving families. It was a new kind of life and would change as it went along, and we certainly had an obligation to make it as successful as possible.

The Authority finally supplied a large basement room in Vladeck Houses which took the place of our small workshop in the new tenement basement, leaving us room for a milk bar which we badly needed at that particular moment.

But this little shop was the beginning of our Home Planning Workshops, started, among other reasons, as a shield against installment buying, along with our Credit Union. What installment buying did to family budgets had always concerned us, but the housing projects are a gold mine for the "peddlers" and other installment sellers. It is so easy. Upstairs and down, the peddlers go calling on mothers who need *everything*.

A group of mothers working with our staff showed off the new model apartment in Vladeck Houses, and the Housing Authority sent each tenant, as they were accepted, to see the apartment. As we had hoped, model apartments eventually became an established practice with the Housing Authority. Our firmest advice to tenants was to build or make old things over in our workshops and/or save money in our Credit Union toward new furniture.

Our work grew fast as tenants moved in. Our workshops were crowded and more space was given us. When Susan Jenkins Brown left us, Karin Peterfy took over the running of our shops, and the Vladeck Houses manager of those days told me that he hated to meet Mrs. Peterfy on the street for fear she would persuade him to give up another basement.

Our Community Studies Department, under Susan Jenkins Brown's creative directorship, had discovered many practical ways of carrying on consumer education as new tenants came in. We knew that every family, no matter how poor, would have to buy something when they moved into their new home. We were at the tail end of the long Depression. As only families with incomes of $1,400 or under were eligible for federally assisted housing at this time, we knew that there would be very little in the way of household goods to move to the new quarters. Years of unemployment, in most cases, had meant no replacements. As one woman put it, "My furniture wouldn't last to move across the street."

Then, too, few of the families had ever had a living room. The small tenement kitchens were often the only place for the family's social activities and had to be used for bathing in the old kitchen washtubs as well, and it was where children had to do their homework. For months after Vladeck Houses was completely full, many of the small living rooms were still bare of furniture.

We were not limited to the skills and resources of our own staff and board in our home planning work. Again, as in our milk study, we had the friendly collaboration of the Consumer Counsel of the Department of Agriculture, this time, Donald E. Montgomery.

A corps of advisers from Washington began to appear at Henry Street. Descriptive literature on good homemaking practices, designs for practical, easy-to-make furniture were put in our hands, and we were supplied with models of such furniture for our model apartments. There was even discussion of a cooperative project whereby the rural community wood-workshops being set up by the Department of Agriculture over the country to give part-time employment to members of farm families could sell their products, through consumer cooperatives, to the tenants of low-income city housing projects. This was a vision for the future which interested us but did not deflect us from our modest immediate job of aiding the Vladeck tenants. Perhaps someday a federal Department of the Consumer will bring such things about.

Most of this preplanning went on during the hot summer months of 1938 since the first groups of Vladeck tenants would receive their admission notices in the fall, and we wanted to be ready. I remember a story told us by one of our friends, a woman from the Department of Agriculture whom I had shown around the neighborhood one hot summer night. We were talking over the possibilities of more convenient kitchen cabinets, which we later built in our model kitchen in our Home Planning Workshops, and she said she had just been discussing kitchen cabinets with a manufacturer. He had said that he had finished a fine new one, fine in that it fitted into a box car without an inch of space wasted. "How does it fit into kitchens?" she asked him. "Oh, that will take care of itself," was the reply.

We built a model kitchen in the Home Planning Workshop when it turned out that the kitchens in Vladeck were so poorly planned. We decided that we had a responsibility toward future kitchens in housing developments, so a committee of neighborhood women worked with us on a questionnaire. We took what the 150 women tenants said they felt was wrong in the project kitchens and built a kitchen that was more practical from their standpoint. We had lower cabinets and more of them, more work space and less waste space, and made a good many other changes, of course using the same floor space. This we built in our workshops, side by side with one of the regular kitchens which had been installed for us there. Then we had an opening party, with the then head of the Housing Authority as guest; a radio announcement by Mary Margaret McBride; followed by articles in eleven architectural magazines, some of which sent architects down to inspect us. All the mothers who had worked on this kitchen were determined that it should help in the building of practical kitchens for other women. We sold our kitchen plans for $1 each and had requests for them from all over the country, so a good many well-off women must have benefited by having cabinets they could reach! Perhaps the trouble with kitchens is that they are made by men and mostly used by women.

Of course a great many of the families who had lived in the old tenements on the site of Vladeck House were old friends; they were "site tenants" at Vladeck who had, if they were otherwise eligible, first chance at one of the new homes. They had stayed in the neighborhood, moving into one of the vacant flats nearby, which sounds hardly possible today, when families on building sites can seldom stay in their own neighborhoods during the building years.

When our carpentry shop moved over to Vladeck basement we had room for a milk bar in which we cooperated with the Department of Agriculture. The Department's Surplus Commodities program was offering what was known at the time as "penny milk," which could be sold through nonprofit social agencies, and we were anxious to have our neighbors take advantage of it. The milk had to be served on the premises at a penny a glass. Douglas Lockwood's teen-age work group got busy again and turned the former carpentry shop into a colorful room with a milk bar. This turned out to be one of the most thoroughly satisfactory of all our many projects of that period. One of our art students painted gay figures from Mother Goose on the walls after the other boys had done the basic carpentry, painting, and lighting.

Children crowded in at noon, often with their luncheon sandwiches, and again after school at 3 o'clock. Many others, particularly old people of the neighborhood, also sought this reinforcement to their meager diets. The National Youth Administration supplied a staff of teen-age girls to help. Many mothers of the neighborhood volunteered to serve during the very busy selling periods, when the milk bar really hummed. Altogether, it was a lively and healthy place for several years.

We tried to persuade the Department of Agriculture to continue the program, but without success. These busy milk bars were not popular with milk dealers, though of course, the milk was supplied by them on a reimbursement basis. However, the school milk program has continued to be followed by the school lunch program. It was a satisfaction when I was visiting a village school in Puerto Rico to see the rows of glasses of milk ready to be served for lunch as a part of the United States Department of Agriculture program. But in our milk bar we had the satisfaction of seeing the eagerness with which old people reached for their penny carton, and the still greater satisfaction of seeing children imbibing milk instead of all-day suckers, Cokes, paper cups of colored ice, pickles, and all the other debris that finds its way into children's stomachs by way of their pennies.

When the surplus milk was no longer available, we planned to raise money to supplement our customers' pennies, but we finally gave it up because it required so much help, as well as the subsidy for the milk. War conditions began to bring neighborhood changes in employment and we were somewhat comforted, in finally losing this thoroughly healthy experiment, by the fact that it was jobs that were taking away our neighborhood volunteers. So many mothers from our clubs had "manned," as it is unjustly termed, our bar. As jobs became available, everyone in the neighborhood, young and old, mothers, grandmothers, adolescents, got jobs as fast as they could. Even if there was a male wage earner in the family, the women, girls and boys worked to make up the arrears left by the long years of the Depression. They had been starved for work as well as food and all the ordinary replacements of a home had given way to the primary need for food and clothing. The oilcloth on the kitchen table, the linoleum on the floor, their few pots and pans were all battered and worn by the years; a happy refurbishing began as money became more than marginal.

This economic upswing could not but be hopeful and vivid seen at firsthand in a neighborhood such as ours, even when we knew that it was the shadow, and then the reality, of war which was bringing it about. A few jobs were found, and the families started to buy. And so a few more jobs were made and this brought more jobs and—you saw the momentum gathering, unadorned by statistics. You saw plans for the future being born again; and this continued through all the war years, along with their tragedy.

Perhaps the most spectacular project of the Home Planning Workshops during the war was the "Swap Shop" which was launched to help overcome the increased shortages of most consumer goods, which was becoming a hardship on our neighbors. Susan Jenkins, as she was known then, had come across an article describing the workings of the swap shops that were operated all over Great Britain by the British Women's Voluntary Services. "Repair—Make Do!" was their motto. She obtained copious material from the British Information Service and turned it over to Mrs. Peterfy.

A system of "credits" was evolved by a committee of women from the Vladeck Women's Club, who took over the running of the Swap Shop. When all was set and in place, there was a gala opening with the wife of the British Consul General attending.

To go back a bit, as Vladeck House got into full swing, we were pressed by the manager to take on the job of working with the tenants' associations. One association had been planned in detail, before the families moved in, and they were ready to operate and take over in about ten days' time. As other tenants began to suspect the political background of the first group, the local Democratic Club got going and started a rival group which they managed so badly that many of the tenants became aware they were being used for political purposes by both groups and refused to belong to any organization. It was at this point that the housing manager asked us to let the tenant groups meet with us. He felt that we might help to bring some kind of order into what had turned into violent political strife between Communists and Democrats rather than a community organization serving many social purposes. We invited both groups into rooms on separate floors in our emergency tenement, and, gradually, as the different factions met going up and down stairs, Susan Jenkins began to plan things of common interest. She said she felt that her most important meetings were held on the staircase with rival factions perched on the stairs as they worked slowly into more cooperative relationships.

As we gave more Henry Street time to the various tenants associations, we acquired more basement space in Vladeck Houses for our Home Planning Workshops. Shoe repair was added, with an elderly, retired shoemaker whose idea it had been as volunteer instructor. He absolutely refused to take any pay for what he did so well, but finally asked for an assistant, whom we did pay. Afterward a retired tailor ran part of the sewing shop, also as a volunteer. He was taken very ill and had a long spell in the hospital. The doctor who cared for him said he felt that the thing that brought him through was his determination to get "back to his class," which he talked about incessantly.

This is how neighbors build programs and how our Home Planning Workshops and its related activities have developed. Any low-income housing development should have some such creative outlet for the tenants' energies and initiative. I am glad to say that the Home Planning Workshop is still a flourishing department of Henry Street Settlement. I am sorry to say, however, that even with a continuous flow of visitors, many brought by the Housing Authority, it has been copied only here and there, not as a real commitment in low-income housing projects.

Once again, with the Second World War, came war gardens and the intensified production of food. We were already prepared for this work to be done at camp because we had added Sally Dodge to our staff to get our roof greenhouse program going.

One of the things that one can't but wish for a city child is the joy of planting a seed and seeing it come up—it is something that shouldn't be missed in life. Just before the war we had built a little greenhouse on our roof at "301." I had gone for advice to Montague Free, head horticulturist at Brooklyn Botanical Gardens, and he was so much interested in making sure that our greenhouse was placed correctly that he came over and told us just how to do it.

Sally Dodge, who had been trained as a horticulturist, had taken over the greenhouse and its young gardeners. Because the greenhouse was heated, we could start very early in the spring and planting and watering and cultivating became a part of our spring program. Watering became so absorbing a function that we should probably have planted only water lilies. Plants were taken home in little pots for window sills and sometimes carried out to camp for further growing.

Then came the war and Sally Dodge, with assistants, arranged for our war production crews of teen-agers. They went out to live at our camp where both girls and boys had jobs with the local farmers. The farmers were glad to get them and they had healthy and useful summers during the war years.

XXIV

A Leave of Absence in the South Pacific

It is the custom in a little church in Nettlesildt that is in Bavaria for the women to sit downstairs and for men to mount the narrow wooden stairs to the balconies running around the church. A group of us from an International Settlement Conference had arrived late for the Sunday service and went up to the balcony where we faced the rows of men from the neighboring villages, all in Sunday black. This was the early thirties and I found myself trying to pick out those who must have been in the First World War. As I looked, however, from face to face, one seemed too old, the next too young. I had searched for some time before it was borne in upon me that the men I was looking for were missing. Then my eyes came to the end of the balcony and I saw a great tablet at the side of the pulpit reaching from the ceiling to the floor with the inscription, "To those who died for their Fatherland." Inscribed below this were the names of the men I had been looking for; their birthdays and their death dates left no doubt of it and I knew I had in truth been looking for a lost generation. The term had been familiar enough but I think I never quite grasped its reality until that moment.

Less than a generation later we were entering into a Second World War. Other tablets with other names and other dates would be going up again in little towns and cities all over the world.

War, of course, brings changes to a neighborhood that super-sedes all other concerns. Our neighbors took a vigorous part in Civilian Defense, and our little emergency tenement was now needed for another emergency—Civilian Defense headquarters. The white helmets of the Civilian Defense Wardens, hanging in tenement kitchens, were worn by many of the same men with whom we had walked in demonstrations directed toward jobs and relief during the Depression. Jacob Markowitz, a young neighbor, now a State Supreme Court Judge, headed Civil Defense for our district. The whole parlor floor of "305" was given over as headquarters where Jack had a large corps of lieutenants working with him. Under his direction, the Henry Street staff set up model "blackouts" at windows, doors, and all apertures to demonstrate to neighbors and local institutions what they could do in their own homes. The stairways and halls were equipped with the recommended sand and water pails, axes, and other tools.

In the spring of 1942 I took a leave of absence from Henry Street to work for Red Cross in the South Pacific for ten months. I had had experience in World War I in France as director of a hospital hut in a base hospital at Chateauroux and in an evacuation hospital in Solemes. After that I had organized service clubs for enlisted men for the War Department in the Philippines and China, in 1920–22. Our troops had been stationed there with Tientsin as our headquarters ever since the Boxer Uprising. Our soldiers and those of our then allies were there to keep the rail-road free for our diplomatic corps, from Peking to the sea. So, as World War II came closer to the U.S., I was not a stranger to war and its effects, not only on soldiers but also on civilians. As I have said, after my hospital service in France I came home feeling that nothing compared in importance to the building of machinery for peace. And then the Senate rejected President Wilson's terms for the entry of the United States into the League of Nations. The wounded soldiers I had served in France were a backdrop to this political tragedy.

In France I had spent a long, heart-breaking winter working in an orthopedic hospital where seriously injured men were having to learn what it meant to be crippled, sometimes to go on in life without an arm, a leg, or a face. Two young soldiers particularly haunted me. They were brought in to us the day of the Armistice, one with both arms off and one with both legs off. And it had happened to them because word of the Armistice deadline had not reached their outfit in time to stop the firing. I can hear to this day the sound of a thrown crutch falling on the cement floor in our service club after I had announced the news of the Armistice. For the first moment there had been dead and unbelieving silence—and then as a gesture of hope the crutch was thrown away and belief spread.

Some pictures remain clear in your mind as time goes on. It was spring of 1919 when my friend and colleague Berkeley Sloan and I were sent to an evacuation hospital that took care of the men who became ill on their way home. One day we took some roses up to the pneumonia ward. A nurse said to us, indicating a Negro soldier in a nearby bed, "Give him a rose; he is dying." He reached his hand out for the rose and smiled. He died that night. The hospital ward where he died was "integrated" but his outfit in the Army had not been!

I knew that if enough people in the United States had understood and cared, no amount of political maneuvering could have kept us out of the League of Nations. While I had not been a pacifist in the years after World War I, I had felt that working for peace, in whatever way one could, was our first responsibility. But the horror of the Nazi persecutions came to seem to me worse than war—something so hideous and so harmful to the human race that I could concede the necessity of fighting to stop the spread of Hitlerism. Maybe the pacifists are right that nothing justifies war, but as grueling as the horrors of war seemed to me, dying, or even living crippled, still did not seem as horrible as living in torture or in slavery of either body or mind.

Because of my experience in France in the First World War and in the regular Army in the Philippines and China, I knew only too well what such services could mean to lonely and wounded men, some of them back from devastating jungle fighting. I joined the Red Cross to serve as Director of Service Clubs and Rest Homes in the South and Southwest Pacific. My work in the South Pacific was full of deep satisfaction as I saw the service clubs and rest homes opening and came to know the men who were using them. The work was also full of frustrations

The start of one of Mobilization's experimental housing projects.
Left to right: Charles Rodriguez, Bertran Beck, Ruth Brill,
Winslow Carlton. (*Photo courtesy of Mike Zwerling*)

Pete's House
Productions: Rehearsal
in the gym at Pete's
House (*Photo courtesy
of Ken Wittenberg*)

Production given at
the Henry Street
Playhouse (*Photo
courtesy of Ken
Wittenberg*

Three small Settlement buildings, now landmarks, after tenements across the street had been torn down—showing Trees of Heaven

Playground continually being built in front of Henry Street
Community Center in La Guardia Houses. Lilli Ann Killen Rosenberg
in the background. (*Photo courtesy of Ken Wittenberg*)

sework in the home with Miss Delia Battin and family

Raising money for a trip to Washington with National Federation of Settlements legislative conference

A dance class at the Playhouse with Murray Louis leading
(*Photo courtesy of David S. Berlin*)

The Henry Street Settlement Playhouse

which I shared with every responsible person in the Southwest Pacific at that time, for this area was short of everything because personnel and materials were going to Europe in preparation for the "Second Front."

When I arrived in Australia I found that only two service clubs were partially operating in the area. I took plans for expansion at once to General MacArthur and found him as eager as we were to have Red Cross services expanded and as quickly as possible.

After seeing at first hand what the hurdles were as we tried to get service clubs set up quickly, I decided that the greatest one was lack of Red Cross personnel. The number of men and women I had been promised just didn't arrive and so I went back to General MacArthur to ask him whether he would intervene for us in Washington. He replied bitterly that he could not get anything from Washington for himself let alone for the Red Cross. "Everything," he said, "is going in the other direction." He told me to hire as many Australians and New Zealanders as I could and get things done without American staff. At a later time in discussing what was happening with supplies and personnel, he said reflectively, "I think that Churchill will be allowed to set the pace for the war while Roosevelt hopes to call the terms for peace. Churchill thinks of himself as a military expert—he isn't, of course—" he interjected, "while the President wants to feel that he can lift the level of life for the poor after the war."

An informal report of mine to Mr. Charles Gamble, the official Red Cross delegate in the South and Southwest Pacific, tells of conditions after we had a good many installations going. He knew the region as he had headed Socony Vacuum operations out there for many years and was in Washington at this time trying to get us adequate staff. From my headquarters in Australia on December 18, 1942, I wrote Mr. Gamble:

> I don't need to tell you how I felt when the cable came saying that people were actually on their way. We had gone ahead with the operations anyway, hiring what good people we could on a temporary basis.
>
> I sent word through a cable to Paul (I didn't know how else to

get the message over by cable) that I had seen General MacArthur and had told him the story. . . . He said to hire anyone I could to carry on as the work must be done, and that he would turn over sixty Filipinos from the Army to help us up North where the labor problem was so acute. When I got back . . . the Filipinos were parcelled out to our labor-hungry Clubs all through the North. We had hoped that a number would be cooks, but most of them were "trusty seamen." Even so, they were mighty welcome.

I knew that when you got to Washington, somehow help would come to us. And it finally has—a fine group of people on the whole—twenty-one in all. . . .

[But] I have cabled you, asking that more people be sent over by Commercial Transport. For this is still just a drop in the bucket! . . .

When I read about five Clubs in a place like London and hear about the Red Cross people who have been flown over there in the last four months, I question whether anyone in Washington realizes what conditions are here.

In the first place, the men are farther from home, they have been here longer, the discomforts as you go farther North are greater, transportation is more difficult, supplies harder to get, and labor almost impossible to find. We are setting up operations in a primitive country, with a population of seven million people spread over the continent, which means that there are almost no cooks, plumbers, carpenters, etc., from which to choose. Part of the work is in a tropical jungle country in a semi-inhabited island. It is a triumph every time we put in a shower or toilet even as far down south as Sydney these days.

In New Zealand, it is the same as in Australia, in regard to supplies. But our men are in all these places. . . . I have hired everyone I could and have stretched the personnel as far as possible. But we have only touched the high spots so far.

I spent a week in New Zealand, at the request of the Army there, and got two operations going. It was like pulling teeth to get a bit of space. I saw everyone from the leading industrialist to the Prime Minister. But the Army was so eager to have us that a Club and Rest Home were started. I returned to get Hannah More Frazer to take care of the whole country. . . .

Stan Sommer and I went to New Caledonia for a week, and the situation was just as I had felt—a Club should have been there many months ago. Never was one more necessary. All the Commands there wanted us and did everything they could to help us pry away space from civilians, but all to no avail. So, the Army is building for us under the big Flame Trees in town. . . .

Luckily, I could send two beguiling as well as utterly competent girls there, Renee Guttman and Isabel Lee, and they both charmed and coordinated this service club into being with incredible speed in spite of the fact that all the essentials that we had sent from Australia—a dreary list of pipes, nozzles, elbows, showers, toilets, and basins—went down when the ship was sunk. However, in three months the club was packed and serving meals to seven thousand men a day. We had twenty-five thousand men on this small island at that time.

At this point in my letter, I received a telegram saying that five more women and four more men had arrived in Sydney for club work. We were ready to open our club in Sydney by Thanksgiving, thanks to Australian plumbers, painters, and electricians who cheered us by being willing to work practically all night. Everybody got interested. Even the "old boys," whose athletic club we took over, enlarging its facilities, forgave us and came to the opening parties and watched us serve ice cream sodas instead of liquor with amazement.

In my letter of December 18 to Mr. Gamble I was able to report that we had opened our new club in Brisbane, too, on Thanksgiving and that 1,600 men had had dinner there; that the Coolangatta Hotel, right on the beach and in excellent repair, had been full almost from the moment we had opened it, with more and more men from the battle areas using it; and that at our club in Rockhampton, one of our prize operations, we were serving two thousand meals a day and putting on dances and entertainments, but still needed to enlarge the club—the Army said—considering the number of men in the town.

Our club people, I went on, "are also meeting the sick and wounded as they come in from the battle areas. . . . Until just now, two people have been struggling with this program." Then I added, by way of concluding my letter:

I hope I won't come across another picture of Red Cross girls with three or four men reclining in leisurely attitudes in a London park. I don't believe this is good publicity anyway, and certainly should be forbidden reading in Australia!

We were able to get to New Guinea by Christmas. Early in November, General MacArthur had told me that within six weeks the Australians and Americans would have pushed the Japanese back far enough across the Stanley Range for me to bring women into New Guinea to start our clubs there. In an article for the *Survey*, I wrote about my arrival and an unforgettable Christmas party:

> On my first visit to Port Moresby, New Guinea, we had an air raid. Thinking at first it was American planes I heard, I was about to sink in bed with gratitude under my netting, when an alert sounded. Every light went off. . . . There was no blackout in the Moresby area such as we practiced in New York. A single switch . . . put every bulb out of commission at once. With a steel helmet wobbling on my head, I was piloted to a slit trench in front of our tent. . . . We sat in the wet in our coveralls, feet dangling in the trench, as we fought the mosquitoes. As the real attack got nearer, the ack-ack sounded, hunting for Japanese planes. We had watched the search-lights disclose these like reluctant flies before I was dragged into the trench. This was my first raid and I hated to be hauled down under the sandbags.
>
> It must have been two hours before the "all clear" sounded and I could crawl back under my mosquito bar and take on the night's business again. An hour later came another alert and this time it brought no sense of adventure. I had seen an air raid and did not feel the need of another that night.

In looking the next day for a club location in Moresby I found only one structure that was not preempted—a huge grass hut, 80 by 32 feet, which an Army sergeant had built for a mess hall. He had tried to improve on native craftmanship but his roof was not steep enough to shed the rain. However this empty hut gave us our first foothold in New Guinea.

Early the following day, I flew back to Australia, and four days before Christmas, returned. The companions I had picked were Leota Kelly, a regional superviser in the days of the WPA in New York, and Helen Schoeni, who for two years had directed our Henry Street Playhouse. We had set out from Townsville with a special allowance of six hundred pounds of supplies between us. By great good luck we had procured the only purchasable amplifying system in northern Australia.

Arrived in Port Moresby, we had a short three days to get up our Christmas party. Outfits for miles around turned out to help. Some gathered small palm trees and decorated them with tinsel. Others improvised furnishings and equipment—benches from boards and packing cases, even a Ping-Pong table. A platform, electric lights, and a piano all came bumping up to our door— or to the opening where a door would have been.

"Christmas night"—to quote again—"we were ready when our audience spread themselves out on the hillside facing the platform we had placed in front of the club. Lights were strung up so that a civilian orchestra brought over from the mainland could see their scores . . . as well as the mosquitoes!

> But to climax things, an alert sounded, that switch was turned off again, and we were in sudden darkness. The music stopped short—but almost as swiftly resumed. I climbed on the platform with a flashlight to find that our civilian talent had made for a slit trench and in their place was a wholly new band. Eager musicians from among the soldiers had scuttled down from the hillside and sprung to the instruments. Seemingly without losing a beat, there they were in the dark, carrying on as lively as you please. And then came a downpour of rain and it took the fear of spoiling the strings to stop our volunteers long enough for the piano to be heaved inside to the one dry spot in the exact center of the hut. Then we started up once more indoors and in the dark, until the all-clear sounded and lights went on to the tune of Christmas carols.

My worries, however real at the time, were small compared to the good feeling I had when I visited the thirty-four service clubs and rest homes before I came home. The Red Cross was now looking after our soldiers from Melbourne all up the Australian coast to Townsville, to New Guinea, to Noudmea in New Caledonia, to New Zealand. By the spring of 1943, we were serving 800,000 meals a month in our clubs and rest homes. But it was not just meals. It was a place where lonely men (often so very young) found a homey place they belonged in, so far from home. These were soldiers on their way to battle or returning from battle—and soldiers whose mail often had not reached them for months. I remember being taken down into a submarine and seeing a young soldier sitting in a corner on the floor reading letters. I asked him if he had just received mail from home. "Oh no," he said, "I'm just reading old ones over." And I glanced down and saw that the letters he was reading were so old they hardly held together.

As I came into one of the northern clubs, which was in a city from which flyers took off on missions, I saw one of the Red Cross women holding up a pair of soldier's boots and saying, "But he was just here yesterday and asked me to keep these for him." The soldier had always come to the service club between missions— until this last one.

The men I had seen returning from jungle fighting seemed almost devoid of life as they first got off the boats. I heard first hand what the clubs meant to them and to all the other service men I had talked to as the clubs got going. And back of these boys in my mind were literally thousands of young American soldiers I had come to know in France, in the Philippines, and in China. What they now said in the South Pacific was much the same and very good to hear and a comfort to take back home with me.

XXV

The Promise
of the United Nations

With us at Henry Street, postwar planning started even before Pearl Harbor. Paul Kellogg helped us launch our programs for the future at a dinner gathering of economists and planners on December 15, 1941, in the Henry Street dining room. We had arranged the meeting in November before the United States Declaration of War on December 7 gave it an imperative significance.

Dr. Luther H. Gulick spoke and led the discussion. As a member of the National Resources Planning Board, he had just returned from a study of Great Britain's postwar plans. Paul was already shaping up a special number of the *Survey* on the subject.

It seemed right to us that our neighbors should begin to think along with us of a future when the war would be over. The families in our neighborhood were immediately immersed in the tensions of the war and we felt it would be helpful if young and old would start thinking of a world organization to prevent war. My friend, Lillie Peck, then the executive secretary of the National Federation of Settlements, and founder with Ellen Coolidge of the International Federation of Settlements, was present at the December 15 discussion, and was stimulated by the talk of ways and means to achieve peace, to start such discussion meetings with the National Federation of Settlements. At the meetings that followed, it was decided that the National Federation of Settlements should take the lead in involving all the settlements in the country in this kind of thinking. Lillie Peck started with New York, and asked Eduard Lindeman, then teaching at the Columbia University School of Social Work, to help her work out a plan. The first step, for the following winter, was an experiment in group discussion about postwar planning, sponsored by the United Neighborhood Houses on behalf of the New York settlements. Thirteen groups were organized in New York under the leadership of Winifred Fisher, head of the New York Adult Education Council.

As those war years wore on it was good to have people thinking of something positive, because families were so caught in tragedy and uncertainty that it was hard to find a home completely untouched—and many of them were touched forever. The meetings and discussions provided an outlet for emotions and stimulated thought. Throughout this long period, the war was omnipresent and the adult members at Henry Street ended all meetings with a prayer for peace.

Neighbors who became especially interested in postwar planning and the part the United Nations, when it was established, might play in insuring peace, formed a special group with members from our different clubs. "The World Workshop" met on a floor in one of our old buildings, redecorated as a gift in memory of Leo Arnstein, a long-time board member and old friend of the settlement. The workshop was under the leadership of Mrs. Esther Tabor Fox, an expert in this field who had joined our staff, and she was helped by Leslie Kempel, one of our residents, who volunteered her services. They were constantly changing exhibits and many discussions focused on an understanding of the countries where our men were fighting. If your son, or your neighbor's son was fighting in a foreign country, you didn't need a high school education to want to know something about it. The discussions, too, seemed to bring the soldiers' home-coming nearer.

During the last year of the war, when the founding of the United Nations had become a certainty, the members of our World Workshop determined to help make their neighbors understand what such a world organization might mean to Americans and all mankind. Adults were hard to educate, since they had been brought up in a war-accepting world.

But there was always pictorial material in the World Workshop planned by Mrs. Fox and her group of neighborhood women. A series of pictorial charts on "World Organization" and the problems involved were displayed and used as a basis for discussion, and club members of all ages dropped in to study these maps. The exhibits, the maps, and the charts became so inviting that few passed the open door of our World Workshop, or "Post War Room" as it came to be called, without stopping to look. One chart was particularly appreciated. It was a map of the United Nations organization framed by snapshots of boys from Henry Street in their uniforms. The words, "We Work, They Fight," flanked the chart.

As reports of the wounded, the missing, and the killed came home to more and more members of our groups, they became interested in action more than study. By what was still called "Armistice Day" in 1944, our special group of postwar planners had something they wanted to show to the rest of the settlement. They decorated the Playhouse with the flags of all nations, and invited everybody to assemble there. They had organized the settlement's fifteen adult clubs to give a dramatic presentation of the pledges which the United States and its allies had made to establish the United Nations at the Dumbarton Oaks and Bretton Woods Conferences held in September and October, 1944. Each club president spoke telling of the plans formulated at these conferences. A young people's chorus from the Music School rendered songs of other nations, ending with the new United Nations song. For the two following months, moving pictures and talks on the subject were a part of every club meeting in the settlement.

The twelve settlements at that time on the Lower East Side had always worked closely together and their directors had met often to compare notes and plans for action in the community. At this time, representatives of the adult clubs in all the settlements formed a Lower East Side Citizens Committee on World Organization, which held four weekly meetings in April, 1945, at our local Seward Park High School on a "New World Organization Based on Human Rights." The last meeting coincided with the opening of the San Francisco conference, which created the United Nations.

Mrs. Eleanor Roosevelt spoke at our first meeing on April 5, 1945, and presidents of the women's clubs served as co-chairmen of our meetings. President Roosevelt died on the day we had planned for our second meeting. We questioned whether we should hold our meeting and then realized how much President Roosevelt would have wanted us to go on. The deep feeling in our neighborhood for the President turned this into a memorial for him. Late that afternoon, Lillie Peck had stopped on her way home to Henry Street at a little grocery store near the settlement. When she came in, she saw everyone was weeping and, not having heard of the President's death, she said, "What is the matter?" The answer was, "Our friend is dead,"—not the President, just "our friend." As I spoke of the President's death at the meeting that night, looking out over the audience, it seemed to me that everyone was crying. That night's program was very appropriately on "Freedom from Fear and Want," with J. Raymond Walsh and James Marshall as speakers.

The third meeting was on "The New Rules of the Game," with Rabbi Stephen S. Wise and the Honorable Herbert E. Gaston as speakers. At the final meeting—on "The Will of the People"— the Seward Park High School Orchestra gave a salute to the United Nations. Lisa Sergie and Albert Phys Williams were speakers.

All this effort was, of course, to help bring a realization of the importance of the United Nations to our neighbors. We knew only too well that there would be no lasting United Nations until the great masses of people in the world, particularly in the United States with its tremendous power, "understood and believed" in the world organization that was being set up right at our own doors.

Six years later, I represented the National Federation of Settlements as observer at the Sixth General Assembly of the United Nations held in Paris in November, 1951. Mrs. George W. Bacon, an old friend from the First World War when we had organized a *Foyer des Allies* (a club for working girls) in Alsace for the YWCA, represented the National Association of Consumers.

I remember an incident that was so typical of Mrs. Roosevelt. One of the Soviet representatives had attacked the U.S. violently, using some very strange statistics. Mrs. Roosevelt had risen and corrected him very firmly. Later, Betty Bacon and I met her in the corridor and she said, "I've just been back to talk to that young man from the Soviet Union because I hated to be so hard on him, but of course I couldn't let his statement go by."

Even though I had seen a good deal of the United Nations in New York after its sessions had started, my day-to-day attendance at the Assembly improved my own understanding so much that I urged the National Federation of Settlements to set up an annual institute for neighbors, staff, and board members from all over the country, to be held at the United Nations, and to last a week. Which they did. The idea was that those who attended would carry on some kind of United Nations work through the settlements in their own cities.

One thing we did at Henry Street to learn what our neighbors were thinking about the United Nations and what they wanted us to do to help them understand more about it, was a house-to-house canvass of one hundred families. Many meetings at the settlement, or small meetings in neighbors' houses, grew out of this visiting. At one home, our worker started to explain what we were doing, and the woman's reply was, "Oh, come right in. My daughter is a 'Citizen of the World,' so of course I know all about the United Nations."

Children could more readily accept the concept of a world organization in which all countries would work for peace than adults who had been brought up in a world where war had been taken for granted. Because we wanted the youngsters to feel they were taking part in its building, early in the UN's history, Ruth Tefferteller, who was then head of our Children's and Young People's Program, started a children's group which called itself "Citizens of the World."

The little Citizens of the World proved to be an enduring program which went on for many years, with younger children joining as older ones went on to other interests. At the start, Ruth Tefferteller told the children who asked about the new club that they would have the usual trips, parties, folk dancing, creative dramatics, crafts, and special projects of their own, but that everything they planned would have something to do with the United Nations.

Ruth Tefferteller has described some of the club's very early activities. I quote her in some detail because the flavor of the Citizens of the World permeated much of the work of all the

children's programs of those days and for a long time. She recalled:

> At our first meeting, we showed a film from the American
> Association for the United Nations, called *Clearing the Way*—
> the story of how the new UN site along the East River between
> 42nd and 47th Street was selected, and the resistance shown by
> a group of children to this idea when forced to surrender a vacant
> lot used by them as a playground. The change in attitude on
> the part of the children in the film, after they fully understood
> the implications of their "sacrifice," had a telling effect upon our
> "Citizens of the World." They asked if they might see the site
> of the UN—for real.
>
> The following week, the club was scheduled to go on a trip
> in the settlement station wagon, so they were driven to the most
> famous building project in New York City. Along the way we
> talked about getting ice-cream cones in the same candy store
> shown in the film where the young characters in the story spent
> lots of time talking with the chief engineer about their problem.
>
> We found the workmen hard at work. The noisy activities
> fascinated the children. They talked with the drillers and asked
> questions about the building. They saw at first hand that a
> beautiful structure was being built of marble and glass, and they
> were told that this would be the place where people from all over
> the world would gather to talk over problems and differences.
> This was the place where the delegates would try to figure out
> ways to avoid wars.

It turned out that our children couldn't find the same candy
store they had seen in the film, and had to buy their ice cream
cones somewhere else. On the way home, they decided to write
the United Nations and ask what had happened to the candy
store. A reply from the appropriate UN office informed us that
the candy store had also been cleared to make way for the
United Nations.

"Where is the United Nations meeting now?" they asked. "At
Lake Success and not very far away," was the reply. So the
Citizens of the World wanted to go there, and another trip was
planned. The station wagon was waiting for them early in the
morning. Ruth Tefferteller continued:

> We squeezed in to make room for all, and were off, singing
> songs about the UN learned in the clubroom, discussing plans

to have lunch in the delegates' cafeteria. Could they see the simultaneous interpretation receivers in the conference room? Could we buy souvenirs?

The sight of the fifty-two flags waving in the breeze on a promontory near the main conference building brought shrieks of excitement and discovery—so many of them!, and so colorful! Lunch in the delegates' cafeteria was one of the high points. Unusually deep interest was shown in the receiver sets, the arrangement of the conference rooms, and in locating the individual nations by their small placards. The children collected all kinds of brochures and pamphlets, and were particularly attracted to a photographic display in the main lobby on the work of UNICEF. We made a game of reciting the full meaning of the many alphabet agencies—and by the time we reached home, all of them knew that UNICEF meant *United Nations International Children's Emergency Fund.*

Christmas was not far away. The Citizens of the World had a big idea—a Christmas party in honor of the children of the UN delegates. For the next weeks, the "UN Party," as it was called, became the core of their club program. Decorations were made during regular meeting time. A program of entertainment for the guests was developed and rehearsed. This included creative dramatics, folk dancing, and singing. Costumes were made in the clubroom. The "peanut brittle" committee and the "homemade cookie" committee made refreshments in one of our kitchens. As described by Ruth Tefferteller, this first "UN Party" was a tremendous success:

> An Australian boy taught the children a native game. Christmas and New Years greetings in Spanish, French, Chinese and Haitian were written on showcards by our guests and hung on the wall. The "Citizens of the World" presented their entertainment with much pomp and ceremony. Both groups sang UN songs and Christmas carols together. It was a moving sight to watch all of them dance together in "Bow, Bow Belinda," a simple American reel dance. The guests participated throughout with enthusiasm. All the children were supremely happy.

Next came the campaign for UNICEF. Our children's interest had been aroused at Lake Success, when a UNICEF staff member had told them about the agency's work in feeding hungry children all over the world. They invited her to a club meeting. The club invited other children in the settlement to attend, and they all saw her documentary film, which was very clear and designed to appeal to children.

Now the Citizens of the World wanted to raise money to help UNICEF. Raising money isn't easy for nine-, ten-, and eleven-year-olds. Exclaiming, "We have so much to do!" they talked of one project or another and settled, as a start, on a special settlement newspaper to tell about UNICEF and their club's interest in it.

Later, selling UNICEF holiday greeting cards became a very successful project for the Citizens of the World, and still continues, with different groups of children tackling it each year. People ask me whether children as poor as some of ours don't resist raising money for other poor children. We are all agreed that, as far as we could discover, no child had felt like this, nor had any money ever been missing in spite of the relatively large amounts that were later handled. As I recall, the first year the young canvassers raised $37, which they themselves took to the UNICEF office. Since then, collections have grown to something like $1,600!

As soon as the new UN headquarters on the East River, a mile away, was opened, we took our neighbors, young and old, to visit it. At first, our footsteps echoed in the corridors; now some two thousand daily visitors during the busy season are reported. It is good to see the young people crowding off the buses. Here in New York the settlements are lucky because it is easy for them to get their neighbors of all ages to the United Nations. If only the work of the World Health Organization, UNICEF, the Food and Agricultural Organization, and the UN Scientific and Cultural Organization could get through to as many people's minds as do the interminable international quarrels!

Ever since those early days, we worked very closely with the staff of UNICEF, and when they needed children for any special occasions, they often called on us. The Citizens of the World wanted to celebrate Madame Pandit's birthday by making a cake for her themselves. To our relief, their mothers became a party to the plan, and the cake turned out to be an enormous affair. The layers were made in several homes and brought together and frosted in our kitchen. The children took it to Madame

Pandit, who received it in proper style and with her own special charm, and the children returned back home in triumph!

Because the work of the UN and its various important agencies was so little understood, and difficult to interpret and make come alive, we prepared a play of our own. Ann Barley, the head of our Community Studies Department at that time, put her exceptional skill in writing to the task. By November, 1952, her play *Jungle Mission*, was ready. Centering on the work of the Food and Agriculture Organization, it was to serve many purposes beside our own.

The action of *Jungle Mission* takes place in the living room of a viceroy's residence in a Far Eastern jungle province. The play is dedicated to the devotion and humanity of experts from Europe and America and their Asian counterparts. The human problems and adventures of one such mission are dramatized with many incidents based on actual case records on file at the FAO World Headquarters, now in Rome. The personnel of the FAO, whom I had come to know when I was with the American Mission in Geneva, were not only helpful, but glad to have the play for their own educational program. At their request, we presented it in Washington, D.C., in addition to showing it at our own Playhouse for the United Neighborhood Houses and the National Federation of Settlements. It had enough romance in it to carry its message along, and came at a time when there was very little interpretive material of any kind to be had anywhere about the UN.

The work of the FAO had been much in my mind ever since Paul Kellogg and I attended the Third Annual Conference of the FAO in Geneva in the summer of 1947, where I was Consumer Consultant for the United States Mission and Paul was planning a special number of the *Survey* on hunger. While the hunger of the world was a tragic thing to hear reported on for three weeks, there was some hope in the fact that it was world hunger, and not just starvation with national boundaries that was talked about. More importantly, how to deal with it as a world problem was the main concern as they tried to match world hunger with world food, and a World Food Council was created to meet between annual sessions of the FAO.

On the way back home from the FAO Conference, Paul and I visited Berlin, Paris, Frankfurt, and London. We supplemented our observations for an article in these cities by reports of European social workers from Belgium, Czechoslovakia, Finland, and many other countries, at an interim meeting of the International Conference of Social Work. We felt very strongly the responsibility that rested on our country at this time, and to quote from our article, *"Ours the Food, Theirs the Hunger,"** we felt that:

> What no one could fail to sense at the FAO Conference was the tremendous responsibility which rests on the United States in this crisis as the greatest producing and exporting nation. Repeatedly there was an instant hush when the American delegate took the floor. It mattered so much to so many, what he said.

And we could not but feel that:

> Self-interest, if no higher motive, should make us hesitate to bequeath to coming generations in America a world in which they must cooperate with men and women who have been ill-fed as children—and ill-fed because we had not organized our plenty to share it with them.

While in London, we arranged for leaders of the English settlements to send the story of their people's handling of rationing accompanied by interviews with British housewives. They followed through, and "What Every British Woman Knows"† told their story, contrasting their decent distribution during extreme scarcity with our uncontrolled inflation and lowered standards for our low-income families. As Paul Kellogg and I read the material over we felt that we had come very close to the women standing in queues at British markets or back in British kitchens trying to "make do." We wished that the whole batch could be shared instead of our trying to distill what was in them and pass it on as best we could.

We particularly wanted our readers to see the deprivation, the courage, and the striving behind these British stories so that the food provisions of the European Recovery Program would seem important to them. Now, years later, we can look back on the Marshall Plan and know what an important part it played in European recovery.

* *Survey Graphic*, December, 1947.
† *Survey Graphic*, March, 1948.

PART FOUR

The Postwar Years

1945 - 1955

XXVI

Disruption of Neighborhoods and Gang Warfare

As the war ended, "Welcome Home" banners began to blossom on tenement fronts and, at the same time, the disorganization of neighborhoods and increased violence among the very young teens became of greatest concern. To add to the difficulties of this after-war period, another period of unemployment began in our neighborhoods. Soldiers were returning and looking for jobs. War industry was closing down and the automation which had increased under the pressure of war production bore down hardest on young people and hardest of all on those from minority groups. This joblessness after World War II robbed young people of their start in a working life, and sadly enough, has continued to be the pattern of unemployment in the ensuing years as untrained young people have been automated out of our economy.

The age of the young people for whom we were finding it most difficult to get jobs was, after all, the age we had turned to to fight for us. They are not too young or unimportant when we need them, but when they need us it is a different story. After seeing American boys serving in our Army in two world wars, and then the same boys squeezed out of the run of life by depression, automation, or by any form of the business cycle—in other words, by things beyond their control—I find it hard to bear. I remember sitting beside a sergeant at a dance in a

Red Cross service club in Australia, the second year of the war, and watching the Marines just back from Guadalcanal. I said to the sergeant, who seemed very somber, "These boys seem so young!"

"Yes, they are," he answered, "too young." And then he said slowly, "We were chased by the Japs for a week straight, got almost no sleep at all. On the seventh night, as the Japs came at us again, I just couldn't wake some of the boys up. I had to leave them in the dugout with the Japs coming over. Some of them were only seventeen and you know how the young sleep."

The "Welcome Home" signs were soon followed by the hunt for homes as new families were born of the soldiers' return. The results of no building during the war years began to push housing into top concern along with gang warfare, not good or even decent housing but just a roof over your head. At this time, a returned soldier said to me bitterly: "They could build huts quickly enough on Anzio Beach but it's over a year since I came back and I can't find a place so we can get out of a room in her mother and father's and have a place of our own."

Following the five-year gap in home building came the demolition of old neighborhoods to make way for public low-income housing, and in our neighborhood middle-income cooperatives, followed by the movement of displaced families as they looked for shelter of any kind, anywhere. Old tenements in our neighborhood that had been boarded up before the war as too bad for renovation were opened up with a minimum of repair and a minimum of legality!

Puerto Ricans from East Harlem and Puerto Rico, and Negroes from Harlem and from the South began to move in. A new family takes time to get its roots down. It takes much less time for adolescent gangs to form to keep intruders out. They now had a purpose. Protecting your turf goes back a long way in human endeavor—Robert Ardrey's book, *African Genesis*, takes it back to the ape—and we know that protecting it from another color or another tongue adds special impetus.

The first peace-time draft didn't help our neighborhoods. It gave a good excuse for hanging around and not looking for a job, which, at this time, got more social acceptance than was ordinarily conceded in the neighborhood in those days. Employers, too, were reluctant to take on the seventeen-year-olds who would soon be eligible for the draft. One of the most serious effects of the draft on neighborhoods such as ours was the undue proportion of boys between thirteen and eighteen; a less stable age than eighteen to twenty-one. The result was that the youngsters tried to take the place of the older boys with less emotional maturity to manage it, which added greatly to the problems of gang warfare.

For the first time, TV antennae were rising on tenement roofs, and children, by turning a knob, could watch violence at will for hours. To my mind, the influence of violence on TV has not yet been sufficiently taken into account. Mobilization for Youth, in 1957, made a quick study of how much time children in a local junior high school near us watched television and found that 12 percent watched it six hours a day.

Another dreary concomitance of the violence in the neighborhood was that many of the stable families, when they could possibly afford it, began to move out so that deterioration was bound to go at an accelerated pace. Many Henry Street adult club members were particularly affected by the ruling of the Housing Authority that made eviction mandatory as a family's income rose over the amount allowed by the law ($1,400 a year when Vladeck opened), for many members of our adult clubs had lived opposite the settlement in Vladeck Houses. The war had brought wage increases to the fathers of families, and children had come of working age. This often put them over the maximum income for continued occupancy in Vladeck but still not enough to pay for decent housing in the open market. So there was nothing to do but move back into another tenement if they could find one. These were by now largely filled with the newcomers to the neighborhood and returned soldiers. So it very often meant not only getting out of your house in Vladeck but getting out of your neighborhood as well.

Those were hard days as we watched the makeshifts to which families resorted to keep their homes. Older sons and daughters who had jobs left home; women refused jobs they wanted; we knew of men who refused raises rather than lose their homes; and, of course, sources of income were not always reported. The Housing Authority gave families extra time to struggle to find a place as they knew the hopeless task it was, but finally they would reach the end of their legal tether and out the families had to go. For years people with strong associations traveled back to meet with their friends and continue their old relationships, but many of them took what they had learned in their once-active clubs at Henry Street into their new neighborhoods. One of the members made a study of how many of our old members were taking civic responsibility in their new communities. The results, reported at a big reunion, may not have been scientific, but they were stimulating and we were all proud. We could not but feel that their sense of responsibility and their ability to carry things through had been enhanced by their association with each other and Henry Street. But while their leadership may have been useful elsewhere, it was certainly missed in our neighborhood at that particular time.

Franklin Harbach and I had long had an understanding that he would not leave until something much more interesting to him than his work at Henry Street was offered. This, he had always felt, would be hard to find, and, as I was very eager to have him stay. It was not until 1943 that he went to Texas to head up the Houston Settlement Association where a very interesting experimental job could be done. I had just returned from Australia, and Franklin had taken my place while I was away and managed Henry Street's Fiftieth Anniversary. Neither of us had any idea of how hard it would be to replace him with the war still on.

Franklin had worked at Henry Street Settlement for a year in 1926 and left to get a law degree. He returned with his wife to live in the neighborhood and work at Henry Street, in 1929. He started as "Boys Worker," as it was termed in those days, and served as associate director for many years. Franklin had a downright practicality along with his zest for new ideas which served Henry Street and all the young people with whom he worked in good stead. He taught them how to get things done by thinking things through, and it was his skill and practicality which helped get our Credit Union going.

After Franklin left, I was continually called from some meeting at one building or another to help stop a disturbance going on elsewhere. An Irish gang called the McCanns was beginning to

make trouble in and outside the house. And one of our psychological rejects from the Army was out to prove he could win the
war in our house even if he couldn't in the service. The McCann
gang was made up of sons of old residents in the neighborhood,
augmented by some very tough additions. As the violence increased, I combed the city for someone who seemed capable of
handling the situation.

James McCarthy was recommended to me as one whose training and experience would equip him for this job, and I felt that a
worker with an Irish Catholic background might be good as the
Jewish groups in the house and newcomers in the neighborhood
were being attacked by this Irish crowd mobilized only for
trouble. Jim took hold so firmly that he was soon called anti-
Irish! This was only the beginning of the virulent gang warfare
which went on for more than ten years, increasing in violence as
more and more newcomers moved into the neighborhood. It was
Jim McCarthy's work with the McCann gang and their followers
that gave him the idea of the "Street Club Worker," with which
he experimented more formally when he left Henry Street a year
and a half later to go to the Community Council. Later on, he
introduced the idea into the work of the New York City Youth
Board. Still later on he returned again to Henry Street to work
on the early plans for Mobilization for Youth.

When the Teffertellers came in 1946 they couldn't have come
at a worse time for them, or a better one for us. While the
McCanns were not riding quite so high in the neighborhood when
James McCarthy left, other gangs were going stronger when
Ralph and Ruth took over in September, and the neighborhood
was more chaotic than ever before in my time. The Teffertellers
had before them the job of making the new neighbors, Puerto
Ricans and Negroes, a part of the settlement program. It was not
too hard with the children, but getting your own way by violence
is a pattern in the teens and it took the skill and understanding
as well as the devotion of the "T's" to help bring these newcomers
into our programs. The teen-agers were attacked on their way into the settlement and on their way home and in the house if it
was possible to get by with it. I remember a young Puerto Rican
boy, just passing by one night on his way from night school, who
was attacked and beaten up and his school papers thrown on

the ground. Ironically enough, one of his lesson papers had written on it, over and over again, "I am an American."

While the actual physical violence around us was caused by teen-agers, we knew that the grownups in the neighborhood needed plenty of education on how to welcome newcomers as well. It was not only among teen-agers that integration had to be worked on in time of such swift changes.

Our Adult Council was made up of representatives from all the adult clubs, Italian, Irish, Negro, as well as Jewish, and had been under Rose Wasserman's able direction for many years. After much club discussion about the changes in the neighborhood, all the Adult Council members decided that the community needed educating on integration. The Negro in American Life exhibition was one of the results of their concern.

Paul Kellogg had helped start us off on this subject by arranging an exhibition in the settlement dining room of drawings by Winold Reiss. Some years before he had drawn Negro teachers, doctors, and professional people of distinction for a special number of the *Survey Graphic*. The pictures stayed up in our dining room for many months after the opening reception. Finally, instead of going back to the storehouse from which Winold Reiss had lent them to Paul, they became a permanent part of the Schomberg Collection in the New York Public Library at 104 West 136th Street. As they arrived uptown, the local high school principal was already planning to borrow them!

The Adult Council felt that an exhibition at Henry Street of photographs of Negroes who had played an important part in building America would be good to present to the neighborhood at this time. We asked John Becker of the Council Against Intolerance to help and he prepared a remarkably effective exhibit for us. Afterward the Council Against Intolerance put the exhibit into book form so that it could be purchased and used all over the country.

The Negro in American Life exhibition opened on a Sunday evening, February 27, 1944, at our Playhouse, with the Adult Council as hosts. Speakers were Dr. L. D. Raddick, curator of the Schomberg Collection, and Elmer Carter of the Board of Appeals of the New York State Unemployment Insurance Division. Two Henry Street alumni, at that time dancers in the cast of *Carmen*

Jones, Dorothy and Vera McNichols, brought other members of the all-Negro cast of *Carmen Jones* with them to dance. They had been in our club program as little girls and had learned their dancing at the Playhouse. I was always grateful to them for putting into their own words something we hope happens at Henry Street all the time, but it's always good to hear. They were having supper with Paul Kellogg and me after a performance of *Carmen Jones* and I asked the girls how they had known that they wanted to study dancing. "Oh," one said simply, "that was easy. We always had some dancing at '301' and we liked it so much that we went over to the Playhouse to learn more!"

That is why we try to have a variety of interests in our informal children's program, so they will have a chance to find out what they enjoy most and can do best, then they can move on into the arts or other branches of Henry Street where the teaching will carry them further along.

XXVII

Heightened Gang Warfare and the Predelinquent Gang Project

Settlements have sometimes been reproached for not meeting the needs of the worst-behaving members of the community. Sometimes this may be a fair criticism, but usually it is made without firsthand knowledge of the struggles, successes, and failures involved in this effort. If a group is making it impossible for all the other youngsters to benefit from the program, then we must admit defeat in integrating that group with the others, and find some other method of reaching them. This was the case with the McCann gang. We either had to work with most of the groups of Henry Street members *or* to take care of the McCanns. We chose first to serve the needs of the whole group; then we turned to ways of meeting some of the needs of the McCanns.

The little emergency tenement was once more used to meet an emergency. The McCanns had been asking for dances; so we gave over one of the floors to dancing. I took Paul Kellogg to look in at one of these dances, and his comment after watching the group for a while was, "Helen, you have too many problems in this small space!" And so we had, but there is always hope that, in working with a very disruptive group, if we don't succeed with all of them, we can at least draw off some peripheral members who are often relieved to get loose from the stranglehold of a "fighting gang." However, to reach the core group it is usually necessary to follow them into the streets. Over the years the settlements with their limited staffs had tried to do this in some measure, but this kind of approach was not attempted on a large scale until James McCarthy, through the Youth Board, experimented with it in many parts of the city.

As age and inevitable calamities overtook the early McCanns, they were followed by two succeeding age groups of the most vicious and harmful gangs ever known to us at Henry Street. The Mayhews gang was composed of Italian, Irish and Jewish boys. Their viciousness, too, as the McCann gang's had been, was especially directed toward the new boys, largely black and Puerto Rican, coming into the neighborhood. The newcomers retaliated by organizing the "Dragons," a name borrowed from Puerto Rican groups in other parts of the city. Gangs formed for defense generally go on the offensive as their strength increases.

We tried every method we could think of to deal with the Mayhews: in the settlement, out of the settlement, on the corner, with their families, and as individuals. The second so-called generation of Mayhews turned out to be more difficult for the neighborhood, for themselves, and for us, than the first had been. Their depredations had stretched over a number of years when Ruth Tefferteller discovered that two younger groups of boys were calling themselves the Junior Mayhews and the Midget Mayhews. These boys, aged seven to nine in one group and eight to ten in the other, were being trained by their predecessors to take over! She decided, at this point, that we had never started young enough—it should be seven, not seventeen, she said—nor had we brought their parents together often enough as serious partners with us on their behalf. Nor had we given to each such group the leadership time that they required. This was the beginning of what came to be known as the Predelinquent Gang Project, carried on so successfully under Mrs. Tefferteller's leadership for the next six or seven years.

She started with these two groups, the Midget and the Junior Mayhews, without a budget, just her own determined and creative planning. Governor Lehman was the first to give us a start in this project. He and Mrs. Lehman loved to follow what was happening in Pete's House, and the Midgets and Juniors were happening there with a vengeance!

Mrs. "T" first brought their parents together, asking them to be partners with Henry Street in our effort to work with their boys who were already in difficulties. We said very directly that we wanted them to exert their "parental authority," and help us build a relationship between them and their children. This is almost impossible to do if you start after adolescence, especially when, over the years the relationship has been strained by increasing complaints from neighbors and police. Yet younger children crave the security of authority, whether they know it or not. A relationship must be built early to hold intact through the stressful years of the teens. Also we know that if we are to help, some children and some adults require a great deal more time and effort than others, which means more money. If society is willing to spend more on these vulnerable ones in the beginning, then so much in plain cold dollars could be saved along with the prevention of human misery.

In the mid-fifties, when we started this predelinquent gang work, it cost us approximately $500 a year per child. At that time, it cost approximately $2,400 a year for a child in an institution for reform and perhaps $7,000 in a prison! A study which was made of what the City had spent on the older children in the families of the Henry Street Boys, one of our five gangs of twelve children for a year, showed a cost to the city of $79,000 for custodial care alone, not counting the cost of police and probation or the deterioration of the club house.

By the end of three years and with the help of a special grant from the New York Fund for Children, the settlement was working with five predelinquent gangs. The behavior patterns had already changed so completely with the Midget Aces and the Junior Aces as the Midget and Junior Mayhews had at once been renamed that the chain of succession had been broken and there was no longer a Mayhews gang in our neighborhood.

In October, 1961, the Astor Foundation was considering a grant to aid juvenile delinquency prevention, and appointed an advisory committee—consisting of Austin McCormick, the head of the Osborne Association; Milton Rector, director of the National Council on Crime and Delinquency; and me—to suggest the most effective way to spend the million dollars the foundation was planning to put to this purpose. Our committee finally decided that Henry Street's Predelinquent Gang Project was the most hopeful program of all those studied. So we suggested trying it for three years in eight other settlements in New York City, adding to it the important ingredient of special work with children who had been in institutions and had been returned by the court to these neighborhoods. We recommended that the foundation ask the United Neighborhood Houses, under Helen Harris' overall direction, to supervise the project in the other settlements. This was the way the plan was carried out, with Goodwin Garfield as the project director and with Ruth Tefferteller as consultant for the first two years.

At Henry Street we had had the satisfaction of seeing the boys in the first five younger groups go through their teens constructively. As they grew older, got jobs, graduated from high school, or had any other kind of success, Mrs. "T" was always the first to know! No matter where they may have moved to in the city, they were back to tell her about it.

There were very few of these boys who did not make good. Those few came largely from our last gang taken into the project. When we started work with them, we felt they were already too old since they were over twelve. However we went ahead with them because they needed help so much and we felt they would serve as a contrasting group. We tried all the same methods but without the same success; it showed us again the importance of starting very young and giving enough help at that time.

Two summers ago, the tragic murder of one of our former Junior Aces by a member of the last Mayhews gang brought home cruelly what these young boys had been steered away from. Tommy had a good job at *The New York Times*. We were all very proud of him. One evening on his way home from work, he stopped with a friend for a drink at a bar on Second Avenue. Frankie Dominic, who had been the leader of the last Mayhews gang, was there and a fight started. Dominic began to pistol-whip a boy whom Tommy knew. He went to the boy's defense; Dominic turned the pistol on Tommy and shot him dead. Dominic and his friends carried Tommy's body to the river and tied it to a pier, where it was not found until two days later. Our neighborhood spent the summer in dread because they knew too well that Dominic was a killer and might return anytime. He had been wanted for murder before, and after Tommy's murder he left New York where the police were searching for him, going to New Jersey. There he got into another fight in a bar and police were called. He and a cohort managed to get the two rookie policemen into the back of the bar where he shot them both dead. Dominic was finally shot himself in his hotel room by New York police when they came to arrest him for the New Jersey killings.

Characters are not changed by one talk, one arrest, one lecture: an important ingredient in the success of the Predelinquent Gang Project, which we were able to achieve, aside from the youth of the boys and the parental involvement, was the day-by-day painstaking attention given to each detail of their conduct. When things went wrong with any or all of them, parents and leaders and the boys themselves were brought together to discuss the situation.

Nothing went unnoticed. Everything that happened to the boys, everything they did, was recorded by the project staff in a day-to-day chronicle that was essential to the success of the project at Henry Street and to its implementation elsewhere.*

* The long record is available at Henry Street Settlement.

XXVIII

Postwar Unemployment

Adding to the problems of the postwar period, a new kind of afterwar unemployment crept into the neighborhood, increasing with the recession of 1954. This time it was protected sometimes by unemployment insurance, and sometimes by wartime savings, but unemployment just the same and frightening to those who had lived through the Depression. As wartime price controls were removed, under political pressure, long before the economy was stabilized, the instantly rising prices added to the hardship and disorganization taking place around us. One of its worst aspects was that it so quickly affected the building of homes.

Well before the end of the war, settlement workers clearly foresaw the need for economic planning at the federal level. So in 1945 we welcomed the introduction in Congress of what was then called the Full Employment Bill—with its provision for a presidential Council of Economic Advisers. We hoped that its enactment would bring more order into the economic chaos that causes failure from top to bottom, or perhaps we should say from bottom to top, and that it would serve to alter the pattern of beginning decline before spending had been curtailed enough to start the downward spiral. To voice the National Federation of Settlements' strong support of the bill, I appeared in August, 1945—soon after Japan had surrendered—before the Senate Banking and Currency Committee, of which the late Senator

Robert Wagner was chairman. I quote from my testimony because I think it gives a fair description of the economic situation in settlement neighborhoods which was very little understood at the time. The slogan "War Wages" had become a sort of screen to hide the real situation of rising unemployment and high prices. Addressing myself to the need for federal action, I said in the beginning:

> It seemed like old times, Senator Wagner, to get a wire from you last week asking me to testify here today on an employment bill. You may recall that the first time I did so was six months after the stock market crashed in 1929. There were only ten people testifying on the Employment Stabilization Act that time and now there are a week of witnesses, and I expect many more weeks could be taken up with the people wishing to speak in favor of the present act.

Senator Wagner agreed that this was so.

> . . . Today, your concern which is not only with mass unemployment or in shifting from war to peace, but to establish "a national policy and program for *continuing* full employment in a free competitive economy"—to fortify democracy at its roots.
>
> My understanding is that some business groups feel that free enterprise can deal with postwar unemployment without government aid. As I read Senate Bill 380 it encourages business to attempt just that, calling upon federal help only when private industry is unable to keep all our people employed. So doing, the bill takes the line that it is the concern of *all* of us that *all* have work if we need it, and makes it altogether clear that we no longer want to get our unemployment statistics from *breadlines*.
>
> Last year, our War Mobilization and Reconversion Act threw protection over *servicemen on demobilization*. But another myth had sprung up as World War II wore on and a very *different* reception was accorded proposals to throw some measure of protection over men and women laid off when war contracts would be cancelled, and war plants closed down.
>
> The discussion provoked by these proposals last year indicated a widespread belief that high wartime wages had placed war workers in particular, and American families generally, in a position not only to move about at will but to tide themselves over handsomely, months at a time, until work is again plentiful.

. . . Certain it is that this myth did not agree with our own impressions as settlement workers, of the facts of life among our neighbors. . . .

I reported to Senator Wagner and his committee of how, in 1944 and 1945, our National Federation of Settlements had undertaken case studies to get intimate family pictures. Henry Street Settlement tried out the idea first not in its own neighborhood on the Lower East Side, but in a crowded wartime area back of the Brooklyn Navy Yard. On the basis of this sampling, we worked out a questionnaire that helped settlement workers elsewhere find out what the war years had meant moneywise to some three hundred families in twenty urban areas. Those areas included the automobile center in Detroit; Chicago with its stockyards and modern plants; such metal and machine trade centers as Cleveland and Philadelphia; New York and Boston, Minneapolis, Rochester, Birmingham, and other representative communities.

The incomes of almost one-fifth of the families had doubled and eighteen of them reported a trebled income. Well toward a *third* had two wartime wage earners, eight families had three, and their family incomes had jumped accordingly. However, at the other end of the scale, approximately one out of seven households had lower incomes to count on than in prewar days. Some workers who had higher wages than before had no more to take home after payroll deductions for taxes.

Almost half of the families we talked to had come into the 1940s with the handicap of back debts—many of them considerable in amount—contracted in the hard times. . . .

Approximately five out of seven of the families reported heavy medical and dental expenses during the war years—some so extensive, running from $200 to over $800, as to suggest that they were trying to make up for ravages of neglect earlier when they didn't have the money to pay for professional services. . . .

Badly needed replacements of furniture and household goods proved to be a drain on the new wartime wages. . . .

Here again, whatever household buying there has been has had to be done in a market where prices were high and quality low. . . .

Among the families with bank accounts, a fourth of them had

from $1,000 to $2,200; another quarter from $625 to $1,000; the remaining half—$100 or under.

It was said that people didn't want to work in 1928 and 1929 and afterwards. We know now that was nonsense. It was these same people and their kind who, working and fighting, won this war. It seems incredibly stupid if Americans can plan together to win such a war and yet don't plan so that men and women can work steadily.

The bill was passed in 1946 creating the President's Council of Economic Advisers, authorized to report on the economic state of the Union to the President, for transmission to Congress. Leon Keyserling, as the originator of the plan and later as chairman of the council appointed by President Truman, brought his liberal social viewpoint and brilliant mind to its organization. The legislation had—and still has—great potential for stabilizing the economy. But unfortunately, the political and social viewpoint of the Economic Advisers themselves, and of the President, and the Congress, can enhance or diminish its stabilizing potential.

XXIX

More New Housing

We were not only concerned over the years with the work of getting federal, state, and city money for public housing and then getting it built, but with all the complexities of what becomes the final struggle—that of moving families off sites into new neighborhoods and helping them fit into their new environment. We felt we had a responsibility which started in Washington but came to rest on our own corner, or we hoped it would! The announcement of a new public housing project for the neighborhood was, of course, a cause for great rejoicing even though we knew we would have to live through the pitiful business of eviction and relocation.

In the early days of public housing, relocation could be a very ruthless business but as time went on more humane methods were worked out, larger grants for moving expenses and for down payments on rent in other quarters were allowed, and more help was given to site tenants as they searched for new homes, Still, the two or more years before the completion of a project were hard for all concerned. We at Henry Street, as other settlements did, worked along with families as they had to get out. It was difficult for the Housing Authority itself, with its bulldozer deadlines and myriad other problems, but above all hard for the families who had to be moved temporarily or permanently. Large families, especially, were incredibly difficult to relocate in new housing, and hard to house decently anywhere.

One way the Housing Authority struggled to meet this problem was by what came to be called "Rehabs." That is, tenements were bought and rehabilitated so that they could house large families with the idea of a temporary stay of two years when the problem had to be faced again, and hopefully more large apartments would be built in public housing units.

We had a very close association with one of these Rehabs, as all the members of one of our Predelinquent groups, with two exceptions, lived there. These Negro families had been drawn from different parts of the city and the families were very large in numbers and problems—so much so that Ruth Tefferteller put a full-time worker with this gang calling themselves the "Henry Street Boys." Their leader was a student from India who devoted himself to the problems of these families so wholeheartedly that one of the mothers put it to me this way: "He is just like a brother to us and we turn to him for everything." Gradually violent quarrels among the families in this Rehab ceased and they began to get together to talk over their children's problems. Finally, out of this grew an active Mother's Club with one of the most hard-pressed of the mothers as president.

This took time and planning, but how little the cost, as I have said before, compared to the chaos both in the families and in the Rehabs which we found when we took their children into the Predelinquent Project. Things were going so well that the Housing Authority did not attempt to move the families at the end of the second year and let them stay until the building was torn down to make way for more housing. A goodly number of the families were eligible for public housing. The mothers still come back to meet with Mr. Romesh Shah at their club meetings which he continued to attend even after he had his graduate degree and was teaching at Rutgers University.

The first new projects were built from plans made before the war and did not take into account the population trends that came after the war, so there were still few apartments for large families. Many of them moved from one tenement to another as they were pulled down, just a few steps ahead of the bulldozer, until some were moved six or seven times. Meanwhile, many lived in buildings unfit for the rats that infested them, wrecked by vandalism, and sometimes without heat or light.

After the war a burst of new low-income housing projects came on the Lower East Side along the East River. It is such a beautiful location I had wondered why real estate interests had not developed that land for high-rent apartments. But they didn't and our neighbors who had borne the heat of the day in the old tenements have the lovely view on the East River. The new projects are suitably named after Jacob Riis. Lillian Wald, and Bernard Baruch. They stretch along the river from Tenth Street to the new middle-income cooperatives built by the United Housing Corporation at Grand Street and the river. Herbert Lehman and Aaron Rabinowitz had supplied capital, at Miss Wald's suggestion, for the first cooperative housing in our area, the Amalgamated Dwellings on Grand Street. Sponsored by the Amalgamated Clothing Workers Union in the late twenties, it remained the sole middle-income co-op on the Lower East Side until after the war, when favorable state financing laws encouraged their further development.

The International Ladies Garment Workers Union has sponsored most of the later developments, channeling its invested union funds through the United Housing Corporation, as had the Amalgamated Clothing Workers much earlier. The Amalgamated, too, added an extension to its older Amalgamated Dwellings. Now the middle-income cooperatives stretch all along East Broadway, from the East River to Seward Park. Some of them are sandwiched in among the public low-rent projects. Thus these middle-income cooperatives, side by side with the lower-income public projects, have made this section of the Lower East Side a mixed-income neighborhood. It is interesting that they are financed by funds from the two large garment workers' unions, for the Lower East Side was once a garment workers' area.

This kind of mixed-income housing should be one of the patterns for the future. But strongly as I believed this, I was dismayed when I discovered accidentally that a plan for a low-income project across the street from the settlement at 265 Henry Street had been changed by the Housing Authority into a plan for a cooperative. I suppressed my surprise when I was told that our Lower East Side Neighborhoods Association had asked for the change! It turned out that some of LENA's members from business interests had created this impression during a conference with the Authority. My first feelings of disappointment were because settlement services are keyed to low-income neighbors who need them most, and the nearer you are, the better. Yet here was to be a middle-income group across the street with middle-income families living between the low-income families in Vladeck and in La Guardia, which was just what I had been urging as a good neighborhood pattern! So I kept still!

In the early fifties, gang warfare had erupted in the low-income housing projects, along with the rest of the city's slums, bringing a good deal of vandalism along with it. It seems mild compared to the violence of the sixties, but it was enough to help create bad feelings toward tenants of public housing. As we know, this kind of publicity can affect appropriations by Congress or the state legislature. We were concerned on many counts and felt that good relationships among new tenants themselves, and between them and the neighborhood into which they moved, was an important factor in making public housing serve its purpose of improving family life.

When you follow closely the difficulties involved in putting together the land for a new housing site you sometimes wonder that we ever get them built. The following incident directed toward La Guardia Houses illustrates one of the problems of vested interests.

My secretary came upstairs saying, "There is a woman downstairs who wants to see you. She wants you to save the synagogue. She says she will take five minutes." My experience had been that the more anyone protests about just five minutes, the longer they stay. Anyhow, I went down and was enveloped by a stout embrace and reminded of "our old days." Her story was that she had come from "the masses of people" who wanted me to save the synagogue on Montgomery and Madison streets where La Guardia Houses were to be built. "God," she rushed on, "moves in a mysterious way and He has appointed you to save the Synagogue. He does strange things we don't understand but the Bible says so, too." I tried to interject to say it was stranger even than she thought, but words flowed over me as God, the Bible, the masses, and "well-known people," all jumbled together to form a united front which apparently I was to represent in snatching this hideous, old, rundown building from the Housing Authority. Finally sternness seemed necessary to stem the tide, and I told her how dreadful it seemed to me to put so much as a pin in the way of more public housing. Did she think children should be brought up in old tenements to save an old building that ought to be replaced with the money the city had already paid to the congregation? And it was not even a Jewish landmark as it had formerly been a Lutheran church. She stopped dead at this point and said she was a great advocate of public housing; in fact, she lived in the Lillian Wald Houses. Then the story of the disagreement in the congregation came out—what I had guessed to be the old against the younger of the congregation. At this point I was to be mediator between the two. That was really what all the Bible portents meant.

My friend and I parted finally, both talking at once—my saying, "Get your two groups together and decide how the money the city has paid is going to be spent." But she had the last word. "That's a good plan. I knew you'd think of something and we will come back for you to arbitrate."

What really happened finally was that after having the older group threaten to throw themselves in front of any bulldozer approaching the synagogue, it became such a religious cause that politically no one wanted to touch it, especially just before elections. The Housing Authority changed the plans of La Guardia Houses, pushing one building back enough to allow the synagogue with all its housing violations and decreptitude to stand!

As a friendly beginning when La Guardia Houses finally opened, adult groups from the Educational Alliance and the Good Companions of Henry Street joined together to welcome the newcomers. During the first week of moving in, they served refreshments in a room off the La Guardia Houses lobby where hot coffee and snacks greeted the harassed families as they herded children and furniture into their new homes. We felt a special responsibility for the families moving into La Guardia as we had undertaken to manage their Community Center, and had already worked for months on its color and decoration.

Along with this, we had worked out a plan to bring new neighbors together in a way that would hopefully avert the problems that were beginning to be serious in new public housing neighborhoods and help make the newcomers feel a responsible part of their new environment.

I tell of our work at La Guardia Houses in some detail, as I did of the work with tenants at Vladeck Houses, because help servicing these basic needs is still lacking in low-income housing developments everywhere. Dean Mitchell Ginsberg of the Columbia University School of Social Work (later Welfare Commissioner and Human Resources Administrator in New York), cooperated with us in the first year's experiment. It was aimed first at averting the frictions that develop when hundreds of families are moved into a neighborhood at one time, and to develop self-governing groups of tenants. Murray Ortoff, later director of University Settlement, who was teaching at the Columbia University School of Social Work came on our staff part-time, and planned and supervised the work of four advanced students of social work assigned to this job as their field work. We felt that one of the by-products of the project would be to give social work students an introductory experience with the problems of families moving into public housing. This first year's experiment was so successful we were able to get a grant from the Fred L. Lavenburg Foundation allowing us to employ a full-time staff for the next two years, with José Villegas as director. He had been working with the United Nations, and his Puerto Rican background was particularly helpful as La Guardia Houses had 48 percent Puerto Rican as compared with 20 percent Negro families. The work continued as it was originally started, and did even more in bringing new and old neighbors together and creating opportunities for cooperation than we had hoped for it.

At La Guardia we first undertook to reach every tenant with a friendly call or, as it turned out often, many visits in an effort to find out what they particularly wanted and to involve them in helping themselves by organizing floor-by-floor meetings in each others' apartments. This visiting which started with the social work students went on continuously for the next two years. As their interest crystalized, the tenants themselves took up the job of visiting and getting their neighbors interested in the self-help programs that were steadily evolving. Our mimeographing machine was never still and our headquarters never without individual and group conferences as the tenants' ideas took shape. The groups raised funds to help support services they considered important for their families. Their readiness to assume responsibility increased as their sense of solidarity and purpose grew. However, this did not happen without a very conscious effort to encourage, and often train, local leaders as they emerged.

We looked on their fund-raising not only as a way of providing money for services they wanted, but as one of the effective ways of developing leadership and encouraging the taking of responsibility. As the Puerto Ricans outnumbered the other tenants, many things they did so successfully took on some of the aspects of Puerto Rican culture, but many of the things they liked to do —singing and dancing, especially—were basic to Negro culture as well although the tunes might be different!

Under Mr. Villegas' encouragement and very knowledgeable leadership, in eight months the seven self-help groups raised nearly $4,000. The details give the picture: The Tenants Association cleared $200 from informal social activities and participation in community festivals. The La Guardia Cooperative Nursery Committee raised $850 from dances, cake sales, Saturday movies for children, street fiestas. The Domino Club raised $1,200 through dances and excursions. The two baseball clubs together raised about $800 as they, together with our staff, worked for more park space for baseball. The La Guardia Health Service Committee raised $300. The members of the Domino Club and the Nursery Committee formed a Queen Contest Committee which grossed $535 during the first five weeks of a twenty-two-week long contest. The profits of the Popularity Queen Contest were used to expand the nursery school and the health education services of the Domino Club. Additional funds came from a six-day, all-community street fiesta, within the project. All this was spent on community services in the project. The staff helped each group in its fund-raising efforts on the condition that the money would be used to benefit the entire community. With such a focus, the planning discussions were of major value. Added to the other considerations, the social purposes of their activities gave these newcomers a feeling of prestige in the community. Their fund-raising activities were, of course, services in themselves, and the dances provided a much-needed place of recreation near home on Saturday nights. They didn't need to go back to old neighborhoods for social life. The movies for children provided better shows at lower prices, and were better supervised and closer to home than any offered commercially in the neighborhood. Other useful cooperative ventures were a sewing machine, cooperatively purchased, and a set of cleaning equipment, also cooperatively purchased. These needs were uncovered and the solution proposed by a part-time registered nurse hired by the Domino Club and the La Guardia Health Service Committee.

I need hardly say that the growth of each one of the groups was a story in itself—a story that grew from continuous friendly visiting by neighbors and staff, listening, encouraging, helping, informal conferences singly and in groups, discussions, careful evaluation of difficulties, success or failure, and never-flagging enthusiasm. It would be a mistake to think that this kind of tenant development would be likely to come about so quickly and successfully without leadership and encouragement of a knowledgeable kind.

Mothers, for instance, experimented with something less formal than a fully staffed nursery school and less expensive, setting a pattern of services that might be used in other low-income developments where there are large families. The La Guardia mothers served as volunteers in their nursery school and in large numbers in a "baby-sitting station" during the summer under the direction of a trained person. This start later turned into the nursery school in which we used junior high school girls.

The Tenants Association, which was primarily a means of screening and bringing tenants' complaints to management through a committee of their own, fell on bad luck after some months of very successful activity. They elected a difficult and unstable president who was influenced by the manager of La Guardia Houses, who in turn admitted he didn't want a Tenants' Association or anything to do with Henry Street. The association broke away except for the use of our mimeograph machine—the heart of community organizing! When they were completely on their own they promptly got rid of their president, selected a more competent person, and asked us if we would work more closely with them again along the lines on which they had started of "visiting their neighbors to learn what they want a 'Tenants Association' to do."

From the beginning of their term of office, as members of the

Housing Authority, William Reid, Ira Robbins, and Francis V. Madigan worked hard at making the handling of families, from the long waiting lists to their tenancy in the projects, as humane as possible. It is no easy task to fit families into the period of land acquisition, demolition, and clearance, site tenants' relocation, construction of the buildings, and then tenant selection, all of it handicapped by the city's red tape.

While Alice Brophy had successfully brought social work into the thinking of the Housing Authority for some years, the Authority members felt that they wanted to set up what came to be called a "Social Consultation Unit," and I was asked to help get it going. Having seen many of the problems at first hand, I was able to spare some part of my time from Henry Street for six months to help set up what was the formal beginning of their Social Consultation Unit, which Jack Goldberg and then Preston David headed.

It seemed very important to me that social work skills should lessen the unhappiness, and add to successful adjustment as families fitted into their new surroundings. It was all so new— eighteen stories where you can't yell out the window for your children or keep an eye on them, self-service elevators which the young frequently used for games as well as toilets and which were sometimes dangerous for women and old people even in the beginning before the present mugging epidemic, incinerators where children helping their mothers spilled garbage on the floors instead of in the chute. It was wonderful what a few floor meetings did to help neighbors understand each other and these common problems.

I had seen not only the problems firsthand, but also many of the joys a new housing project brings as well. These we sometimes forget in our concentration on what still needs to be improved. I often wish more people could see this side of the picture. There was the neighbor who stopped one of us on the street to beg us to come and see her "little three-room paradise." Bathrooms and sun seemed to come first in appreciation. I remember a mother's tale of her little boy's joy in his first bathtub. And what an elevator meant to mothers with babies and toddlers! A little girl's rheumatic heart had kept one family hunting for first floors and basements for years and now with elevators they could choose. We had to go to see one "beautiful" apartment after another. The children's pride in the furniture and new home was touchingly evident as the mothers showed us around. We worry so much about the pitfalls of installment buying that sometimes we hardly see the new furniture the families show us and the pride it can bring along with the monthly payments. When I visited one of our former neighbors who had moved her big family to the Williamsburg Project in Brooklyn, I exclaimed at the size of the new dining room table as I squeezed around it. The reply was, "Well, I just said my littlest one was going to have room for his elbows on the table and sit up with the rest of us."

One of our difficulties at Henry Street had always been that we found it next to impossible to convince our neighbors that we could not get an apartment for them if we tried hard enough. One day I found a little note on my desk left there by one of the staff, which said, "I went to see Mr. and Mrs. Davis about the apartment and they say they know they have one too many babies for that apartment but if the Housing will only excuse the littlest one, they promise not to do it again!" I sent this on to the Housing Authority, just as it was and they did excuse the littlest one!

The trees were another great cause for rejoicing. One neighbor told me of a tree episode as we rode along in a Madison Street bus. "You know," she said, "we look right out on the top of one of the trees and what do you think—a mother bird built a nest in it where we could see and she laid her eggs and then the birdies were born. And then one day one dropped out of the nest while we were watching and it was too soon, it couldn't fly, so my John ran quick and brought the birdie up and we fixed a box and got an eye-dropper right away and fed the birdie milk with vitamins [a modern touch] and the children and their father and I watched it grow. And we could hardly keep away from the window watching the babies in the nest being fed. Then one day when our birdie was stronger and the others were beginning to fly, we put it on the window sill. It chirped and, what do you think, Miss Hall? Its mother came and showed it how to fly. It was strong enough now. But we sure do miss that little birdie," she ended wistfully.

XXX

The Beginning and the
Slow Understanding of
Narcotics Abuse

Gang warfare, on which the settlements had focused so heavily, reached its height in the middle fifties, and little by little became less of a problem as neighborhoods settled down, gang members grew up, and the city's Youth Board developed its street club program. But gang warfare was followed gradually, in our neighborhood and others, by what became the overriding problem of the late fifties—drug addiction of the young—a problem that has increased steadily through the sixties. We watched it increasing among the very young, along with acts of individual violence. Mugging, stealing, and burglary of all kinds perpetrated by addicts desperate to buy their drugs became everyday news. A kind of unremitting viciousness has changed the climate of neighborhood life, as women in particular, but people in general, are afraid to be out on dark streets, afraid of dark hallways and stairs, afraid to enter the self-service elevators in the low- and middle-income projects.

We at Henry Street became aware in the early fifties, through our Mental Hygiene Clinic, of the beginning of drug use among teen-agers. The boys who first came to the clinic for help were afraid of being drawn into the habit by their older teen-age brothers who were beginning to experiment with drugs and were getting hooked. At University Settlement on the Lower East Side, Charles Cook, then director, was starting to work with the police in tracking down pushers. At the same time settlement workers on the Lower East Side got together to exchange ideas as to how we could best tackle this new trouble that was beginning to be a problem for us all. There had always been a few older men who were then referred to as "drug fiends" drifting up from Chinatown, but the teen-age drug-taker was new. The insidious business spread slowly at first, but had gathered momentum by the mid-fifties.

At Henry Street, we approached the problem in a number of ways. Because Ralph Tefferteller had had a friendly relationship with so many of the boys who were beginning to experiment and get hooked in their very early teens, we were close to the problem from the beginning. After the steadily increasing numbers of addicts began coming to him for help, Ralph made himself available any time of the day or night. Very often when we came home late from a meeting in one of the other buildings, a forlorn figure would be sitting on the stoop at 265 waiting to see Mr. "T." Earlier or later, they turned to him for some kind of help. If it was for hospital treatment, he was often in a quandary, for at that time drug addicts were not taken into many hospitals. You often hoped they would have some other physical trouble which the hospital would feel obliged to treat.

Ralph Tefferteller worked closely with Dr. Howard Brown at Gouverneur Clinic on getting help for some of his most desperate addicts. In those years, only the city's specially set up Riverside Hospital on North Brother's Island and the federal government's narcotics hospital in Lexington, Ky., were geared to treat addicts, and they were not immediate answers. The latter was far away and admission to Riverside required time.

As the problem grew, mothers, sisters, wives, and girl friends began to come to "Mr. T." in dismay and misery. They wanted help for their particular addict and they wanted to understand what was happening.

To help with this part of the problem and bring some understanding to the neighborhood, Ralph cooperated with LENA in starting a Narcotics Information Center, with Edward Brown, a Presbyterian minister who had been at Riverside serving on one of its clinical teams, taking over its direction in 1959. LENA had been organized in 1955 on a broad front to include not only the settlements of the area, but all community-minded civic, church, business groups, and neighborhood groups. Operating on a small grant from the Aaron E. Norman Fund through LENA, and from the Church of Sea and Land, whose minister, David Romig, was deeply concerned, LENA opened its first Information Service Center in a little store-front on Madison Street; then moved to an old tenement stoop apartment on Henry Street where it stayed until they could afford to move to one of their present locations on East Broadway and Rutgers. In the beginning, our neighborhood agencies shared their staffs in manning the center and conferring with addicts and their bewildered families. Parents groups were formed to hold meetings on the problem. As grants from Mobilization for Youth and the New York City Department of Mental Health became available, the center was able to expand its work. In 1967, the agency was refinanced through the New York City Office of the Coordinator of Addiction Programs and the New York State Narcotic Addiction Control Commission, which expanded their needed services.

Over the years, the Service Center has attracted experts and many interested persons from other parts of the city to its Board of Directors. Arthur Harlow, who was at the time chairman of the Narcotics Committee of Henry Street's board, was deeply interested in the problem. As director of Group Health Insurance, he was involved in its health aspects and in any way that GHI might help. Fairfield Dana, from our board, followed as chairman of our committee after Arthur Harlow's death.

The Rutgers Street headquarters seemed ample when they moved in, but by the winter of 1968–9, with a $400,000 yearly budget, they had six centers in the immediate neighborhood used for different aspects of the work.

Early in our struggle, we also tackled the problem of police protection, or lack of it, from pushers. We were greatly disturbed by members of families who came to Ralph Tefferteller to tell him that a man in the neighborhood (one of three brothers, all with equally unsavory occupations) was shamelessly standing on the corner of Henry and Montgomery Streets a half block away from the settlement and giving heroin free to thirteen-year-old Puerto Ricans to get them hooked as future customers. We not only were outraged at the performance, but hated the thought of helplessness this flagrant behavior must give our then new neighbors. At one time, neighbors reported that they saw the man shake hands with a policeman in a passing patrol car.

We decided to put an end to this performance if we could, at least on our corner, and after considerable investigation were given the name of someone high up in the Police Department who, it was said, could be trusted to follow through. With two members of our board, Winslow Carlton and Jack Markowitz, Ralph and I went to see him and not only told him the story but who the man was and a few other pertinent details. He said he would put two detectives on the case. At the end of a month, he called us into his office again and said he was awfully sorry, but his men hadn't been able to catch the man doing anything. He explained they could have made an arrest for gambling, but he supposed that wasn't what we wanted. We agreed it wasn't.

Mrs. Robert Potter, another very active member of our board who had followed this affair, told a Deputy Commissioner of Police, Alexander Aldrich, what had happened, and after conferring with us, he sent a truck with one-way glass windows to our corner and in three days the man was arrested, caught in the act. Bill Calise followed the case in the courts to see whether he would be let off again. He had had a record of seventeen arrests and had gotten off an equal number of times. The excuse, when we probed for it, was that he was an informer for the police. This time he was sentenced, but not for a long term. We finally came to the conclusion that the police would not be our main source of strength in controlling the use of drugs in our neighborhood.

For years, a bedraggled, forlorn group of addicts hung around our corner, going in and out of the little candy and stationery store, making the people who ran it miserable. Later, it had a new owner and was closed after it was revealed that it was in on the racket.

All the time that Ralph Tefferteller was trying to relieve the individuals' suffering and help their families, we were, of course, looking for a cure. Riverside, the City Hospital for young addicts, was not much more encouraging than Lexington, Ky., which reported less than 10 percent success. When I was in California, I spent a day at Synanon and, later, we went to see the first

Synanon setup in Westport, Conn., and we were able to get one of our neighborhood boys in there. The methods employed are similar to Alcoholics Anonymous, where the treatment is by the addicts to each other, but different in that they live and work together. It is a voluntary acceptance of a communal life as long as the addict is in need of help. The Synanon people seemed hopeful as to proportion of cures, but at that time were reluctant to give any figures. Our enquiry took us also to the Rockefeller Institute, where we learned in detail of the experimentation they were doing with Methadone, the therapeutic drug administered to heroin addicts which keeps them functioning. Methadone seemed to us then the most hopeful thing in the field, and it still seems to be the most important breakthrough, although it is still considered experimental as to its long-term effects.

Six local agencies, with Dr. Howard Brown as chairman and Simon Slavin as secretary, undertook to establish an ambulatory clinic for methadone patients in cooperation with Dr. Vincent Dole. This was developed some time later by Dr. Trumall at Beth Israel, which is still the largest treatment center for heroin addicts in the city. However, the real problem today is a matter of numbers. We are still treating so few addicts in any way, compared to their number and their devastating effect on the city.

The most far-reaching contribution made by Henry Street was the book, *Addict in the Street*, edited by Jeremy Larner, and based on the seven years of tape recordings that Ralph Tefferteller had taken of the stories told him by the neighborhood boys who had been coming to him for help ever since the ugly business began. Published by Grove Press in hardcover in 1965, and later in paperback, *Addict in the Street* opened many people's eyes—and ears. For a number of years, it had been difficult to arouse public interest in addiction and as a matter of fact still is. Most people were too far away from it to realize how fast it was increasing, how young its victims were, and how dangerous the addict who was hooked and had not money for a "fix" was to the community.

It was in 1957 that Ralph Tefferteller made his first tape recording of a drug addict and, as he recalls it, he made it primarily for his own enlightenment. This led to other tapings. One of the first, dealing directly with our local teen-age addicts, was made by a group of young girls who came to Mr. Tefferteller in 1958 to get his help for their boy friends and brothers who were caught up in the racket.

During the following years, Mr. Tefferteller continued his tape recordings steadily. Often in the middle of the night, in a small office at 265 Henry Street, he recorded the misery and frustrations of individual addicts, and sometimes also recorded talks with relatives and friends. During this time he was able to get nearly two hundred addicts into local, state, or federal treatment programs, inadequate as they were. Along with this went a steady flow of boys finally admitted into hospitals for detoxification.

The book that grew out of these tape recordings enjoyed such success that it showed how far behind we were in our understanding. In February, the same month that *Addict in the Street* was published, the *Atlantic Monthly* featured on its cover an article by Mr. Larner describing Henry Street's work with addicts and including excerpts from the book. In New York, the *World-Telegram* serialized the book in part, starting the first day with a page one streamer headline and concluding with a lead editorial. There followed reviews from coast to coast, others in Canada and Mexico, interviews on TV and radio, and transmission of some of the tapes, reviews in such far-off countries as India, publication of the book in paperback in England and, in translation, in France and Italy. I quote from book critics, because they give an idea of how much this kind of interpretation was needed at the time: In *Commonweal*, Saul Maloff wrote:

> . . . no one who reads *The Addict in the Street* will ever be quite the same again. By the simple expedient of taking, not categories of human beings (Underprivileged, Culturally Deprived, Slum-Dwelling, Youthful Addicts), but this boy and that girl, this son and that mother, and letting them make themselves known by speaking about themselves in the presence of a tape-recorder, Ralph Tefferteller . . . has rendered a Sociological Class into unforgettable human scale.
>
> By judicious editing of the tapes—cutting them to eliminate redundancy but otherwise not tampering with them—novelist Jeremy Larner transforms talk into speech while retaining individual peculiarities and all other spontaneous marks of an unmistakable person making language of his life. . . .

Ralph Tefferteller knew his subjects intimately and over the span of much of their lives; and they trusted him as much as it was possible for them to trust anybody. He wasn't fuzz, or in the invidious sense a social worker, or Authority. He was a man who cares about them. . . .

They emerge in these pages from the dark places to which we banish them from our sight, and come alive in the sound of their speech, breaking the silence we had pledged them to, echoing in the chambers of the mind and the heart.

"This book," Alan Pryce-Jones wrote in the *Herald Tribune*, "helps us to do what Dickens did in *Oliver Twist* and elsewhere: it compels unwilling eyes to see what is there."

In the *Saturday Review*, Harry Elmer Barnes wrote:

So far as I am aware, there is nothing in previously published literature . . . that so vividly and factually describes the mental reactions, social patterns and pathological behavior of youthful addicts. . . . A rational solution of the narcotics problem is likely to be long delayed. The extensive circulation of *The Addict in the Street* would constitute a strong push in the right direction.

Reviewing the paperback edition, *Publishers' Weekly* declared, "[this is] a book of such raw misery and power and so great an indictment of the present narcotics acts that one wants to go out and demand new laws!"

"These raw chunks of autobiography," Nat Hentoff wrote in *The New York Times Book Review*, "both annihilate any pseudo-hip myths of romanticism concerning the life of the junkie and also emphasize how agonized drug addicts are. . . ." "*The Addict in the Street*," a reviewer in Canada's *Mental Health* commented, "has special value to the helping professions. . . ."

And from Senator Jacob Javits:

This verbatim transcript of the horrible treadmill of narcotics addictions is an electrifying document . . . more effective than any clinical study could be, this is a powerful wedge against public indifference and misunderstanding. I believe it will help bring wider recognition of how baffling this social disease is, how inadequate our tools against it are, and how much greater resources must be devoted to enlarging our knowledge about it.

In neighborhoods such as ours, heroin still seems to be the preferred drug, while there is experimentation with pills of all kinds. LSD, speed, and similar halucinatory drugs seem to be more concentrated on campuses and in the suburbs, but the smoking of marijuana is widespread everywhere.

Efforts to cure drug addiction have increased over the years as its devastating results are seen not only on the individuals involved but on our communities but they are still tragically inadequate. While the experiments with Methadone on heroin addicts do seem the most helpful breakthrough so far, those dealing with addicts know that continued experimentation and a multiple approach is still absolutely necessary. With the still-increasing crime rate and the high proportion of addicts involved, it should be obvious that we need to continue to do more.

I will let the addicts speak for themselves from *Addict in the Street.*

> I started nine years ago with marijuana. I started off in a pool-room. I used to go in the poolroom when I was under age, and the Spanish fellas used to be smoking marijuana there. Before you know, a couple friends of mine started, and I started too. I followed them. From there I went to snorting heroin and then using the needle. We all switched together, after about six months of pot and six months of snorting. I guess we just got tired of marijuana and were looking for a higher high. It was always a group, at least two or three of us together. We used to shoot up together, in hallways and on rooftops. . . .

> I was thirteen years old when I had my first fix. I went directly mainline. I went with a guy, one of my friends—not really a friend but supposedly—we went to the other end of the neighborhood to pick up some things for some other kids. We got a free bag, and he asked me if I ever got off before. I said yes, so he said okay, let's split the bag. So we went up to the roof and that's where I got my first fix. It was 1953, the Saturday before Easter Sunday. Nine years and a week ago. . . .

> I've been on drugs now almost eight years. I've been arrested four times; I was convicted on three of the charges. Of the eight years I'd say I spent about two years in jail. In the past five years I haven't stayed a whole year out of jail. Since 1958 I've been

continuously involved with the law or the court—arrested, out on bail, awaiting trial, or in jail.

I was arrested two months after we talked last April. On the new charge, I did three months, and then I got six months for violation of parole. I was released two weeks ago; I've been living at home and haven't used anything since I've been out. . . .

How expensive for the community and useless for the addict.

I'm twenty-one years old; I started with pot when I was fourteen. I used to go home from Junior High and get real high at lunchtime. I used to buy it from a man in the park. Pot keeps you cool. I used to eat a lot; I felt good. The man who sold it was a friend of mine, about twenty-four years old. There were a lot of dealers, but his pot was better. He didn't ask any of us to deal, because in pot only one dealer can make money.

In heroin it's much different. When you're using drugs it's really a dirty job, you know? When I was about sixteen I went to heroin. After about two weeks I wanted to use it every day. I started mainlining because I found that you get your high faster. But I can't explain it because it's too dirty. People don't care about their mothers. . . .

They say if you felt anything for us, you wouldn't do it. But it doesn't go like that. It has nothing to do with it. Because I wouldn't do anything to hurt them. It's not a matter of hurting you or not hurting you. It's something I do, I don't know why I do it, but I do.

I would do anything for them, but when they say, if you felt anything for us you wouldn't do it, it's not an honest reason. It's no reason to stop. Because I do care for them. but it just seems it hasn't anything to do with it. . . .

I'm not gonna look ahead too far, I'm just gonna take each day. I don't really want to look ahead, because I've seen back. So you can't tell anything, really. The first couple of years doesn't mean too much. If you completely forget about it, you have a pretty good chance. If you don't use it but you still have it on your mind, chances are you're gonna go back.

XXXI

The Founding of the Lower Eastside Neighborhoods Association (LENA)

Much of this review of postwar activities has been concerned with the violence and disorder around us, and in its deteriorating effect on the community as a whole. The Lower Eastside Neighborhoods Association (LENA) and Mobilization for Youth grew out of this concern of the settlements and their conviction that such widespread violence could be controlled only by measures involving the whole community.

LENA grew directly out of a meeting at Henry Street in September, 1954. A few of us met over a small map of the Lower East Side to plan new ways of dealing with the gang war around us. The immediate precipitating event was an attack on a twelve-year-old Puerto Rican girl who had been knocked down and kicked in the stomach as she came out of school at noon. The assailants were the girl friends or "Debs" of the second generation Mayhews gang, fifteen-year-old boys, at that time, whose activities had been gathering momentum for some months. The police told the girl's mother that she must spirit her daughter away from the neighborhood for safety! The police seemed to feel that Henry Street was not safe for this twelve-year-old girl and that East Harlem was better, which was a startling assumption, to us.

As we studied the map that day, we came to the conclusion that the Lower East Side, from Fourteenth Street down, was too interdependent and too interdelinquent for us to stop at any one small neighborhood. If our planning covered only a limited area it was unlikely that the young people themselves would oblige us by choosing the same boundaries, and the basic problems of tenements, health facilities, playgrounds, schools, and police protection certainly crossed the smaller neighborhood lines.

Our group that morning consisted of Father Kilmer Myers of St. Augustine's Episcopal Chapel on Henry Street, now Bishop of Northern California, which at this time served a predominantly Negro group of teen-agers, Jacob Markowitz, William Calise, and Ralph Tefferteller and Milton Yale of the Henry Street staff. Settlement leaders on the Lower East Side had been working closely together for many years and as a result of this meeting we promptly drew the other settlements into the planning.

We all pledged ourselves to the job of finding leadership from all our ethnic groups in every Lower Eastside neighborhood, and from all the interest groups which make up a community. Subsequently, we called the organization the Lower Eastside Neighborhoods Association, which with those initials, at once became LENA.

It did not seem feasible to cover the whole Lower East Side geographically at once, but rather to spread out gradually as leadership was found in the different neighborhoods. This was not to be a coordinating council of agencies but a group of people, and so during the next four months we went into a "still" hunt for people. And I mean "still" in more ways than one for we were looking for hard workers in the neighborhoods with a concern for the community, not just the talkers.

We were particularly eager to tap at once the leadership among the Puerto Ricans and Negroes. We were able to involve seven Puerto Ricans on the first board—but I have to say that this early group didn't stay with us, as most were ministers and their small churches were their first concern.

While we searched for people we built ourselves a large folding map of the Lower East Side, 8 by 16 feet, on which its social institutions were made large enough for all concerned to find themselves. The late Albert J. Kennedy, of the National Federation of Settlements, volunteered his expert knowledge of city planning, and with the help of Lilli Ann Rosenberg of our Art

Department the map was ready for the enlarged organizing meeting which took place at dinner at Henry Street Settlement, on January 8, 1955. From then on we lugged the map to all our meetings as a visual illustration of what we were trying to accomplish, using it as a focus for the diverse interests of our organizing members, and for all the others we hoped to involve.

It was easy to see the physical strengths and weaknesses of the Lower East Side as they showed on the map. For instance, our local hospital, Gouverneur, was at the extreme edge of the community away from transportation; the bright green we used to designate parks was obviously lacking in many areas and there were few recreational facilities in others. So the map took on meaning to everyone.

Events moved so fast that within three months we knew we had to have at least one person who worked at nothing else but LENA, and that person had to be very skillful and experienced. There was a small fund at Henry Street, known as the "Headworker's Fund" which was initially given to Lillian Wald to be used for purposes of her own choosing. During my incumbency I guarded it fiercely for purposes of my own choice. We drew on this fund for the first three months' salary for LENA's director, while we got our breath and started to look for support in earnest. Mrs. Rose Porter was a good sport and agreed to start on this basis and we were very fortunate to have her for our first five years.

It is unreasonable to expect a neighborhood organization such as LENA to be supported financially largely by low-income neighborhood people. It may be wholesome that some support comes from the neighborhood but we do not expect the big city-wide welfare councils to be supported by their membership alone. With the Anti-Poverty funds of the sixties coming into depressed neighborhoods, there is less pious talk to this effect and more realization that if the people living in such neighborhoods could support a council, in any substantial way, they wouldn't need it so much. This long-held attitude, especially on the part of foundations, may have been one of the reasons that local neighborhood councils like LENA have come and gone so fast. LENA has lasted longer than any other within my knowledge.

End of a Christmas party in the Playschool (*Photo courtesy of Ken Wittenberg*)

Leaving our Playhouse for one of the many bus trips
to Washington to fight for low-income housing:
Langdon Post, Mrs. Simkovitch, Helen Hall, Julius
M. Goldsmith chairman of the Lower Eastside
Housing Conference

Breaking ground for Rutgers Houses during double ground-breaking ceremonies on Monday, June 5, are (left to right): New York City Housing Authority member Ira S. Robbins, Miss Helen Hall, Manhattan Borough President Edward R. Dudley, City Housing Authority Chairman William Reid, Assemblyman Samuel A. Spiegel, Francis V. Madigan, vice chairman of the Housing Authority (*Photo courtesy of L. Marinoff*)

Junior high school aide in our nursery school (*Photo courtesy of Esther Goldman*)

Cover of *The Addict in the Street* (*Photo courtesy of Sande R. Jones*)

Suzuki violin pupils in our Nursery School with VISTA Volunteer, Doris Schark (*Photo courtesy of Ken Wittenberg*)

Families arriving at Echo Hill for a
day in the country and returning
(Photos courtesy of Ken Wittenberg)

A Boys' Club going down Henry Street passing the Settlement's original building on right, and showing Wall Street section in the distance (*Photo courtesy of William E. Barksdale*)

LENA's financial support came chiefly from three sources: some from Foundations; dues from membership organizations and from individuals; and at an early stage, a grant from the New York City Youth Board from its community organization budget. Eventually, LENA received an important grant from Mobilization for Youth, to help develop its Neighborhood Councils program.

We decided early in our planning that co-chairmen ought to be a practical way of handling the work ahead. Roughly, the idea was to have one person from the local community and one from one of the agencies involved in getting LENA going. The latter would be able to supply some of the clerical help and the inevitable mimeograph machine.

William Calise and I were chosen as co-chairman of the first board of LENA. Bill protested at first, feeling that a "professional" ought to do the job, but was finally convinced not only of the importance of his leadership qualities but of what his particular knowledge of the community could contribute. He had grown up on the East Side and knew every nook and cranny and the people in them. We also pointed out that he was "indigenous," and that while the word was not yet so popular, it was beginning to be stylish. Some months later Bill represented us at a meeting at a university, and when he came back he said, chuckling, "I know what you mean now about being 'stylish'; they certainly warmed up when they discovered I was a native."

LENA's Youth Division was one of its most important projects for the next few years, and we were able to draw many young people into helping solve our gang problems. They sat in on councils and committees and worked closely with Father Myers and Ralph Tefferteller, who became co-chairman of the Youth Division at that time. There were subcommittees on football, basketball, dances, a restudy of cellar clubs by local people, and ad hoc committees of young people when trouble errupted in one part of our "turf" or another! During the height of gang fighting, a boy called "Reds," a sixteen-year-old gang member, thought to be involved in a fatal shooting incident, went into hiding, and the police put on a search for him. Believing in LENA, his family urged him to come to us and tell his story. We were having an emergency meeting of the Board of LENA at the Educational

Alliance to discuss this latest gang outbreak when one of our members, a minister from St. Christopher's Chapel on Henry Street, walked in with Reds in tow. He had decided to give himself up to us rather than to the police. While he was telling us his story, two detectives walked into the meeting with guns in hand. Reds had to go with them, but I remember my sense of relief when I saw Bill Calise go out with him and knew that he would see Reds through, no matter what happened.

Other divisions focused on Housing, Health, Community Education, the Arts, local business support. The people serving on these committees were planned as a cross section of LENA membership and handled the problems and emergencies in those areas with assistance from LENA's staff, and reported back to the Board. To identify and draw into LENA's work the often untapped leadership in a neighborhood, local councils were started in each of the five chief neighborhoods. Their representatives have served on the central board and on all of the divisions. It often takes time and skill to find this leadership among the very poorest of the community, especially if they are newcomers. Then there is the job of making sure that the activities are stimulating enough to interest a real cross section of the neighborhood.

As headlines continuously reporting crimes have a deteriorating effect on a neighborhood, it is healthy to have a community of people think well of themselves and to have others think well of them. One of LENA's telling accomplishments in this direction has been its Evenings by the River concerts. They were held in cooperation with the Musician's Union, Local 802, in the beautiful but, until then, seldom-used Parks Department Amphitheatre on the East River at Grand Street, which holds 2,500 people. For many years Mrs. Eleanor Roosevelt and Newbold Morris—both dearly loved on the Lower East Side—came to the first concert of each season, which meant a grand sendoff. It was Newbold who had put us in touch with the Musician's Union and had helped us get funds for the first season's concerts. The citywide radio coverage of the concerts by our city station also helped the neighborhood's image throughout the city.

LENA's story is a long and interesting one—only suggested here. Our success has been in large measure due to LENA's widespread acceptance in the community. To quote a neighbor, "They are not just 'finks'—they are part of the neighborhood and to be trusted." We've also been successful due to the fact that from the beginning we had ready access to city officials who really knew we represented the community, and were willing to listen and often to act on the never-ending problems we brought to them. Our leadership has followed the pattern of change in the neighborhood. Our executive secretary in 1968, Alwin Davis, was black; and LENA's board represents in large measure the black and Puerto Rican members of our community, along with Jews and Italians of long standing on the East Side. It is the mixture that has to get along and LENA's board has been a good place to practice!

The years since LENA's founding have been busy ones, involving many different people throughout the years. Two of our community councils—Two Bridges and North East Neighborhood Association—have been very successful indeed. The former, initiated by Geoffrey Wiener at Hamilton-Madison House just as LENA started, was helped by leadership from the staff of Hamilton-Madison House for many years. NENA, with the leadership of Ana DuMois on the LENA staff, was responsible for starting a new health service in this area, having obtained a special grant for the purpose, and is now functioning on its own budget although allied with LENA through LENA's board.

Martin Livingstein was our second director, and Marta Valle, who was later head of the Youth Services of the City, was our director in 1966. Paul Kurzman, assigned from LENA's staff for Two Bridges, and Ana DuMois took responsibility for the whole organization during our long hunt for a director in 1967, which ended in Alwin Davis's appointment. A year later he resigned and left us looking again for a director.

LENA's basic budget has been supported by Anti-Poverty funds through the local Community Corporation for two years and with grants for special purposes. Its future is precarious at a time when the community needs it greatly. However, the life of community organizations are generally precarious and LENA has lived through many crises and I am hopeful will continue to do so as long as it is useful to the Lower East Side community. And at a time of such hostility and violence, an organization that attempts to bring people together for social planning can be of great service. Perhaps more than ever before.

I am glad to be able to add a happy postscript to LENA. The

Lower East Side has been designated by the United States Department of Commerce as the nation's first Economic Development Area under a 1969 amendment to the Public Works and Economic Development Act, and LENA has been asked to bring the different elements in the neighborhood together to implement a plan to create several thousand new, stable, and well-paying jobs for the unemployed and the underemployed of the Lower East Side.

XXXII

The Beginning of
Mobilization for Youth

Mobilization for Youth has had a major and far-reaching impact
on the treatment of the problems inherent in slums. It grew
out of a board meeting at Henry Street Settlement held on
May 13, 1957. It was the board's custom then, after a business meeting and dinner, to assemble again to discuss informally one or another phase of the settlement's many-faceted
program. Juvenile delinquincy was the subject of the evening's
discussion, and the following guests took part in it: Mr. Harry
S. Jacobson, Mr. Alfred Winslow Jones, and Mr. Jacob M. Kaplan.
Father Kilmer Myers, Vicar of St. Augustine's Chapel, had been
invited to join the Henry Street staff in developing the presentation, as he was very much involved in the problem of gang
warfare in the neighborhood. The board had been kept very
aware of the problem and were deeply concerned. Two years
before, Ralph Tefferteller, in discussing the problem at a board
meeting, had brought a bag of weapons taken from the young
boys as they came into Pete's House, and spread them out on
the floor—knives, steel knuckles and guns, and other combative
oddments.

After hearing in detail the latest aspects of the problem and
of the methods that were being used to deal with it, and also
how inadequate we felt it was, it was proposed that all our ideas
on the subject be put together, and that Henry Street Settlement

should consider embarking on a demonstration on the Lower East Side. Mr. Kaplan offered to underwrite the preparation of such a plan, and members of the staff agreed to prepare the proposal.

We started immediately, and the proposal was top priority on my agenda for the next ten months. The first plan was ready by April of 1958, after constant deliberation and consultation by members of the Henry Street staff and board.

We had turned to many people that winter for advice as the plan developed. These included Helen M. Harris, director of United Neighborhood Houses; Alfred Winslow Jones, who was author of a sociological study of a community entitled *Life, Liberty and Property*; Professor Robert M. MacIver, director of the Juvenile Delinquency Evaluation Project of the City of New York; James E. McCarthy, former deputy director of the New York City Youth Board, at that time director of the Big Brothers; Mrs. Rose Porter, director of the Lower Eastside Neighborhoods Association; Judge Sylvia Liese of the Family Court; and a number of others. Sylvan Furman, who became head of the Manhattan Society for Mental Health, and Susan Jenkins Brown, head of our Community Studies, provided editorial service over these months.

I personally took this first plan for discussion and criticism to the executive directors of the other settlements on the Lower East Side, and to the director and board of LENA and other agencies and churches on the Lower East Side especially involved in juvenile delinquency and gang warfare. We also sent the plan for criticism and suggestions to other experts in the field outside the community. From April on, there ensued widespread discussion on the Lower East Side.

In this first plan, Henry Street Settlement was suggested as the fiscal and administrative agent for the project as it had been first envisaged. The project director was to be responsible to the director of Henry Street Settlement and a coordinating council was planned for administrative unity, with representation from the participating agencies.

Much of the discussion, that summer of 1958, centered around the feasibility of LENA's being the executive agent instead of Henry Street. This problem was finally resolved in November,

1958, in another administrative plan, suggested by Simon Slavin in one of our many discussions. It had the same social objectives, but with a completely separate Board of Directors for Mobilization for Youth, to be set up in the beginning by Henry Street Settlement. This board was to consist, at the start, of an officer of the board and the executive director from each of the six participating settlements—The Educational Alliance, Grand Street Settlement, Hamilton-Madison House, Henry Street Settlement, Lillian Wald Settlement, and the University Settlement—the co-chairmen and executive director of LENA, the vicar of the Lower East Side Mission of Trinity Church and a lay representative of Trinity, the director of the Research Program, and the project administrator, and ex-officio, the treasurer of Henry Street Settlement because Henry Street had to be willing to handle the funds given to Mobilization until it was tax-free. Our board agreed to this although some members still felt that Henry Street should have taken the major responsibility. However, Winslow Carlton and I both felt that responsibility on the part of the other agencies would ensure wider participation and that this would also encourage government financing. We had felt from the beginning that anything as comprehensive as we had in mind would have to have federal financing.

In June of 1958 we obtained another grant from the Kaplan Foundation to hire James McCarthy on a full-time basis. (As I have said, he had been on the Henry Street staff when the McCanns were first bringing gang war into the House.) You need "full time" even to read what you must do in order to get a grant from some government agencies. Jim McCarthy and I started one evening at 7:30 to read one such, and it was 11:30 before we finished just reading it!

In July of that summer, James McCarthy and I took our plans of that date to the National Institute of Mental Health in Washington. At this meeting they showed interest in the proposal and also asked us whether they might perhaps have us try out our Predelinquent Project which was embedded in the plan. We said, "No," as we felt that what was most important and experimental about Mobilization for Youth was the attack on the multiple causes of delinquency over a wide geographical area in a city slum, bringing to bear every device and every known—or to be devised—method to change the social climate of the area. We wanted to get away from a piecemeal approach and to deal with the community as a whole. It was an effort to saturate a whole poverty area with services enough to change its living conditions. This had never been done before and we felt it was worth fighting for. In our planning we had not started with measuring the costs of the project but with what was needed to be done, and all through our planning we kept our eyes on the need and not what it would cost, or even where we would get the money.

When we had finished our preliminary proposal in April of that year, a research design for the project had not yet been prepared, but we had known from the beginning that there should be competent research along with our action plans. By the time our second request went in to the NIMH,* at Alfred Kahn's suggestion, we had involved Lloyd Ohlin, director of the Research Center of the Columbia School of Social Work, and his associate, Richard Cloward, and they promised to prepare a research design for the project if we could raise the money to pay for it. Winslow Carlton and I went to Stephen Currier for a grant to cover the cost of such a design, which he immediately made available through a gift to the Columbia University School of Social Work. This assignment was to develop an action research plan which would, hopefully, be acceptable for government financing.

From 1958 on, Winslow Carlton, with James McCarthy as executive, took the determining part in the continual planning of strategy and interpretation, to government agencies and to members of Congress. This long struggle is a story in itself.

Very fortunately we were able to reach the late congressman John Fogarty informally, through James McCarthy. His uncle, a priest, had been Congressman Fogarty's teacher. Congressman Fogarty was chairman of the House Appropriations Subcommittee dealing with welfare, and he became very much interested in the Mobilization for Youth approach to delinquency as he became familiar with it. He was to be a source of great strength in our long struggle to get appropriations, and he was our guest of honor at the formal launching of plans for Mobilization for Youth at Pete's House on February 2, 1959.

---

* National Institute for Mental Health, in the Department of Health, Education and Welfare.

Later, through the President's Committee on Juvenile Delinquency, Robert Kennedy, then Attorney General, was also to become very much interested in Mobilization for Youth, coming to see us at Henry Street, and later at Mobilization headquarters —giving us real encouragement and backing.

The action plans, which had been announced in February, and the research design accompanying them were subjected to intensive review by NIMH committees for several months. We were finally told that the preponderant opinion among the mainly friendly critics who studied our proposals was that a more coherent program was needed, one that could be evaluated better by the research people. Consequently, we withdrew our application to NIMH, and in May, the board of Mobilization for Youth voted to ask for money to replan the project. Finally, on December 15, 1959, the National Institute for Mental Health made a grant of approximately $450,000 for a two-year period, to prepare a new Action-Research Design for submission at the end of that time.

It was not until November, 1960, three years and four months from the time that we had started, that Mobilization for Youth was ready to move out of Henry Street Settlement into its first headquarters at 214 East Second Street. In the meantime Lloyd Ohlin had gone to Washington and Richard Cloward had taken his place as director of research. James McCarthy, Richard Cloward, and George Brager became the directors of Mobilization for Youth as they started on the assignment of developing an Action-Research Plan, which was finally accepted at the end of another two and a half years, support coming in 1962 from four sources: NIMH; the President's Committee on Juvenile Crime and Delinquency; the city of New York; and the Ford Foundation.

On May 31, 1962, President Kennedy launched Mobilization for Youth, with the announcement that $12.6 million of federal, city, and private funds were to be spent on "the most advanced program yet devised to combat delinquency on a broad scale." This was setting the stage for the Anti-Poverty programs which were to follow two years later, when many of the concepts developed on the Lower East Side for helping people lift themselves out of poverty were set in motion across the country in like neighborhoods.

Dealing with the problems of a wide slum area and the concentration of multiple services to meet these problems was, of course, the most important innovation in the Mobilization for Youth program. It broke the back of "littleness" so to speak. Of course we expected that many new ways of dealing with the problems of a neighborhood such as ours would grow out of it, and they have. However, the overriding importance of Mobilization for Youth was the fact that, two years after we had launched our plan, it was serving as the starting point for sixteen other cities, and that it became the forerunner of the Anti-Poverty program as that developed in Washington. While at that time each city adjusted the plan to its own needs, they were spared the long initial struggle it required to get the idea of widespread community planning accepted and going, not the *five* years it took in the case of Mobilization for Youth; the spade work for this basic idea had been done.

After its first two years of operation, Mobilization for Youth came under bitter attacks from a number of sources. The organization was accused of having Communists on the staff and being extravagant and careless in the handling of funds. That criticism would follow the expenditure of, at that time, such an unprecedented amount of money in one community was almost inevitable. And mistakes are bound to be made when new ideas are being tried, when concepts are being translated from the blueprint stage into the creation of an untested structure. Mobilization for Youth had to hire over three hundred people at once and weld them into a functioning staff.

Unfortunately, in the beginning there was a lack of realization that innovations in a community cannot exist in a vacuum, as well as a lack of understanding of the way communities, such as ours, interact. The so-called "target population," the poorest of the community, is woven into the fabric of community life, however tenuously, into relationships with the school system, with the police, with landlords, with local and city politicians, and with local churches and other agencies of all kinds. However unsatisfactory many of these relationships may be, they do exist. Instead of using the knowledge and resources and goodwill of the community, staff members at Mobilization had often shown hostility and arrogance toward the other agencies in the community, which left Mobilization with few friends able and willing to defend them when the attacks came, except the settlements. I look back with warmth toward those who did stand by us, the Citizens Committee for Children being one of them. Settlement people felt that the idea was more important than any mistakes that might have been made, and those serving on the board of Mobilization also knew that many of the attacks were untrue, or unfair, and they certainly turned out not to be sustained. And the board knew, too, that important innovations had already been made. We were also aware that back of some of the attacks was the fact that through the organization of community people for social action and protest, we were in the position of using public funds to attack public agencies, which was generally resented. It must be faced that much of the so-called community action was not spontaneous but organized, led and stimulated by staff members from Mobilization, and later Anti-Poverty agencies. That the community groups learned through this process and sometimes followed through on their own is important, but it is wise to understand what the actual process has been.

This still remains a dilemma. At the time, however, it looked like outrage, not philosophy, that motivated some of the anger against Mobilization. As we consider this use of public funds we may feel that it could, in the long run, be used for political purposes and become a danger to the community. However, this is hindsight and was not a part of our thinking at the time.

Winslow Carlton, who was the president of the board of Henry Street and president of the board of Mobilization for Youth from its inception, handled the onslaught with courage and good sense; and Mobilization survived its attackers and its own mistakes.

While I disagreed with some of their methods and their over-hopefulness about being able to research everything, I considered the first three directors intelligent and creative men, who had great dedication. When such difficulties occur it is always well to remember that in big new programs mistakes will continue to be made. Many inexperienced and often inadequate people are involved in working from allocation to allocation; from termination date to termination date; through government redtape, enough at times to strangle all movement. We should remind ourselves, too, that we are apt to accept as normal the miscalculations that may send multimillion-dollar rockets off their course or cause them to blow up on landing. And we might remember also that the highly advanced automobile industry still makes thousands of cars that have to be recalled each year.

So, fortunately for the children in the slums, Mobilization for Youth, the forerunner of the War on Poverty, survived its attackers. Its board was reorganized and a new director, Bertram Beck, took over, with remarkable skill, the difficult job of bringing stability and acceptance to the organization. We were fortunate because what happens in the long run to the work undertaken by such projects as Mobilization for Youth must determine the real value of the over-all plan. I am glad to say that many of Mobilization for Youth's projects and innovations have played an important part both in present-day thinking, and in acting. Its legal services; its job training and placement programs; its tutoring programs; the organization of welfare clients, out of which has grown the national Welfare Rights Organization and the active involvement of so many neighborhood people in so many different ways. As a part of this, the training of the indigenous worker or paraprofessional starting under Frank Riessman at Mobilization has developed into an important movement in social work.

I am not attempting to write about the accomplishments of Mobilization, its many experiments, its failures, its successes, and all their sociological significance. There are volumes written about it already, and hundreds of papers. However, historical accounts of Mobilization for Youth are, today, apt to leave out its origin and any mention of the more than three years which got it going. I wish this were not so, because from my standpoint, one of the lessons to be learned from Mobilization for Youth is the importance of continuous experimentation by private social agencies, in the field of social change, and the recognition of how much can be stimulated with very little money. The private agencies' freedom to act can be of enormous value in organizing for change and protest. Our Henry Street board raised $42,000 and the settlement contributed board and staff time, office space, and other overhead expenses—and much determination—for over three years to get this project going, which had by 1968 brought over $30,000,000 in services to the people of the Lower East Side and had helped to change the outlook toward slum neighborhoods in the United States.

XXXIII

Still Unfinished Business and Chaos

Many years ago, a little girl at University House in Philadelphia put the case for health insurance very succinctly: "We're God lucky at my house," she said. "Me mother got sick on me father's payday!"

While the Depression put unemployment insurance first on the list of New Deal musts, old age insurance and health insurance were recognized at the same time as two of the basic underpinnings of family life. This also was President Roosevelt's hope, as he expressed it to a little group of us who, in 1934, went to urge him to push the unemployment insurance bill through that year. "No," he said, "I do not want to push for unemployment insurance this year, I want to get the cherry in one bite!—unemployment insurance, old age insurance and health insurance."

But President Roosevelt counted without the American Medical Association. I couldn't but think of his hope when I went to Independence, Missouri, thirty-one years later to see President Johnson, as the guest of former President Truman, sign the Medicare Bill. This was a gain for persons sixty-five and over, but my satisfaction in seeing this comparatively small breakthrough was tinged with bitterness as I looked back on my years of experience with the health needs of my neighbors. My experiences in England added to my bitterness, where over the years I had seen at first hand what the British Health Services meant to working people.

Over fifty years ago, in 1917, the National Federation of Settlements passed a resolution in favor of some form of compulsory health insurance. It was not an accident that settlement workers who lived in city slums, and were faced daily with the waste and tragedy of sickness, should lead in taking this stand.

To put it simply, the last fifty years have been the story of a small, articulate, and well-financed group working against the comparatively inarticulate needs of the great majority of poor Americans, and those who are poor when it comes to illness. It is a long story of health shibboleths and roadblocks measured against suffering and vulnerability.

At University House in Philadelphia, we had a medical and dental clinic run by two fourth-year students in each discipline, under the supervision of the medical and dental schools of the University of Pennsylvania. Our clinic was open five nights a week and the students were on call for emergencies in the neighborhood. They were the best-loved people on our staff. I remember the young boy whose arm had to be amputated, and who refused to let the famous surgeon at the University Hospital do it until "his" doctor at the settlement assured him it was necessary. That was a "doctor-patient relationship" springing from a free, unencumbered association.

When I got to Henry Street in 1933, I found that a family without money enough for a doctor and the patient too sick to get to a hospital would have to call an ambulance from a hospital or the police department. It came with a driver, and, until 1942, a doctor—now an attendant and a separate police car with an officer in attendance comes. Strangers, of course, and often frightening to an already frightened family, or, as was often the case, an old person living alone. The policeman always looked so big and unnecessary in the little tenement rooms. As a matter of fact, I have never been able to get a sensible reason for the policeman and I have been in homes too often when this trio arrived not to know that it was a far from comforting way to treat a family in trouble—and think of the unnecessary expense to the city. But there they were and there they still are at this writing—all out for one neighborhood call which they cannot treat when they get there. They have to make an on-the-spot decision as to whether the patient is sick enough to be admitted to a hospital; if the decision is no at the moment, but the patient takes a turn for the worse, the process is repeated again unless the family has found a doctor in the meantime. This cumbersome and wasteful system in reality forces the family to make its own diagnosis. Some families wait too long, often to the lasting hurt of the patient, hesitating to call an ambulance out, while others call an ambulance for minor sickness, having nowhere else to turn. And, of course, many times the responsibility was thrown back on some private physician in the neighborhood who perhaps could ill afford to bear the economic burden thrust upon him by his own kindness, or the family hustled around and perhaps borrowed money.

In 1935 we had made a case study at Henry Street Settlement of 241 families on home and work relief. We made the study in cooperation with the Home Relief Bureau shortly after its Medical Bureau was in operation. The families were selected at random from the relief rolls in the Yorkville and Lower East Side districts.

The most challenging generalization from our study at that time was the simplest one: that 19 percent, or less than one-fifth of the unemployed wage earners in those home relief families, could be said to have a good bill of health. The fact that those better able to work had often been transferred to the rolls of the WPA affected this showing. So a similar case study was made of the heads of families on work relief in order to complete the picture. Here 49 percent, still less than half, were found to be in good health.

The more we studied the past history of these unemployed men and their families, the more we were made aware of the hit-and-miss nature of the medical care that had reached through to them—good here, bad there, but nothing that they could count on, and certainly not preventive care by any stretch of the imagination.

By 1938, the Home Relief Bureau in New York had worked out a system of panel doctors to treat home relief families and to answer sick calls. Even if this was not satisfactory in many ways, if you were a nurse or a settlement worker in those days and were called into a home because of sickness, you almost hoped that the family was on home relief because you knew you would be able to get medical care for them.

Today, a very small home care unit with doctors visiting the homebound, largely old people, operates from some hospitals. At our local Gouverneur Clinic, approximately forty patients were being cared for through this system in 1967. This gives an idea of how small a beginning we have made in this practical application of a service to the poor to which the rich are entitled by their financial status.

To go back again to 1938: In that year a New York State Temporary Commission to Formulate a Health Program was appointed by the Legislature. Our Lower East Side assemblyman, Leonard Farbstein (later U.S. congressman), was on this committee and he was deeply interested. Knowing of the settlement's concern with the health field, he came to me for suggestions as to who would be the best person to consult on this subject. I suggested Michael Davis, one of the leading experts in this field, who was glad to work with him. Assemblyman Farbstein presented what turned out to be an excellent report, but unfortunately a minority one. In testimony to the commission, speaking for the New York settlements and the National Federation of Settlements, I emphasized three outstanding needs as we saw them in New York at that time: the need for medical care in the homes of low-income families; the need for better health examinations in the schools with a more adequate follow-up; and more free dental care. Needless to say, no health insurance bill for New York went through as a result of the commission's work in 1938, in spite of all the interest stirred up at the time.

Those of us involved in the fight for basic social security in this country so often found ourselves hampered by misconceptions about what was happening in England. We seem to know more about the surface of the moon today than we have known in the past about how working people in England were faring on the social insurances! When I had gone to England in the summer of 1932 to learn from working people themselves how Unemployment Insurance was working, I had found how inextricably the insurances were bound together in their protection of family life. The National Federation of Settlements sponsored the publication in 1938 of a survey made for us in England by Douglass W. Orr, MD, and his wife Jean Walker Orr. They were Barnett Fellows, an exchange arrangement of many years standing between English and American settlements in honor of

Canon Barnett, founder of Toynbee Hall in London. The Orrs found almost universal agreement in England that the Health Insurance System was satisfactory to doctors, insured persons, and the general public. The main question at that tme was how to extend it.

Entitled *Health Insurance with Medical Care—the British Experience*, the Orrs' report carried a Foreword by David Lloyd George. As a leader of the then powerful Liberal party he had health insurance pushed through Parliament well before World War I. Twenty-five years later, Lloyd George's comments on how well the system was working carried a lesson for American lawmakers—and still should. In his Foreword, he wrote:

When in 1911 I laid before the British Parliament my proposals for a scheme of National Health Insurance, they encountered a stern and growing volume of bitter opposition which surprised me by its intensity. Concessions and modifications, some of them unfortunate, had to be made to placate this interest and that, and even then it was a matter of the utmost difficulty to pilot the measure successfully to the Statute Book. Probably it would be true to say that a referendum of the whole country taken at that time, would have shown only a minority of the people in favor of the new system.

In the quarter of a century which has elapsed since it became law, this once-abused scheme has become one of the most popular elements in our administrative system. The nation would as soon think of abandoning it as it would of abolishing the Post Office. The medical profession, which at the outset viewed it with unconcealed distaste, now finds it a highly satisfactory source of an income considerably in excess of that which they formerly secured from the section of the public which it covers. The insured classes enjoy by means of it a degree of medical attention previously unknown, as well as a measure of financial security in sickness to which they were once strangers. It has become the keystone of our social structure for the maintenance and improvement of the nation's health, and round it have clustered a host of ancillary schemes for extending and supplementing the services it renders. . . .

It is curious that the value and popularity of this well-tested system is not better recognized, particularly in the United States, where so much attention has for years been given to problems of health and hygiene. Its reputation in America suffers both from lack of information and from misinformation. Defects or occasional rare abuses which come to light are exaggerated, and serve to obscure for the distant looker-on its immense positive worth and the high esteem it has won. Undoubtedly the present system is capable of improvement and revision; but in the general opinion of this country, the reform most urgently needed is a very considerable extension of the scope of the National Health Insurance, to bring within its purview all those masses which are at present out of range of its benefits. Such an extension is being urged alike by the medical profession and by the general public; and the demand for more and yet more of the same treatment is an unchallenged testimonial to its merits.

The Orrs' book, Lloyd George declared, "sets out in a lucid and dispassionate and very readable form the results of their investigations." And in conclusion he wrote:

> I commend it warmly to the attention of the public, both in Britain and in America. To our own people it will give a remarkably clear and helpful picture of the complex of our existing health services, and of the nature of the problems involved in their further extension and reform. To Americans it should be of the greatest value in clearing away misconceptions and ill-based prejudices against Health Insurance, and placing at their disposal the practical results of our experience as a guide in their own approach to this vital social issue.

Through Dr. Orr's book, we were of course trying to clear away some of the road blocks to Health Insurance in this country.

There were two rusty clichés in this country which we found repeated so often that we attempted to throw light on them by settlement studies. One was that the sanctity of the doctor-patient relationship would be impaired. In 1938, our National Federation of Settlements made a firsthand study in twenty-three cities located in sixteen states of what their neighbors do when they are sick. This inquiry revealed that two-thirds of those interviewed had no family doctor at all, the same results as an earlier such inquiry made at Henry Street had shown. Even in the case of the third who claimed to have a doctor, the connection was often nebulous and unsustained. Obviously, you do not often have a doctor-patient relationship with a doctor whom you cannot afford to see.

Then there was the free choice of physician with which health insurance might interfere. Opponents of health insurance who put such stress on this have often claimed at the same time that out-patient clinics and hospital wards could be looked to to supply the needs of the low-income sick. Yet there is seldom free choice of doctor and scant doctor-patient relationship of the sort they prize, in either a clinic or a ward. They refuse to face the truth that both the relationship and the free choice can be counted upon only in upper-income brackets. These arguments, though used so often, were—and are—obviously spurious because they do not apply to the poor.

As a part of our effort to educate in the field of health, we produced a Living Newspaper in our Playhouse in 1939 called *Medicine Show*. Later, when the war was over, Henry Street did a study of wartime wages and expenditures which the National Federation of Settlements later sponsored nationally. One part of this study dealt with health and it showed that it was sickness that had put the greatest drain on the savings of war workers.

A National Health Bill (S.1606:H.R.4730) about which, at the time, we felt hopeful was introduced into the Congress in 1946 by Senators Wagner and Murray and Congressman Dingle, and I testified for the National Federation of Settlements in its support. At this time, besides our own observations and studies, we had the overwhelming evidence of inadequate medical care as shown by the results of medical examinations for military service in World War II.

Later we had the example of how prepaid medical care, with no choice of physician, served the needs of ten million Americans in our armed forces. As I observed it while with the American Red Cross in the South Pacific, competent medical men were still competent, incompetent men, still of that stamp. The quality of the doctor was the determining factor, not government regimentation nor the method of his payment.

Again in 1949 there were four major bills dealing with health, and that very fact, and some of the points on which they agreed, showed that the furious discussion in the preceding fourteen years, since the Social Security Act of 1935 had not included the protection of health as one of its major provisions, had perhaps borne some fruit. All four bills acknowledged at least that the American people required some modern organized help in meeting their health needs. A second point of agreement was that federal funds must play a large part in any wider distribution of medical care, and also there was agreement among the four bills' sponsors, that 80 percent of the population, made up of families earning less than $5,000 yearly at that time, should be drawn into a plan that would help safeguard their health.

Leaving aside the technicalities, the basic points of difference were that the Taft Bill and the Hill Bill could not be carried out without a "means test." The Flanders–Ives Bill, not only relied on federal subsidies to private prepaid health service plans, but called for a 3 percent minimum voluntary payroll tax on "the subscriber's family income."

These were offered as alternatives to the compulsory insurance provisions of the National Health Program embodied in the Wagner Bill (S.1679) which required a 1½ percent contribution by the employer and no means test. The Hill Bill, as well as the Flanders–Ives Bill, proposed giving subsidies to voluntary plans.

However, health was not on the "must" list for that session of Congress. I could not but think that sickness would be on the "must" list of millions of American families that year because they could not choose as the Congress could. It was not on the must list then and it hasn't been on the must list since.

Henry Street made a study of what families did "when sickness strikes," a report made in 1950 and published in the *Survey* in 1952, under that title.* We endeavored to get a blueprint not only of what medical and dental care and drugs were costing our neighbors, but how far voluntary health insurance plans of various kinds had reached down into neighborhoods such as ours, and how much protection they assured and to whom. The 553 schedules that we used as a basis for our findings included members of our adult clubs and the parents of children coming to Henry Street Settlement. Lest this should prove too selective, we made a door-to-door canvass of families, covering two square blocks. We found that 52 percent of the families had no insurance

* "When Sickness Strikes a Family," *Survey*, 1952.

plans for medical or hospital care, while only eleven families had any comprehensive protection.

On the whole, our inquiry covered employed people, eager to be on their own and self-dependent. Families are aware that sickness is no respecter of provisions in a health plan, but they had turned to plans with limited provisions when these seemed to be all that was within their reach.

This report was included in "Building America's Health," a report to President Truman by the Commission on the Health Needs of the Nation, appointed by the President on December 29, 1951. I served as a member of the Panel on Financing a Health Program set up by the commission, which was responsible for Vol. 4 of the report.

Using the schedules we had worked out at Henry Street, the National Federation of Settlements three years later sponsored a survey conducted by fifteen widely scattered settlement houses. This national study of 334 families, issued in 1954, disclosed that 37 percent had no health insurance coverage, as compared with 52 percent in Henry Street's study three years earlier. There were indications of an increase in health-care plans as part of union agreements with employers. This trend has continued in the fifties and sixties, while the voluntary insurance plans bitterly opposed by so many physicians have made an important contribution, not only in providing actual health services, but in experimenting with the principle of insurance as applied to illness.

In New York, there are two major plans, Group Health Insurance (GHI) and HIP (Health Insurance Plan of Greater New York). Both organizations were pioneered by Winslow Carlton. HIP had a small forerunner in the Corlear's Hook Medical Association, initiated in 1939 in our neighborhood by George Baehr, at that time Mayor La Guardia's physician, and David Heyman, president of the New York Foundation. It was their idea that I might help get the tenants of Vladeck Houses, the low-income project which had just opened across the street, interested in joining a voluntary health plan. We discussed it over lunch at Henry Street and it moved forward quickly with the New York Foundation making a grant to launch it. It proved itself successful but was discontinued when the two major city plans were initiated four years later.

We continued to watch the progress of health care in Great Britain as it evolved into the British Health Services and the government took over comprehensive responsibilities for the hospitals, as well as total family care. In 1954 the National Federation of Settlements sent another Barnett Fellow, George Goetschius, to Great Britain to gather firsthand evidence for us as to how the new plans were working. As Dr. Orr had done before, he talked to British working people along with doctors and government officials and was assured of the tremendous strides forward that had been made since the Orrs had made their study. I myself made a quick review of the situation some years later, staying with doctor friends who helped me get an inside view of opinions of both doctors and patients, and I did not wonder that Great Britain's health status had continued to improve over the years. This visit of mine, as a matter of fact, was particularly directed toward finding out what was being done about teen-age drug addicts, and I was told by none other than the head of Scotland Yard that there were not any! Unfortunately this is not true today.

On former visits to London I had been interested in a notice on the front page of the *London Times*, where they publish personal notes and such, to see one that read plaintively, "Guys is on the Danger List"—"Guys" being one of London's largest hospitals. However, when I went back after the hospitals had been absorbed into the Health Services, I looked, but "Guys" appeared to be off the danger list at last! And a visit there substantiated this.

In 1949 the discouragement was very widespread in this country when the National Health Bill did not go through. It was at this point that President Truman felt it might be politically expedient to try to get health insurance as a part of social security for persons over sixty-five years of age. Insurance for old people might have more emotional appeal and be more difficult to defeat. And it could at least break the deadlock on health insurance through social security. It is shocking to think that even this far-from-comprehensive piece of legislation took approximately fourteen years to get through the Congress. By this time, the AMA had been joined in its opposition by the private insurance companies and Blue Cross and Blue Shield, all of which helped prolong the struggle. On the other hand, old people themselves were becoming better organized and were able, as time went on, to reach the Congress through their own organizations. If they had not spoken up for themselves, they might not be getting Medicare yet.

When I went to Independence, Mo., to see President Johnson sign the Medicare Bill, I brought back one of the signing pens to our Good Companions at Henry Street. It is framed, and hangs on the wall, and I have inscribed it to the Good Companions, where it certainly belongs, for they had never missed an opportunity to speak, write, parade, or go to Washington for Medicare.

XXXIV

An Unfinished Story of a Community's Fight for Its Hospital

Very soon after I came to Henry Street I was alerted by our visiting nurses to the poor care their patients received at Gouverneur Hospital, the small city hospital that served a large area of the Lower East Side. As I looked back, the first thing I came across in my file on Gouverneur is a letter written in November, 1933, from the chief nurse, Anna James, thanking me for a dinner at Henry Street and asking me to come over to talk to her group of nurses.

My association with Gouverneur has continued from that time on, largely as an exercise in frustration, for the campaign for the improvement of the services of that hospital and for the construction of a modern community institution is a prime example of "unfinished business." Indeed, the entire health care field comes under that description—not from the aspect of scientific advances in medical care but from the slowness in advances in its *distribution*. Gouverneur Hospital is also one of the best examples I have experienced of neighborhood people working together over a long period—more than *thirty* years—under great difficulties, for we had to contend continually with the crosscurrents of citywide politics and with changes within city administrations, and particularly with opposition from powerful members of the medical profession itself.

Basically one of the problems has been the conflict between

those who want to centralize all hospital care in large institutions and those who think that health care should be easy to reach for people in a poor community. But above everything else has been the persistent effort on the part of the medical establishment to keep health care out of the hands of government —city, state, or federal. Another point of controversy has been whether the people of a neighborhood should have anything to say about their health care. Our neighbors' work to change Gouverneur Hospital started thirty years before "maximum feasible participation" of its beneficiaries was required in the federally supported Anti-Poverty programs.

The fight for an improved, neighborhood-oriented Gouverneur Hospital was a neighborhood enterprise from the beginning. We argue on the Lower East Side at the drop of a hat or before the hat is dropped—but not about Gouverneur. Everybody agreed that it was a terrible hospital, but it was also agreed that good medical care made quickly available was preventive care and that was what we wanted. We fought for a new hospital building from 1934 on, but not because it was a building we wanted—we wanted good care above all, and medical authorities in the city insisted that we could not get decent medical services until we had a better physical plant. May I say in parenthesis that many years later Dr. Howard Brown was to amply disprove this contention when he was made director of the Gouverneur Out-Patient Clinic and produced good clinic care in the old building just painted and cleaned up.

Gouverneur Hospital had been located since the 1880s in two old, dilapidated buildings on the East River at the end of Gouverneur Street, in sight of Henry Street Settlement.

In spite of all the early assurances we were given that Gouverneur would soon be replaced, as time went on we found that the new hospital either didn't get into the city's capital budget or did not stay there when it did.

Robert Wagner had given us solid encouragement when he was borough president of Manhattan. When he ran for mayor in 1953, I remember handing him, at a big outdoor rally, a paragraph to insert in his speech, promising us a new hospital when he became mayor. He smiled and handed the paper back saying, "I was going to say that, anyway." And he did. This often repeated promise the neighborhood people took to heart, and they reminded him of it at each crisis throughout the years. Many of us realized the pressures he was under, for we knew that the then Hospital Council of Greater New York, an unofficial but powerful body, and others influential in the city's medical hierarchy, were dead set against neighborhood health services. They did not hesitate to let it be known behind the scenes or, for that matter, in front of them. Episode after episode has demonstrated this kind of opposition. I remember an order that came to the governing board of Gouverneur from the then retiring Commissioner of Hospitals not long before Christmas in 1948. It directed the evacuation of all general patients by January 1, so that the buildings could be used for tuberculosis patients from Bellevue Hospital, the city's biggest in Manhattan. There had been a recent newspaper attack on the overcrowding of TB patients at Bellevue, and this was a way out, and would also do away with our neighborhood hospital.

When we learned of this plan, we quickly arranged a meeting with the Hosiptal Commissioner and some five or six people from the neighborhood. We met in Dora Tannenbaum's office (she was then head of the Grand Street Settlement) and vehemently protested the Commissioner's evacuation order. When he questioned our right to say anything about his order, someone with him pulled his sleeve and said, "Commissioner, I wouldn't speak this way, because these people can get thousands marching down to City Hall in a minute." It was a very flattering supposition. However, the meeting was at eleven o'clock in the morning and the order was rescinded by three o'clock that afternoon. On January 4, 1949, we received the following letter of thanks from Gouverneur's Committee of Attending Physicians:

January 4, 1949

Dear Miss Hall:

As President of the Medical Board at Gouverneur Hospital I wish to tell you how much the Medical Staff appreciates the effort which you and the community have demonstrated in saving the hospital from being converted into a hospital for tuberculosis. On December 15, 1948, when the Executive Committee met with the Commissioner of Hospitals, we were told categorically that by the first of the new year Gouverneur Hospital would cease to exist as a general hospital. Two days later, when I was informed that this move was indefinitely postponed, I wondered what had occurred, but have since learned that you and other social service interests succeeded in keeping Gouverneur in its present status.

A review of the monthly activities of the hospital—clinical visits, cases treated in the emergency room and the bed census which has been constantly above normal, would have easily shown what an unwise move it would have been to remove the only general hospital from the community.

We all realize our shortcomings which in no small way are of an architectural nature. We all feel that the community and staff, who have served so faithfully, deserve a modern institution. We sincerely hope that the construction of a new hospital will not be long delayed.

Again let me thank you for your magnificent effort and with best wishes for the New Year, I am

> Sincerely yours,
> Frank J. McGowan, M.D.

The settlements had spearheaded the drive for the hospital with wide general support from their neighbors until the Lower Eastside Neighborhoods Association was organized in 1955. LENA's Health Committee promptly took on the job and kept the neighborhood alerted.

Wishing to make none but sound recommendations, LENA enlisted as its medical adviser, Winslow Carlton, the president of the Board of Henry Street Settlement, who was a recognized authority on organized health services, beginning with his pioneer work in organizing Group Health Insurance, Inc. He later designed the Health Insurance Plan of Greater New York (HIP), and served as consultant to many hospitals, medical schools, and legislative groups. LENA's Health Committee at that time was under the co-chairmanship of Dora Tannenbaum and Dr. Sidney Rosenfeld, both devoted to the cause. Dr. Rosenfeld, a local physician who was both loved and respected in the neighborhood, had been a member of the Corlear's Hook Medical Association, with the largest panel of patients of any doctor in the neighborhood.

In the early years we had met with little direct opposition, so we often thought that things were moving forward, only to find that nothing had been done after promises had been made. Hospital Commissioner Kogel's Annual Report of 1949 recommended a four-hundred-bed replacement of "obsolete" Gouverneur. In 1947 and again in 1950, the Hospital Council, which was later to change its position, had recommended a new hospital. On February 17, 1950, Mayor O'Dwyer's Committee on the Needs of the Department of Hospitals also recommended a four-hundred-bed replacement. The following request from the Gouverneur Lay Advisory Board during Mayor Impelliteri's days, asking for just enough renovation to operate until the new building was ready, is an illustration of the constant work that went on over the years.

PETITION

To the Honorable Mayor Impelliteri and Board of Estimate
Dear Sirs:

The hospital facilities of the Lower East Side are shamefully neglected.

The Gouverneur Hospital has unused ward space because facilities are lacking with which to equip and operate the wards.

The Gouverneur Hospital runs the risk of disaffiliation with the New York University–Bellevue Medical Center, the right to train interns and the risk of losing resident interns because of lack of facilities.

The Gouverneur Hospital cannot contribute its rightful share toward training nurses because of a lack of facilities.

The patients of the Lower East Side cannot get adequate treatment as in-or-out patients because of lack of facilities.

We respectfully petition the Mayor and the members of the Board of Estimate to provide in the budget for the rehabilitation of Gouverneur Hospital in order to increase ward space, training facilities, and service to patients.

Sincerely yours,
Woolf Colvin, Chairman
Lay Advisory Board of
Gouverneur Hospital
Principal, Seward Park High School

In November, 1952, the members of the Borough President's Planning Board III, covering the Lower East Side, learned in a letter from their chairman that he had appeared before the Planning Commission of the City of New York and before the

Board of Estimate to urge that the item for a new site, design, and plans for a new Gouverneur Hospital be restored to the Proposed Capital Budget for 1953. He had also called on, among other officials, Borough President Robert Wagner and Dr. Marcus Kogel, Commission of Hospitals, and had reported that the former had promised to move at the December 1 meeting of the Board of Estimate to restore to the budget the $1,500,000 needed to acquire a new site. Every member of Planning Board III was therefore urged to send a special delivery letter to each member of the Board of Estimate, giving his personal views on the need for a new hospital.

Enclosed with the chairman's letter was a copy of the strong memorandum which Dr. Kogel had sent, on August 2, 1952, to the City Planning Commission. In blunt language the Commissioner of Hospitals had written:

> The utilization of the Gouverneur Hospital is extremely heavy. This institution has been in operation for over half a century; it is dreadfully run down and has none of the service elements which are considered so essential for the operation of a modern hospital. The volunteer professional staff is in revolt at the conditions under which they are required to work and the whole community is seething with resentment at having to put up with such conditions. The housing developments in the area serve an income class that has no alternative but to use municipally operated hospitals. The replacement of this hospital deserves the highest priority. Funds should be provided in 1953 for the acquisition of the complete site and for design; and the construction funds should be made available in 1954.

From Robert Wagner on, the borough presidents of Manhattan have seemed to a greater or lesser degree on the side of having a new community hospital in the place of Gouverneur: after Robert Wagner, Hulan E. Jack from 1954 to 1961, Edward H. Dudley from 1962 to 1965, Constance Baker Motley in her short time from 1965 to 1966, and Percy E. Sutton, who took office on September 13, 1966. They were, of course, aware of large constituent backing for this project on the Lower East Side. Our local politicians of both parties have given it lip service at least, and some of them a great deal more than that.

Just before election day, Gouverneur always became a cause

and it was a good time to push ahead if things were slowed down or a crisis was imminent.

As one of his first acts after Mayor Wagner had made him Commissioner of Hospitals in August, 1954, Dr. Basil McLean startled us all by announcing that there was no need for Gouverneur Hospital and that he was rescinding his department's request to the Board of Estimate. The announcement was made at a time when the blocks surrounding Gouverneur Hospital were being cleared for the erection of housing projects, as George Freedman, a local resident, director of the New Era Club and self-appointed historian of Gouverneur Hospital, pointed out in a letter of invitation to one of our continual "protest" meetings which started up with a vengeance at this very direct attack. An Emergency Conference for a New Gouverneur Hospital was to be held at the New Era Club. Among those invited were physicians, representatives of the *East Side News*, the East Side Chamber of Commerce, settlement houses, civic organizations, parents' groups, schools, churches, synagogues, etc.

It appeared to us that Dr. McLean was taking his lead from the Hospital Council, which as reported above, had in 1947 and again in 1950, favored the building of a new Gouverneur Hospital but was now using blocking tactics. While the Hospital Council had never been an official city body, since its organization in 1938 it had had a great deal to say about the construction and geographical distribution of both voluntary and city hospitals. Physicians representing the city's most prestigious voluntary hospitals have always been prominent in its counsels, and they have been listened to at City Hall. Assuming broader responsibilities for comprehensive health planning, the council changed its name in 1967 to the Health and Hospital Planning Council of Southern New York, Inc.

By 1954 we knew that the Hospital Council was having a study made of the need for Gouverneur Hospital, and that the first results of the study, as reported to the council, indicated that it was needed. This report was never issued, but in October of 1954, we were told there was to be a re-study which would not be ready until the following spring! The results of this re-study were to say that the needed beds could be put in *either* Bellevue or Gouverneur!

We wanted not only a new hospital but one in the right location. So we took the huge map of the Lower East Side which had been prepared as a build-up for the founding of LENA down to City Hall to spread before officials of the City Planning Commission. The map showed the old Gouverneur to be at the extreme edge of the area and beyond easy reach of transportation, and it was agreed that a search would be made for a more central location. Although it was agreed then that the site would be changed, and there was much talk and much visiting of sites, it was not until three years later, in 1957, that we were finally told that "a site would be acquired" and the planning begun in earnest at an early date. This, despite the fact that $1,500,000 had been included in the 1953 capital buget for the acquisition of a site! The site finally settled on was between Madison and Henry streets and Clinton and Rutgers streets, on a bus line and a subway route and within walking distance of several low-income projects.

While this effort for a modern facility went on, we continued trying to get decent patients' care in the old buildings. Dr. MacLean took pains to look into the reports of bad service at Gouverneur and came down to listen to neighborhood groups. In a letter in which, at his request, I had reported a bad situation, I wrote:

> This is a very mild situation compared to any number that have been brought to my attention in the neighborhood. It is impossible to mention Gouverneur Hospital, as you saw the other day at the meeting, without getting stories of serious neglect.
>
> I am looking forward very much to having you and Mrs. MacLean as guests at Henry Street. I will telephone your office and hope to arrange a mutually agreeable time.
>
> Thanks for listening to us all the other day.

In March, 1954, I became chairman of the Lay Advisory Board of Gouverneur Hospital, succeeding Dr. Woolf Colvin, principal of Seward Park High School, who was transferred out of the neighborhood. In November, 1955, I received a copy of a letter to Dr. Steinholtz, administrator of Gouverneur, from Dr. Kenneth B. Babcock of the Joint Commission on Accreditation of Hospitals, which gave us some good news.

The Board of Commissioners of the Joint Commission on Accreditation of Hospitals has approved the recommendation that the Gouverneur Hospital receive FULL ACCREDITATION. As you know this is a result of the evaluation of the hospital survey conducted on August 23, 1955, by Dr. F. C. Fitts, a field representative of the Joint Commission. Your courtesy to Doctor Fitts at the time of his visit is appreciated.

If you look over the long record of this neighborhood's efforts to get decent health care for themselves and their children you will find reports on petitions, marches to City Hall, meetings with public officials, parents' meetings, and continued activity among the settlements, churches and neighborhood groups of all kinds —efforts that never stopped. As an example, on June 15, 1955, Simon Slavin, executive director of the Educational Alliance in the settlement group, sent me a copy of a resolution their Adult Council had adopted. It read:

ADULT COUNCIL RESOLUTION
ON GOUVERNEUR HOSPITAL
PREFACE—This Resolution was adopted after a report of a delegation of ten members who had visited Gouverneur Hospital on April 23rd, 1955.

The Adult Council of the Educational Alliance favors the construction of a new Gouverneur Hospital. After sixty-eight years of the old hospital, a new building is needed to serve our community where more and more housing projects are going up and the number of East Siders is rapidly increasing.

In the meantime, we feel that service should be improved, especially in the emergency ward.

In January of 1957 we were once more assured of success in getting our hospital, as the following from LENA's newsletter tells so glowingly:

A NEW HOSPITAL—AT LAST!
A New Gouverneur Hospital was virtually assured when the Board of Estimate voted early this month to include in the 1957 capital budget an appropriation of $2,400,000 earmarked for the selection and purchase of a new site. Only City Council approval —due by December 27th—is required to confirm the appropriation, and city officials expressed confidence that the Lower East Side has at last secured its new hospital.

For more than ten years, neighbors and community organizations have fought to replace Gouverneur Hospital, built in 1901, with a new facility located more centrally in the neighborhood it serves. Earlier this year a LENA petition drive netted over 24,000 signatures of adults living south of Houston Street. These were presented to Mayor Robert F. Wagner and Boro President Hulan E. Jack in August when a neighborhood delegation called to request their support.

Recently, representatives of LENA, the Eastside Chamber of Commerce and the Lower Eastside Democratic Association appeared at a Board of Estimate hearing to press for the hospital's inclusion in the Capital Budget. Mayor Wagner and Boro President Jack reiterated their endorsement at that meeting, and the Board's action followed.

The old hospital's fate was sealed when the Hospital Council of New York issued a report in which it called Gouverneur "obsolescent" and recommended that it be replaced or abandoned. Some, including the Hospital Commissioner, urged the expansion of Bellevue's facilities to serve the entire Lower Eastside but community groups argued successfully that a hospital, however good, located at such a distance could not adequately serve the neighborhood. The City Planning Commission (James Felt, Chairman) also supported approval of a new Gouverneur Hospital.

Unbelievable as it may seem, by the next year, 1958, it looked hopeless again as we began to dig into what was really happening or *not* happening! In September the Good Neighbors Council of LENA, made up largely of fathers and mothers of the neighborhood, held a meeting at Henry Street to discuss complaints about the hospital's admission policy and service to patients in the Emergency Room, and appointed an investigating committee of seven, five of whom were Puerto Ricans.

One of the encouraging things in this utterly discouraging business was the understanding and support we got from James Felt, who was chairman of the City Planning Commission at that time. He had taken great pains to study the situation and he never failed to help where he could. In September, 1958, he invited Winslow Carlton and me to present our case for the new Gouverneur Hospital to the commission's members. We had brought with us an expert witness, Dr. H. M. Bluestone. Dr. Bluestone had been director of Montefiore Hospital for many years, and was in wide demand throughout the country as a hospital consultant. He started "organized house-care" based in the hospital, primarily for chronic patients who didn't need in-hospital daily care, but did need special help and care at home, and occasionally treatment at the hospital. This is now part of most communities' health programs.

But as usual crisis followed crisis. On June 22, 1959, four of us—Winslow Carlton, Judge Jacob Markowitz, Dora Tannenbaum, and I—sent the following telegram to Mayor Wagner:

> WE HAVE FOUND THAT THE WORDING OF THE RESOLUTION RE-GARDING GOUVERNEUR HOSPITAL WILL DELAY OBTAINING SITE FROM YEAR TO TWO YEARS. WE WERE ASSURED IN HULAN JACK'S OFFICE THAT THE WORDING WAS PURELY TECHNICAL AND NOT DONE PURPOSELY TO DELAY HOSPITAL AND THAT THE RESOLUTION WOULD BE CHANGED AT BOARD OF ESTIMATE MEETING OF JUNE 11. NOTHING WAS DONE. NOW WE ARE TOLD THAT THERE MUST BE A LETTER FROM DR. JACOBS* TO CHANGE RESOLUTION. IT IS OBVIOUS THAT ONLY YOU CAN OVERCOME THIS DELAY AND SEE THAT THE RESOLUTION GOES THROUGH AT THE BOARD OF ESTIMATE MEETING OF JUNE 25, AND THAT WORK IN ACQUIRING THE SITE FOR GOUVERNEUR HOSPITAL GOES ON AS YOU PROMISED SO LONG AGO.

In October of the same year, Samuel A. Spiegel, a leading Democrat, later to become a judge, wrote Mayor Wagner, urgently requesting a meeting with a delegation from the Lower East Side present, in regard to the proposed new Gouverneur Hospital, because "the situation is desperate and there is un-warranted delay." The twenty Lower East Siders included two judges, three congressmen, a state senator, a city councilman, a publisher, members of the settlements, a high-school principal, an executive of the borough president's office, and representatives of LENA and of other community groups.

But on November 16, 1960, we were back again at a Board of Estimate hearing. Members of the neighborhood crowded into the room to protest the fact that while money for drawing plans for a new Gouverneur Hospital was indeed in the capital budget, 1965 (five years later) appeared as the time for building. (LENA had immediately reached out into the neighborhood, as usual

---

* Morris Jacobs, MD., was appointed Commissioner of Hospitals by Mayor Wagner.

through widely distributed flyers, by this time in both Spanish and English.) As well as protesting a five-year delay, we tried at this Board of Estimate meeting to dispel once and for all the persistent rumor that all we wanted was to replace an old building with a new one and then go on with the same kind of services. This had continued to be repeated, no matter what we said or did. We were pressing for a new building because that was one way to better health services. We had kept abreast of neighborhood changes as well as progressive thought in the distribution of medical care.

A number of us testified at this Board of Estimate hearing, and our statements, along with the responses we evoked from the mayor and the acting president of the Borough of Manhattan, were later distributed to the neighborhood by LENA. Excerpts from the record follow:

> MISS HELEN HALL: Sir, I am here representing the Lower Eastside Neighborhoods Association, and there are a lot of other people here with me.
>
> I would like to start out by saying that we were very much disturbed to see that 1965 was put in as the time for the building of Gouverneur Hospital. The site has been selected and largely taken over. The plans have already gone to architects for preliminary work, and we now hear nothing is to start until 1965.
>
> We do feel that this is tantamount to saying there will be no Gouverneur Hospital. We are well aware, of course, of the many different viewpoints in medical care, and realize that this makes it difficult for the Mayor and for the rest of you. However, we do feel that Gouverneur Hospital has had a long history, and that it has been in and out of the City budget a great many times, and we feel that there have been commitments made so that it should be considered as a serious matter by all of you here. . . .
>
> . . . We are suggesting a community hospital, and something quite different from the kind of hospital that Gouverneur is today.
>
> I would like, also, to say, gentlemen, that if you try this kind of neighborhood hospital, or community hospital, which we are suggesting, you are building it in a community that is stabilized, in a community that is not going to change tomorrow. We have large housing projects of low-income people, we have a large population, and more to be expected because we're building more low-income projects.
>
> Of the population that uses Gouverneur, the hospital we have

now, almost 40 per cent who come to it are old people, and are young mothers with children.

MR. WINSLOW CARLTON: Mr. President, gentlemen: I want to make it clear that I'm appearing here this morning not as the Chairman of the Board of Group Health Insurance, but in my capacity as a medical care consultant, which is my main business. And I am consultant to the Lower Eastside Neighborhoods Association's Health Committee.

I've come to urge, Mr. President, the building of a new and truly modern community hospital in the Seward Park area of the Lower East Side, to replace . . . Gouverneur Hospital which is obsolete in plant and equipment, in staffing and in services.

A truly modern community hospital is not just new bricks created on an old plan. That's like trying to create a new man by putting new flesh on an old skeleton. A truly modern hospital is a fundamentally different kind of institution from an old hospital, like the present Gouverneur.

Now, for one thing, a new hospital is designed to reach out into the community through its combined health center, clinics, and its out-patient department. And, also, through its close daily collaboration with the local doctors who serve on the staff. That is, such a hospital should be and can be a health facility, not just a sickness facility. This is particularly important in Gouverneur Hospital's community, because of the very many young children, as Miss Hall has said, and the very many elderly people, both of whom, especially, need this reaching out, protective, preventive, positive health care. Our modern community hospital also reaches out by providing the sick with the kind of care and in the kind of place best suited to their needs.

The Department of Hospitals, as you I am sure all know, has made good progress with its home-care programs. This is especially important again in Gouverneur Hospital's area because of the many old people.

Our truly modern hospital is also one that is attached in a daily operation to a big central hospital. . . .

It's the traditional relationship of son to father. Concretely, it means that the father or the central hospital has the highly organized and specialized doctors and technicians and the highly specialized, usually expensive equipment they need for the very difficult or intricate cases. . . .

At this point I'd like to refer to some of Mr. Riegelman's remarks on the subject of Gouverneur Hospital. He quoted a statement from the Heyman Commission report which is a very odd statement, because it sets up a straw man.

The report speaks of the impracticality, the waste involved in setting up an unaffiliated small hospital with a cobalt bomb and a few other things that would be extremely expensive and probably not adequately employed, if it were, in such a hospital, where, to my knowledge, nobody on the Lower East Side, certainly, had ever proposed setting up such a hospital.

For the last five years, at least, since I've been connected with the Lower Eastside Neighborhoods Association, they have been talking about a satellite hospital, a community hospital, not an unaffiliated, old-fashioned City hospital. Nobody wants that. And I don't understand why the Heyman Commission took off on this point.

Now if you build this hospital the way that we are suggesting, you will not be acting in a vacuum. You will truly be demonstrating how a central hospital and a satellite hospital can operate, how a regional hospital system can be built in the City of New York.

CONGRESSMAN FARBSTEIN: I am Leonard Farbstein. I have represented the Lower East Side in one office or another for the last twenty-eight years, and I think I know the neighborhood as well as anybody within the hearing of my voice.

Now, if you will only look forward a little bit, you will come— you must come to the realization that the Federal Government at the next session will pass an Old-Age Medical Care Bill attached to Social Security which undoubtedly will be taken advantage of by the people in my neighborhood. As has been said by previous speakers, there are more old people in my neighborhood than there are younger ones. It's a peculiar situation, but it's so because the neighborhood is a very old neighborhood.

If you say you are not going to give us the hospital, at least tell us about it. This way it's every year we have a meeting with the Borough President, another meeting and another meeting, and we are told we are going to have it, and then we wind up that it's subsequently extended.

ACTING PRESIDENT OF THE BOROUGH OF MANHATTAN: I assume you are directing your remarks to the previous speaker who had made reference to it, because I don't know of anyone on the Board of Estimate who has even implied that we would not continue with the construction of Gouverneur Hospital. We did make a commitment to the community—at least, speaking for myself.

THE MAYOR: I will be glad to say that I am for the hospital, too.

CONGRESSMAN FARBSTEIN: I am certainly very pleased to hear

this. But why at this stage of the game, in 1960, suddenly we hear that it is to be put over to 1965? Why?

THE MAYOR: That is just in the proposed Capital Budget from the Planning Commission. We haven't acted on it as yet.

ACTING PRESIDENT OF THE BOROUGH OF MANHATTAN: I would like to point out for your information, too, that preliminary plans are being prepared now. I had a conversation with representatives of the Public Works, and they tell me that preliminary plans are presently being prepared, that they should be completed by early March, and the final plans will be completed by the end of the year, and that they plan on construction for 1962 or early '63.

I would like to point out, too, that the only thing that we do approve here is the single line that appears in the Capital Budget, and that is for the money of $747,625 which is sufficient for preliminary and final plans.

I want to assure you that we will press for early construction of Gouverneur Hospital.

CONGRESSMAN FARBSTEIN: I want to assure you, Mr. President, that I certainly appreciate hearing this statement made publicly by you, and hearing the statements made publicly by the Mayor, to the effect that the building of a new Gouverneur Hospital will be prosecuted as quickly as possible, irrespective of the rumors that are rampant today amongst those who are supposed to be knowledgeable on the subject.

THE MAYOR: Progress has been made. The land has been acquired, plans are now in operation, and the money in this budget we are talking about is to pay not only for the preliminary plans but the final plans.

ACTING PRESIDENT OF THE BOROUGH OF MANHATTAN: I should like to point out that you yourself stated that this thing has been in the making for the last fifteen years. Now, you did get a commitment from this Administration, and it is evident that something is being done. We recognize the need for this hospital in the community.

I want to assure you, as soon as the plans are completed— there must be plans—we will do everything possible to expedite the construction of the hospital.

In spite of what was said at this meeting in November, 1960, Mayor Wagner's new Commissioner of Hospitals, Dr. Ray E. Trussell, taking office March 1, 1961, only four months later, took a different stance. On March 6, 1961, the *World-Telegram and Sun* reported:

Aroused Lower East Side community leaders today demanded that Robert F. Wagner keep his promise to build a new Gouverneur Hospital for the area's 200,000 residents.

The outcry came as a result of a blow struck last week by Dr. Ray E. Trussell, the new Commissioner of Hospitals, against the community's long-standing campaign for the hospital.

The Commissioner said he favored closing Gouverneur Hospital and he strongly hinted that the 75-year-old building would not be replaced in the community.

However, on March 7, 1961, the *World-Telegram and Sun* reported further:

Mayor Robert F. Wagner said today he would keep his word and build a new Gouverneur Hospital in the Lower East Side, despite indications that his new hospital commissioner opposes the move. . . .

"NO CHANGE OF MIND"

Asked by this newspaper if there had been any change in policy regarding his commitment to erect the proposed $8.6 million, 300-bed replacement for the old hospital, the Mayor released the following statement through Frank Doyle, his executive secretary:

"There has been no change of mind, no change of policy."

"What will the Mayor do if Dr. Trussell suggests closing the hospital?"

"He hasn't had an opportunity yet to talk to Dr. Trussell on this but he will shortly," Mr. Doyle replied.

On March 8, 1961, the *World-Telegram and Sun* continued the story:

A leading health authority today urged Dr. Ray E. Trussell, newly appointed city Hospital Commissioner, to keep the Lower East Side's 63-year-old Gouverneur Hospital open until a new one is built.

Winslow Carlton, Chairman of the Board of Group Health Insurance, Inc., and President of the Henry Street Settlement, said the city should spend "whatever is needed" to make the present hospital operable. . . .

Yesterday, a split in city administration policy became apparent when Mayor Robert F. Wagner renewed his pledge to the 200,000 residents there to erect the proposed 300-bed, $8.6 million hospital. . . .

RESIDENTS PLEAD

Lower East Side residents, meanwhile, renewed their pleas for a modern plant to serve their community of more than 200,000 low- and middle-income families.

Following a decision by the Medical Board of Gouverneur Hospital to discontinue its in-patient service, Mayor Wagner yesterday announced a four-stage program which will eventually shut down the institution completely.

Wagner said the continuance of the hospital has been a controversial issue because of its age and its lack of adequate plant facilities. . . .

The Hospital's Medical Board of attending physicians had fought hard to keep the in-patient service open until the new hospital was built. However, on March 13, 1961, the *World-Telegram and Sun* wrote:

> Over the weekend Dr. Trussell met with more than 30 doctors, members of Gouverneur's Hospital Board, headed by Dr. Herbert F. Newman. The Commissioner, it was understood, is attempting to persuade these doctors that Gouverneur cannot properly operate under present conditions.

On that same day, the *New York Post* reported:

> Neighbors of the hospital, rallied by thousands of leaflets distributed by the Lower East Side Neighborhoods Assn., are to march on City Hall at 10 tomorrow to urge Mayor Wagner to "staff the old and build the new" Gouverneur.

But LENA did more than stage another demonstration. On March 10, it sent to the new Commissioner of Hospitals a comprehensive memorandum not only protesting the threatened closing of Gouverneur, but setting forth the kind of community hospital that was needed on the Lower East Side.

The LENA memorandum recalled that for the previous ten years

> the civic, religious and welfare organizations of the Lower East Side have repeatedly and consistently called to the attention of the City Administration the obsolete condition of Gouverneur Hospital and the need for its replacement.

"Our requests have been met," LENA continued,

with emergency patchwork improvements in the old structure and until 1959 with evasions and postponements of action on a new hospital. In 1959, the Department of Hospitals requested, and the Board of Estimate approved, a capital budget item sufficient for preliminary planning and site location of a new hospital in the Seward Park area, and in 1960, a capital budget item sufficient to acquire the site and to complete the plans for a 250-bed hospital. At the 1960 hearing, the Mayor reiterated his ten-year pledge of support for the new hospital, first made when he was Borough President of Manhattan, and he was joined by the Comptroller and the Acting Borough President.

We have consistently held that our community needs a municipal hospital for both in-patients and out-patients. We were, therefore, deeply disturbed, first by the report of the Hospital Council in 1955 that proposed as an alternative to a new Gouverneur Hospital, the concentration of all municipal hospital beds for the entire east side area south of 42nd Street to the Battery in Bellevue Hospital; then, by the categorical recommendation of the so-called Heyman Commission in 1960 that Gouverneur be abolished and its municipal bed complement added to Bellevue, and most recently, by the recommendation of the Hospital Council that the present Gouverneur Hospital be closed because of its loss of accreditation. . . .

We are convinced that the great majority of the 200,000 people who live on the Lower East Side (the area bounded on the north by 14th Street, on the south by Brooklyn Bridge and City Hall park, on the west by Broadway, and on the east by the East River) need a hospital centrally located within that area, central, at least, as to public transportation facilities. . . . We are also deeply convinced that the quality of the Lower East Side as a residential community will be substantially improved by our having a modern Gouverneur Hospital within the area. . . .

"We cannot reconcile ourselves to the idea," LENA declared, "that Gouverneur's immediate problems cannot be solved and that therefore the Hospital must be closed forthwith.

We ask you to remember that for a decade we have been calling the City Administration's attention to . . . the repeated warnings given by technical investigators, that we have pleaded for the kind of medical school affiliation that would raise the quality of house staff and ancillary services. We cannot but hold the City Administration responsible for this most recent blow to Gouverneur, its loss of accreditation. . . .

If the Hospital is now closed and its services removed from the people of the Lower East Side, its loss will inevitably be laid at the door of the Wagner Administration. We regret to say, we think the attribution is justified, because if action had been taken earlier, the present situation would not have occurred.

Addressing itself to "the central issue," LENA granted that many medical educators and others devoted to the cause of high quality medical care support centralization, but pointed to fallacies in their plan to have Bellevue serve the entire Lower East Side, south of 42nd Street, and to concentrate the municipal out-patient services at First Avenue and 26th Street, with perhaps an "outpost clinic in the Gouverneur area." LENA noted that the three medical schools at Bellevue had in fact asked for three hundred more beds than the latest Hospital Council survey had recommended for the entire area, and it questioned the wisdom of the planners' judgment that if patients did not choose to go to Bellevue they could choose one of the voluntary hospitals that lie on the periphery of the Lower East Side. "Although," LENA's memorandum read,

. . . they grant the self-evident fact that their plan would impose some inconvenience on many Lower East Side residents, they aver that centralization is necessary because well-trained interns and residents will not come. They also speak disparagingly of City hospital administration, of the lack of adequate equipment and of technical ancillary personnel, especially when there is no prestigious medical school to ride herd on the Department of Hospitals.

"We recognize the force of some of these points," LENA conceded.

Despite the best efforts of many qualified and devoted attending physicians at Gouverneur over many years, we have seen no improvement in the quality of care in the old hospital—indeed, as the general demand for interns and residents has risen over the past fifteen years, quality has declined. Consequently, we have sought from advisors whom we consider qualified, advice as to how our people and our community might obtain a high quality of medical and hospital care within our area. We have sought a way to bring health care *to* our people, as our social agencies bring them social services, as our churches and temples bring them pastoral care. . . .

. . . We know at firsthand the problems of mothers with three, four, even five children under seven years of age when one of them gets sick; of elderly men and women who need weekly clinic care; of families when an accident befalls one of their members. We daily see families in obvious need of elementary health education and preventive services, whose educational and cultural level is such that they cannot bring themselves to take a long trip to a great, complicated and strange institution like Bellevue, or even to the Health Center at 25th Street. In our view, these are precisely the people for whom the municipal hospital system exists. We think the system should be designed to serve them.

Spelling out its conception of the new Gouverneur, LENA called for the kind of hospital for the Lower East Side that would be similar in principle to the Hunterdon Medical Center which Dr. Trussell had directed.

"In this case," LENA specified,

Gouverneur would be satellite to Bellevue and its professional staff would be nominated by one of the medical schools that now have services at Bellevue. . . .

This would mean that the in-patient services of Gouverneur would include the basic medical and surgical specialties but not those used relatively infrequently or requiring elaborate special equipment and specially trained ancillary staffs. The lines of demarcation between central and satellites services would be determined by the medical school and the Department of Hospitals within each major field. The same principles would govern the subdivisions of the out-patient department.

. . . In this connection, we would hope that the health protective services and health education provided by the Health Department's District Health Centers would be made part of the program. We would also hope that home services to the Welfare Department's clients would be provided from the hospital, to the end that home, clinic, and hospital care of Welfare cases would be coordinated. If, in addition, Welfare Department social services were also tied in with the provision of health services, total care of these families would, we think, be greatly improved.

LENA pointed to "a growing need for locally based psychiatric services, such as a mental hygiene clinic, 'day' hospitalization, and 'night' hospitalization; and stressed that narcotics addiction is rapidly spreading among adolescents in the area, indicating a great need for an organized medical approach to this problem."

The type of hospital it envisaged, LENA held, would serve as a magnet to draw well-trained physicians into the Lower East Side community.

> At the present time, few of the doctors located in the area have any meaningful association whatsoever with either a voluntary or municipal hospital. We understand that it is very difficult for doctors to keep up with the advances of medicine without participating in organized hospital services, and that modern medicine requires the kind of consultation with and referral to a wide variety of specialists that is facilitated by a good hospital. In this case, "the good hospital" would be not Gouverneur alone but Bellevue as well. We would, therefore, hope that the kind of hospital we have in mind would include our community physicians both now and in the future.

The Hospital Council, LENA recalled, had said in a statement issued the previous year that "approximately 90 percent of all services rendered by physicians take place outside the hospital." "Therefore," the council said,

> . . . It is the obligation of hospitals to reach out to the community and to afford to every physician who practices in the community an opportunity to join a hospital staff and participate in its work within the limits set by his experience and competence. Hospitals do not fulfill this obligation by appointing to their staff only the best qualified physicians.

A hospital in the area was also needed, LENA continued, because of the growing demand for semiprivate accommodations. Increasing numbers of people were covered by voluntary health insurance, entitling them to such accommodations, and it appeared likely that the elderly would, before many years, be covered by government health insurance. A hospital such as Bellevue that provides only ward beds enforces economic segregation. "Our community," LENA observed, "has emerged from the state of being 'an economic ghetto' and we think it of first importance that the new hospial should not be an (economically) segregated facility."

Were the Lower East Side to get the kind of hospital envisaged, LENA predicted, the entire community would rally behind the new Gouverneur and contribute markedly to its success as "a health facility, in the human as well as technical sense of that term. . . . Even the present Gouverneur, with all of its obvious shortcomings, had had many volunteer workers serving both in the hospital wards and as aides to clinic patients."

While LENA did not presume to speak for the medical educators, it pointed out in its memorandum to Hospital Commissioner Trussell that the addition of a new Gouverneur to the Bellevue medical center complex would provide "an exceptional opportunity to train undergraduate medical students in the practice of neighborhood medicine through the clinics, home care and emergency services." And that "rotation of interns and residents from Bellevue would provide these young doctors with experience in a different kind of medicine from the kind that they see at a great general hospital. Physicians already in practice would, of course, also be benefited by their association with teaching services in a hospital of this character."

A hospital that maintained a close association with the homes and lives of the people of its area would also, LENA suggested, provide opportunities for certain kinds of investigative medicine, principally those with what might be called a "social" component such as, for instance:

> Health maintenance of ambulent geriatric cases; the treatment of malnutrition; experimenting with a combination of psychiatric, somatic and environmental treatment of various forms of retreatism.

The implementation of such a program, LENA conceded, would oblige the city to provide a certain number of full-time physicians and probably more technical and ancillary personnel than is commonly furnished in nonteaching hospitals. While income from semiprivate patients and some ward patients would at least in part offset these additional costs, LENA declared:

> It seems to us clear that if extra cost is required in order to bring high quality, modern care to the people of our community, the community at large, through City, State and Federal Governments should, and will, find the money. The kind of health facility and health services that we are asking for would not only save much suffering but would prevent many cases of dependency arising from untended or inadequately treated physical or mental illness.

LENA was asking not only for a modern hospital for its own community, it said in concluding its memorandum to the Commissioner of Hospitals, "We are also asking that the City . . . make here a demonstration in modern health care. This could be a model for our City and conceivably for many other communities as well. We offer you whatever assistance and support we can give in bringing this to pass."

LENA's reasoned plea notwithstanding, the in-patient services at Gouverneur were closed before the end of March, 1961, the out-patient and home care continuing.

In spite of this, our efforts to get the new hospital under way were redoubled. On Friday, July 28, 1961, we thought we had cause for rejoicing. The newspaper headlines read:

> *Herald Tribune*: GOUVERNEUR HOSPITAL BUILDING PLANS OK'D
> *The New York Times*: EASTSIDE TO GET 204-BED HOSPITAL
> *Daily Mirror*: OK PLANS TO BUILD NEW GOUVERNEUR HOSPITAL

The Board of Estimate had approved preliminary plans at a late session the night before. The unusual step was taken of immediately authorizing $300,000 to complete final plans. At that point, the hospital was to cost $7,895,000, and was to be eleven stories. It might be pointed out again that, throughout its history, movement forward was apt to take place just before election. This was the end of July.

The *Herald Tribune* had noted on July 28:

Hospital authorities, including Hospitals Commissioner Ray E. Trussell, have advocated the permanent abandonment of the (new) Gouverneur site as a hospital location.

Mayor Wagner overruled his new Hospitals Commissioner after hearing repeated protests from community organizations.

The best thing that happened to us in 1962 was the selection of Dr. Howard J. Brown to run Gouverneur's out-patient clinic. There is no question that an affiliation contract with Beth Israel at this time did away with much of the red tape which strangles the city's functioning at every turn, and made it possible to hire full-time medical staff. This affiliation had come about under Dr. Trussell's plan to strengthen the municipal hospitals by putting them where possible under the medical direction of established voluntary hospitals. The affiliation with Beth Israel, even though it cost the city much more, worked well for Gouverneur's out-patient department. Dr. Brown, who had been named to the staff of Beth Israel, was allowed a free hand in building his staff— and in relieving doctors and nurses who did not meet his standards of patient care, with special emphasis on courtesy and considerate treatment. On March 16, LENA joined with Henry Street Settlement in giving a welcoming reception for Dr. Brown and members of his staff.

Almost from the moment Howard Brown came to Gouverneur, the whole atmosphere of the place changed. It did not take many months before the attitude of the neighbors changed too; instead of criticisms of the care heard on every side for years, came stories of kindness and consideration and success. It was gratifying to see good news travel so fast. Dr. Brown himself became well known to the patients. He attended small and large meetings where he could talk to his neighbors and answer their questions and get their viewpoints. He not only came himself but other members of the Gouverneur staff also came.

Daily attendance at Gouverneur's clinics zoomed. At last the old people of the Lower East Side—and the young too—had doctors to see them, prescribe for them, and advise them at no cost below a certain income level. Patients were treated with a consideration too seldom shown in municipal hospitals and all too often wanting in voluntary hospitals.

Dr. Brown had been given the job of making plans for the new Gouverneur, but in spite of that the new hospital continued as a mirage. Despite all the encouraging headlines and the pre-election assurances we had had in July, 1961, we began to realize that once more things were not moving ahead and that it was not just red tape that seemed to have brought things to a stand-still. At this point it appeared to many of us that only the mayor could put a stop to the underground operations against the hospital, and we had had enough! So I went to see Mayor Wagner and gave him a picture of what was happening as the neighbor-hood saw it. Since he was under the weather, I saw him at Gracie Mansion and had the chance for a good talk. He promised that he would carry the ball from then on. I wrote him on October 19, 1962, as follows:

> Dear Bob:
> Thanks for seeing me the other day and I hope your cold is better.
> Since then I have met with the Executive Committee of LENA and told them that you will handle the next stage of the long story of Gouverneur and that we do not have to have another demonstration or meeting or even come to see you again. How-ever, the group was very much concerned about the time element. This is understandable as we realize that the plans were again deferred this summer and that they should have been ready by next month. This of course could go on and on as it has in the past.
> I am sure you know that there has been no other thing which has caused so much suspicion and distrust in the neighborhood as the long delay over Gouverneur and I cannot imagine anything that would be more stimulating and inspiring to the neighbor-hood than to see their Community Hospital really going up. We would appreciate reassurances on this point, too.
> Sincerely,
> Helen Hall

In spite of the mayor's assurances at this time I received a telephone call on December 20, 1962, to warn me that at that moment an amendment had been introduced at a meeting of the City Council to delete Gouverneur Hospital from the capital budget already passed by the Board of Estimate. It has generally been a formality that the City Council approves the budget the Board of Estimate has passed, so none of us had been alerted to this scheme. At the same time, I was told that uptown members of the Reform Democrats were carrying the ball for the deletion. I immediately telephoned members of the Reform Democrats in our neighborhood, who knew that this was no way to influence votes for them in *their* neighborhood, and they went to work. I then reached leading members of the regular Democrats who also got on the job. It seemed that Dr. Trussell had been invited to the City Council meeting to "explain the situation" and also that our Lower East Side member of the City Council was brand new and was caught completely off guard. This particular delaying tactic was caught in the nick of time, but unfortunately many others were not!

For the next two years things seemed to go ahead with Dr. Brown working on the plans, and a ground-breaking ceremony on April 29, 1964, might fairly have seemed like the end of the long struggle for Gouverneur, and at the time we almost thought it might be. The impressive architectural drawing of the new hospital, even situated on the right site, which appeared in the newspapers the next day was cheering, but by that time we had learned that headlines didn't make hospitals. We remembered the headlines in 1961, and the June 16, 1963, headline:

$14,000,000 HOSPITAL TO BE BUILT ON THE LOWER EAST SIDE.

The ceremony was held indoors at the Educational Alliance because of the weather. Dr. Trussell, who was still Commissioner of Hospitals, presided. He said that the hospital was a "new and exciting concept, perhaps the first of its kind in the United States." It was certainly exciting to us, but certainly not new, for it contained the chief elements of the plan we had been working on for so long, the outlines of which we had sent to Dr. Trussell when he first took office as commissioner in 1961. Borough President Dudley, Dr. George James, Commissioner of Health, Dr. Alonzo S. Yerby of the Department of Health, and Bradford M. Clark of the Department of Public Works were there to give us the blessings we were unfortunately still to need!

Now Lower East Side eyes were on that hole in the ground, but the construction proceeded so slowly that again everyone began asking why. We all turned into sidewalk superintendants as we saw the lack of progress. Finally, Kenneth Wittenberg, a brilliant young photographer who, because he had begun in our photography shop, was accustomed to taking pictures to illustrate our points, took some of two public schools close by which were started long after Gouverneur Hospital, to show that one was almost finished and the other way above ground while Gouverneur was still in its hole. At one time, nature joined the forces against us by producing water where rock should have been. Considering everything, this was hard to believe, so Ralph Tefferteller climbed down with the engineers to investigate at first hand. This involved more months of delay while we were told that foundation plans were being changed.

In the meantime, as Dr. Brown had been given the responsibility for working out the detailed plans of the upper structure with the Department of Hospitals, Health, Welfare, and Mental Health necessary for the comprehensive kind of health care which was envisaged, he was pushing as hard as he could to have them ready to set on the foundation when they had solved its water problem.

We were barely above ground in 1966 when Mayor Lindsay appointed Dr. Brown as Health Services Administrator, which made him responsible for both the Departments of Hospitals and Health and the Mental Health Board. Although everyone hated to have him leave Gouverneur, there was rejoicing because the whole city would have the benefit of his services.

It had been suggested a number of times that Gouverneur Hospital be named after me and it came up again in December of 1963. I have been questioned so often about my refusal that I am putting my letter to the mayor in this record. It had always seemed to me that, aside from its basic importance as an example of comprehensive community health care, the campaign for Gouverneur, I hoped, would show how a thoughtful, sustained effort on the part of a neighborhood might lead to success. It was a very broad partnership of people with roots in the neighborhood, grass and otherwise, who had worked hard together over the years.

Dear Mayor Wagner:

A reporter from *The New York Times* called my attention this morning to a release from your office suggesting again that Gouverneur Hospital be given my name.

As you may remember when you first suggested this at a LENA Awards Night meeting two years ago, I said that I felt the name Gouverneur had come to represent to so many people a successful community effort and for that reason it was important to keep the name.

There is, however, something I would like to ask you and the Board of Hospitals to consider; that is, to have put on one part of the outside of the hospital, the names of many people who for over 15 years worked to get a community hospital in their neighborhood. LENA, I know, would gladly undertake to do this and I would help. The neighborhood effort was so long, and so sustained, and so thoughtful that I feel it should be commemorated in this way and that it would be deeply appreciated and be an inspiration to other communities in the country.

It doesn't seem possible, but a few days before Mayor Wagner went out of office we discovered almost by accident that the final corrected plans for Gouverneur had not been signed by the mayor and that no further move could be made without the mayor's signature on these plans. As soon as we heard this, Lloyd Paperno, co-chairman of LENA, and I went immediately to see Mayor Wagner and discovered through some telephoning in his office that this was so, that the plans had *not* been signed. Mayor Wagner promised to sign them before he left office. A telephone message, dated December 31, 1965, in my files, reads as follows:

Tom Lawless called to say that the Mayor signed the Gouverneur Hospital authorization.

The work could not have gone on without the mayor's signature; another mayor might have wanted to start all over again and might well have hesitated over this controversial bit of signing.

Dr. Brown caused amazement and great dismay when ten months later we learned that he was not going ahead with the plans for the new two-hundred-bed Community Hospital which he had helped plan, but that he wanted to convert it to chronic care, primarily for the aged, which Dr. Trussell had also proposed earlier. In a letter to the borough president, Dr. Brown wrote that:

> . . . it would be a disservice to the City and to the residents of the Lower East Side to build 180 acute beds at Gouverneur instead of the 300 chronic care beds envisioned in my proposal.

Only a few months earlier, Dr. Brown had himself described Gouverneur as "a model for national reform in the field of community hospitals." He further had said that:

> . . . after the decision was reached to build the new Gouverneur Hospital, the City had decided to make it one of the most unique community hospitals in the country.

We talked with Dr. Brown himself, and Father William Reed, co-chairman of LENA, Winslow Carlton; and I also discussed the problem with Dr. Brown, Mayor Lindsay, and Commissioner of Hospitals Terenzio, but, sadly enough, with little meeting of minds.

Borough President Sutton was very much interested and immediately helpful. He asked Dr. Brown and Dr. J. C. Haldeman, of the Hospital Review and Planning Council, to meet with Dr. Sheps, head of Beth Israel, and a community group from LENA in his office. Typical of the situation, we discovered at this meeting that the Hospital Review and Planning Council had gone along with building one hundred new beds at Beekman Hospital (a voluntary hospital) at the same time they were saying we did not need a new Gouverneur. In other words, we needed to increase the voluntary hospital beds but not the municipal. The meeting ended with the promise that a smaller group would try to work out a solution.

In the meantime, LENA decided to circulate petitions to the one hundred or more small organizations on the Lower East Side, with which they were in touch, so that once more the neighborhood would know what was happening and could express itself. And so the process of alerting the neighborhood and opening channels for grass-roots expression started again, two years after the ground-breaking ceremonies. It was not done with quite the same spirit as usual because nobody wanted to be against Dr. Brown. But Gouverneur Hospital was in jeopardy, so once more they went to work.

Mobilization for Youth cooperated with LENA to reach representatives of small groups, staging the usual meetings, the tables at stores for signing of petitions, and the neighborhood discussions everywhere.

Borough President Sutton came down to the East Side to receive the petitions at the site of the hospital. He stood on the top of a truck while the representatives of the groups which had gathered the signatures handed him the twelve thousand petitions. As I got myself down off the truck, one of my oldest neighbors said briskly, "Now we go to City Hall?" I said, "Not this time." "And why not?" she said reprovingly.

It took another month or more before a compromise was worked out, with Dr. Cecil Sheps and Winslow Carlton playing a constructive part in the negotiations. This involved keeping 120 beds for acute medical care of adults and children, and eighty-five for extended care for older people. Except for emergencies, no surgical or obstetrical cases could be treated in the new hospital but would be taken care of in the now "parent" hospital, Beth Israel. This plan was ratified at an opening meeting of LENA which the Borough President attended and at which Dr. Sheps presented the compromise proposal to the group, and the building of the hospital was to continue with all speed. But I have to add that this is not happening; and while the roof is on, the windows in, Gouverneur Hospital is still not ready to serve its neighbors.

XXXV

Some Beginnings of the Consumer Movement

People have often asked me why a social worker should be so much interested in consumer problems. I must say I have often asked myself the same question. Not because I am not convinced that I should be, but because it's been such slow, uphill work I sometimes wish I were not.

The title "consumer" for an organized movement was first used in 1891 when the New York Consumers League was founded. A few years later Consumers Leagues were formed in Massachusetts, Illinois, and Pennsylvania, and in 1899 the National Consumers League came into being under the executive leadership of Florence Kelley. The league's early purpose was to enlist consumer support for the elimination of sweatshop working conditions. The league issued a label to manufacturers agreeing to conform to minimum standards and sought to educate consumers to demand labeled goods. As additional state leagues were established, the purpose broadened and efforts were made to secure a $6 a week minimum wage for employees by publishing a "white list" of employers agreeing to do so. It was soon recognized that a labor standards program relying solely on consumer education and voluntary patronage of fair standard firms was hopelessly slow and the leagues turned their efforts from 1909 toward the promotion of state minimum wage legislation, laws limiting hours and improving conditions of work. It wasn't until the 1930s that consumer league programs sought, in addition, to promote consumer standards and protection.

Organized efforts in behalf of the consumer which began to gather momentum in the 1920s and early 1930s were greatly stimulated when in 1933 President Roosevelt appointed the Consumers Advisory Board to the NRA and named Mary Rumsay as its chairman.

My own concern with consumer problems started in 1934 during my first year at Henry Street when I was appointed to the new Milk Advisory Committee to the Milk Control Board set up by the New York State Department of Agriculture. Dr. John L. Rice, New York City's Commissioner of Health, and I were to represent consumers, and the rest of the eighteen or so members were milk producers and distributors. While the committee was only advisory, the law was such that no milk price rise could take place without our having been consulted. Miss Wald had, in an earlier day, worked to improve the sanitary code and the conditions under which milk was allowed to come into New York City. However, the cost of milk was the problem we were asked to consider in 1934.

At one of the early meetings of the Advisory Committee I had occasion to say, "Consumers won't stand for another price rise." At which the head of one of the milk companies turned to me and said firmly, "You know, Miss Hall, that consumers aren't organized and they can't do a thing about it." At this point, a "Consumer" was born. As far as I was concerned, the hungry children of my neighborhood sat in on these meetings from then on—and were very unwelcome, as were both Dr. Rice and I, as we fought against the continuous efforts to raise fluid milk prices.

Fortunately, Dr. Rice and I had one of the most ardent consumers in the world right at our backs—Fiorello La Guardia. At one point when things got tough, I appealed to Mayor La Guardia to come to one of our meetings in Albany to help. Much to the consternation of his staff he said he would come, and canceled his appointments in New York City. On the day of the meeting, his car broke down on the way to Albany. He climbed up behind the police motorcycle escort and arrived disheveled but as pugnacious and dramatic and effective as ever. The rise was stopped, at least for the time being.

Just as I was feeling good about it, another meeting was called to which I was not invited and a price rise did go through! However, my lack of notification provided the technical ground for an injunction suit which La Guardia promptly instituted. This held up the rise for approximately six weeks.

I also sent a statement to the Advisory Committee, protesting their sanction of the price rise and the failure to notify me of the meeting. I reminded the committee that ". . . the law under which we are acting designates the purchasing power of the public as one of the chief factors to be considered in fixing prices." This early statement, dated May, 1934, expresses my basic reasons for my work in the consumer interest.

"We are told," I went on,

> that there has been an increase of approximately 50 percent in malnutrition among school children since 1927. When recently we made a survey of eleven blocks close to Henry Street Settlement, we found that 54 percent of the wage earners were earning less than $15 a week. No one could go over these family budgets without knowing that 1 cent on the cost of milk would have a direct bearing on the health of the children.
>
> When the 1-cent rise was announced, one mother said, "Well, that means a pint less for us."

"These household facts," I argued, "should be laid alongside the facts as to the cost of production on the farm, and the cost of distribution of the bottle of milk between the farm and the tenement kitchen. . . . The farmer's stake is not antagonistic to that of the consumer. One wants to produce what the other wants to buy. . . . [But] if the farmer gets approximately 4½ cents a quart for fluid milk and the mother pays 11 or 12 cents for Grade B milk, then the burden of proof is on those who say that the 6½ or 7½ cents difference . . . cannot be cut down." Then I pointed out: "It has been cut down in Chicago and the cut from 11 cents to as low as 6½ cents has brought with it a material increase in consumption with small variation from the stipulated price to the farmer."

Another meeting of the Advisory Committee was called, to which I was invited, but the price rise was again voted by the majority. To comfort myself for the ultimate failure, I counted up what that six weeks of delay had saved the milk consumers of the city and it came to something like $1.5 million, a small part of New York City's milk bill, but perhaps indicative of what saving of pennies can mean to family food budgets.

A survey by our Henry Street nurses had shown the relation of milk consumption to income and to price changes. But I needed a broad statistical base to carry my point with the Milk Advisory Committee. I saw the need, too, for a thorough investigation into the economics of milk distribution. Failing to arouse the interest of the Milk Control Board of the State Department of Agriculture, I went to Washington to see Fred Howe, then Consumer Counsel of the Agricultural Adjustment Administration. He told me his office was launching a study of just this kind— the relation of milk consumption to family income—in four cities, and he said that he would be glad to extend the study to include New York City. We discussed the way to do it and what kind of help settlements and other organizations could give to the inquiry. However, just as I was leaving, he was called away. When he returned, he said he was awfully sorry, but that his office could not make the study in New York.

"But why not?" I asked.

"The agricultural interests there have not asked for it," he replied. "Under the regulations they would have to support it."

"But," I said, "you are a Consumer Counsel, are you not, and consumers are asking for it?"

"Yes," he said, "but I am a Consumer Counsel in the Department of Agriculture."

I decided then that if we really wanted to protect the interests of the consumer we would have to have a consumer agency free of other overriding interests in government. But in the meantime we needed our statistical base.

I reported my failure in Washington to Mayor La Guardia and he offered to help, and arranged for cooperation from the Departments of Health and Accounts and the Board of Education. We worked out a plan to have the United Neighborhood Houses, through a committee chaired by Helen Harris, then head of Union Settlement, get information through the settlement houses working in cooperation with their local public schools. The mayor assigned us one hundred CWA (Civil Works Administration, precursor of the Works Progress Administration) workers and two city statisticians. We set up headquarters at 99

Park Avenue, where I had my own uptown office and which served as headquarters for our Henry Street Visiting Nurse Service at that time. Mr. Joseph P. Kelley, a volunteer member of the staff of the Henry Street Settlement, and a cousin of our board member Nicholas Kelley, offered his services as director of the survey.

In Washington, the office of the Consumer Counsel of the Department of Agriculture gave us every encouragement. They looked upon our survey, correlated as it was with their national study, and based on similar questionnaires, as a valuable addition to their own work.

The findings of our own survey, tabulated by the city's Department of Accounts and reported directly to Mayor La Guardia, were later reproduced in a summary table, accompanied by three pictograph sheets illustrating various aspects of the study.

The survey centered in the low-income neighborhoods around the settlements. In all, 146,000 persons in 21,559 families were covered; these families included 11,504 children under five, and 53,559 between five and sixteen years of age. Families averaged 5.14 persons. The usable returns were about 44 percent of the questionnaires distributed.

Incomes over $50 a week were only 1.58 percent of the total, and more than three-fourths of the families had $25 a week or less. Yet this income range bore comparison with a large portion of New York City incomes during these Depression years, and factors affecting milk consumption in these groups were of city-wide significance.

Some of the findings: Per capita consumption of milk went up steadily with income, up to $50 per week. The lowest income group ($5–$10 a week) spent *16.22 percent of its income* for milk. Most of the milk was bought at stores, as the legally fixed price was 1 to 2 cents a quart cheaper than home-delivered milk. Consumption of butter and cream also increased with income, the sharp rate of butter increase suggesting that butter substitutes rather than butter were used in the lowest incomes.

Conclusions: The average of none of the groups met the recommended amount of milk consumption, usually given as a quart a day per child, a pint per adult. The 16.22 percent of income spent for milk by the 13.69 percent of the families in the lowest group was a testimony to the success of health education

and milk advertising. But the high percentage-to-income consumption of milk in the lower income groups reflected a sacrifice
of other diet essentials.

These findings turned out to be comparable to those found in
the federal survey of milk consumption in other cities published
later in the *Consumers Guide,* official organ of the Consumers
Counsel Office.

As I look back on it, I realize we must have worked with
considerable speed, thanks to our ebullient mayor, to our new
colleagues in Washington, and to the great interest felt by members of the mothers' clubs of the settlements, who helped to
produce the data. The survey was launched in May and completed in August, though it took some months to compile and
reproduce. It was a satisfaction to have the printed report with
its charts—in great demand for years to come. Farmers, unions,
and many other groups awakening to the need for consumer
responsibility used it as illustrative material.

The survey also helped to educate at least two milk companies.
One day I had a telephone call from a member of the Henry
Street board asking me whether I could see her at once. Her
first words as she came into my office were, "Helen, why do you
hate —— Milk Company?", mentioning the name of a large milk
concern. I replied that I didn't, I only hated to have the price
of milk go up with children hungry in our neighborhood, and
I reached for our milk charts. She then explained that a foundation supported by this milk company might withdraw the nurses'
salarys which they had contributed to the Visiting Nurse Service
for a long time. However, when we had finished our examination
of the charts, she said, "Would you mind taking these to show
the foundation why we are interested in the price of milk?" Of
course I was glad to go, and they *were* interested and did not
stop our nurse's salary.

Interestingly enough, the only piece of paper I saw in the
stylish foundation office I visited was a small leaflet issued by
our Milk Consumers Protective Committee. On the cover of the
leaflet was a cow being milked and inside I knew were printed
the profits of milk companies (which was public information of
course). I also knew the leaflet had taken practically our last
cent to get made! While I was there the head of the foundation

studied the charts very carefully and then he said a little ruefully, "Maybe, after all, milk should be a public utility."

Another time, Mrs. Mary Simkhovitch, director of Greenwich House, a settlement, and a member of the Milk Consumers Protective Committee, telephoned me and asked me to lunch with other members of the committee and meet one of her contributors, the head of a large milk company. He had always supplied ice cream for all their Christmas parties and now had threatened to stop because of her work to keep the price of milk down. When, during lunch, we produced our charts showing, we hoped, why settlement people should be interested in milk, the president of the company turned to two young public relations men who were with him and said, "Why didn't we do something like this? We ought to know this, too!" And Greenwich House Christmas parties were saved!

By this time, a new force had entered the consumer field, namely, Consumers Union, primarily a product-testing agency with a broad consumer concern. They had recruited the aid of Dr. Caroline Whitney, a highly trained economist and statistician, to draw together a group of people who were concerned with the cost of milk, which became the Milk Consumers Protective Committee and progressed under Dr. Whitney's capable leadership. A large meeting protesting a particular price rise was held early in the fall of 1936, at which the late Stanley M. Isaacs, then president of United Neighborhood Houses, presented our findings. This time we *had* our figures and the price rise did not occur. The vice-chairman of the Milk Consumers Protective Committee, Meyer Parodneck, a lawyer, estimated that the savings to New York's milk consumers this time was about $12 million a year! Our milk survey had proved its value.

Other milk events followed in rapid succession. Chief among these was a new relationship with a number of upstate dairy farmers, whose low income from milk had led some of them to withhold their supply in a "milk strike." Their attention, and ours, was focused again on the "price spread" between what the farmer got and what the milk consumer paid. This "distributor's margin" had a way of always being the largest part of the consumer dollar, and always less subject to the fluctuations, down at one end and up at the other, to which both farmers and consumers were subject.

We were invited to appear at a number of dairy farmers' meetings upstate, and dairy farmers came to the city to take part in our sessions. During the next year or so, many of our new farmer friends were guests at Henry Street, were vivid speakers at our club meetings, and fascinated our city mothers as they told of how hard their wives worked.

Meanwhile, following on the milk survey, a "Housewives Milk League," made up of members of existing mothers' clubs, was organized at Henry Street, and similar leagues were set up in other settlements. Occasions were not wanting for our Housewives to show themselves in force, at public hearings called by legislative investigating committees or by the officials of the federal-state milk control agency which succeeded the state's Milk Control Board. At these meetings, milk price rises or general questions relating to retail price-fixing for milk were usually the subjects of consideration.

I remember marching, early one morning, one of the heads of a delegation of Housewives from Henry Street, down to a hearing at City Hall, clutching the center of a fifteen-foot-long banner which was stoutly held at each end by the presidents of two mothers' clubs. Paul Kellogg walked along with us that morning. He saw meaning in every homely happening in a neighborhood such as ours, and especially where we touched base with any form of government, from the police to the President. To his mind, this was helping to make democracy work. His viewpoint always heightened the color and added meaning to the life around us for our settlement family, and for our neighbors, and for me. White armbands identified the women as they marched, some two hundred strong by the time we reached the hearing chamber, for we picked up delegates from the other settlements as we went along.

We arrived right on time, only to be greeted with the news that no consumers were to be heard that morning. This was discouraging as most of the women could not leave their homes and children all day. But our protest only brought from the chairman, a state senator, the reply: "We treat everyone alike. We hear all the distributors first, then all the producers, then the consumers. We always do it that way—treat everyone alike." No appeal to logic would have made an impression, but the sight of our big delegation with their armbands finally did. The consumers in this instance got second place, and their "housewife research" proved what they had to say: that their families could buy less milk than the health authorities set as a minimum for growing children.

Retail price-fixing was abandoned in New York right after the hearing, which gave the women a great sense of satisfaction— even though the subsequent fall in prices proved to be only temporary.

The Milk Consumers Protective Committee held its own public meetings, too. The most dramatic of these took place in Foley Square, on a cold, sleeting day in November, 1937. It was to be the climax of a baby carriage parade, organized by the League of Mothers' Clubs of the Settlements throughout the city. The Milk Consumers Protective Committee had been trying to organize a consumer–farmer milk cooperative as a means of applying a yardstick to the cost of fluid milk but had been unable to get a license for the cooperative from the State Department of Agriculture. The League of Mothers' Clubs undertook the baby carriage parade as a means of bringing attention to this situation, and "Cora, the Co-op Cow" gave special drama to the occasion. She had been transported from her warm stall in Columbia County by E. Claude Jones, one of our dairy farmer friends from the Hillsdale Producers' Cooperative, to show the solidarity between farmers and city milk drinkers. The climax came when Cora, carefully blanketed, was milked, to the cheers of the audience; and a wide representation from the press gave her full publicity. And the result was the license we had been asking for came in three weeks.

Caroline Whitney and Meyer Parodneck drew up the articles of incorporation for the Consumer–Farmer Milk Cooperative, the plan being to buy milk directly from the producers' cooperatives sympathizing with our efforts, starting with the Hillsdale Producers' Cooperative. Incorporators and the first Board of Directors were drawn from the active leaders of the Milk Consumers Protective Committee, with representatives of settlements, including Mildred Gutwillig, Director of Recreation Rooms and Settlement, and Winifred Frazier of the United Neighborhood Houses.

Meyer Parodneck had had previous experience with a consumers' milk cooperative, knew its legal requirements and had a good business head, so he took responsibility for the technical phases. Caroline Whitney proceeded to help organize the future customers, at first largely in settlement house neighborhoods. Members of the settlements took on the job of persuading their local stores to handle Consumer–Farmer Co-op milk. It was a stimulating activity, providing many lively discussions at club meetings and on street corners.

During June, 1938, the first nine thousand quarts of Consumer– Farmer milk were sold in New York City, and in subsequent months the cooperative took a firm hold. Then in November, Caroline Whitney died in childbirth. The mourning was wide-spread and at her memorial services there was an outpouring of settlement members from all over the city. The late Dr. John Lovejoy Elliott, founder of Hudson Guild and head of the Ethical Culture Society, conducted the simple service. Asked to make a brief statement on behalf of the settlements, I said:

> I have tried to find words today not only for those of us who worked closely with Caroline Whitney, but for the mothers of the East Side and West Side, and in all the tenements of New York. They know that she fought for them—so that their children would be better nourished. . . .
>
> She had knowledge, brilliance, and imagination, but what counted most was her caring. She cared so much it made everything else possible. Such an ardent spirit is rare, and very precious. There is comradeship among those who work together that matters very deeply. We know that no one can replace you, Caroline—but we promise to close ranks and carry on.

As I spoke I was able to look out over the audience and see the familiar faces of members of the mothers' clubs—from East Harlem, the West Side, the Lower East Side, from Brooklyn— who made up the bulk of the audience. They were solemn, and rapt. They were there to show their gratitude, because they sensed that Caroline Whitney had possibly sacrificed her young life through overexertion on their behalf.

Her husband spoke to me afterward. "It is not news to you," he said, "that during this past year I have tried again and again to keep Caroline from giving so much time and using up so much of her energy in this work. I did not succeed. When I saw these women pouring in here today, and looked at their faces as you spoke, I saw why she felt that she *had* to do it, that she could not stop. This has helped me."

We very fortunately succeeded in persuading Meyer Parodneck to become executive director of our tiny Consumer–Farmer Milk Cooperative. It has been through his extraordinarily brilliant and incisive mind, his knowledge of the milk business and of law, and above all his untiring devotion and service to a cause he believed in so strongly, that the Consumer–Farmer Milk Cooperative has given the consumer a voice in the milk business since that time.

A small by-product of my service on the State Milk Advisory Committee turned out to be what at first were called "8¢ milk stations." At one point when I was discussing poverty and babies and milk, an official of one company said placatingly, "All right, we will sell milk at 8 cents to your people. You can set up milk stations and we will sell at cost." It didn't take long for some of the settlements and a church to find room for a milk station where milk was delivered early in the morning, off the milk truck, and people stood in line to get it. And they have been standing in line to get it to the present day; not now, of course, at 8 cents, but 2 cents below the store price. The milk companies which made the first offer and got us going finally gave up the job, but fortunately, by that time, the Consumer–Farmer Milk Co-op was able to service the milk stations and has carried on with them ever since. But, and this is a sad part of the story, it soon became a part of the city-wide Teamsters Union contract that we could not expand the number of our milk stations. In this way, the union was serving the milk companies' ends. We did everything we knew how to expand this service in our poorest areas, but unsuccessfully. It was not until December, 1967, when the entire milk industry, including dealers and unions, were under indictment by the New York County Grand Jury, that the restrictions against expanding the number of milk stations were removed.

This is not the whole story of the Consumer–Farmer Milk Cooperative—only a very small part of its beginnings. The whole story would be as lurid in some of its parts as a gangster novel, including hijacking of one of our first trucks by competitors, and a constant struggle with the authorities to maintain and to extend our license to operate. It proved to be an extraordinarily useful education-action program for many low-income groups. As they worked to protect their interests as milk consumers, they became aware of their stake as consumers, in a broader sense that covered the whole market basket, and including installment buying for their homes.

During the early years of our milk struggle, many new allies came to join us, numbers of whom were concerned with consumer problems other than milk.

Grading of meat landed in our laps in New York City in 1937 and 1938 through the zeal of Mrs. Frances Foley Gannon of the New York City Department of Markets. Standards had been developed by the U.S. Department of Agriculture for the grading of a number of meats and meat products, but their use was optional. Packers preferred to use their own glowingly descriptive titles on the meat that reached the housewife. Responding to widespread complaints, the city's Department of Markets proposed that the City Council require that all meat products coming into New York City be graded by federal standards. Meat crossing state lines had to be federally inspected for health and sanitation reasons, so why not require that it be graded at the same time?

There had been much complaining among our Henry Street mothers, at their club meetings, about the difficulty of identifying meat quality and paying high prices for poor meat. "I don't mind buying a tough piece of meat if it's the right price," one woman said. "I know how to cook it so it's good, but it makes me mad if I get charged for tender meat."

The United Neighborhood Houses' Consumer Committee, under the chairmanship of Mildred Gutwillig, appealed to the settlements for aid on a local meat-grading bill. Armed with descriptive literature from the Consumers Counsel office in Washington, the Consumer Committee spread the word through the mothers' clubs of all the settlements. Of course, compulsory meat grading was a popular issue among the women, for meat hits the family pocketbook hard. As was to be expected, the butchers' and packers' associations were dead set against it. When public hearings were held before the City Council, the chamber was filled with experts for the meat interests, armed with their descriptive charts and arguments: grading would skyrocket the price of meat; more government interference; corrupt bureaucracies would spring up; housewives could trust their butchers; and so on. At one such hearing in the council chamber, the main floor was jammed to overflowing by the meat industry representatives. When the housewives appeared they were shunted up to the gallery where they were very inconspicuous. An articulate spokesman for the industry denounced the grading bill at great length and wound up by declaiming dramatically, "The Department of Markets insists that our housewives want this costly, pernicious grading. As I look over this assembly I see no housewives! If they wanted this ordinance they would be here. Where are all these women who are so set on meat grading?" The gallery sprang to life. "Here we are!" came as one voice from above. The assemblage burst into laughter, led by the councilmen and by the ardent opponent of grading himself. "Guess that's one on me," he murmured.

Meat grading was not understood by some members of the council itself; it was even argued that "hanging" meat for unspecified periods was all that was needed to make it edible. Certain council members kept putting this idea to all the witnesses favoring the bill. Mrs. Gannon answered that "the quality is *in* the meat." Then one of the housewife witnesses gave this answer: "You can hang a rock for as long as you like but you'll never be able to eat it!" "Maybe you'd like to hang some of us," said another councilman gently, after the laughs had subsided. "Oh, no," said the woman, "then you wouldn't be able to vote for the bill!"

By this time some of the large middle-class women's organizations, who had taken sporadic action on consumer problems, had become aware of the fact that the settlements had a responsive grass-roots constituency—that they represented large numbers of low-income consumers for whom protection was needed, and that despite time-consuming tedium their members and neighbors could be relied on to turn out in large numbers at public hearings and meetings where it was highly important that the consumer interest be shown.

The interest of these organizations in consumer affairs had been stimulated by the work of the Consumers Advisory Board to the NRA under Mary Rumsey, particularly by Professor Paul Douglas' plans—mostly unrealized—to support county consumer organizations from 1933 to 1935. When the NRA was declared unconstitutional, these plans generally collapsed. But from then on, organizational concern with consumer problems was stimulated by the new Consumers Counsel to the U.S. Department of Agriculture, Donald G. Montgomery, who held that post from 1935 until the outbreak of World War II.

Partly, at least, under his influence, late in 1936 the newly appointed chairman of the Consumer Section of the New York City League of Women Voters brought together representatives from a number of organizations, including the settlements with their "grass-roots" clubs, mainly to strengthen support for the principle of consumer representation in government at federal, state, and local levels. The immediate occasion for this development was the appointment by President Roosevelt of George Berry as Coordinator for Industrial Cooperation following the demise of NRA and with it, the Business, Labor, and Consumer Advisory Boards.

A broad range of local branches of national organizations responded, in addition to the League of Women Voters: American Association of University Women, General Federation of Women's Clubs, and the Consumers' League. Consumers Union was also represented, and at the city-wide level, the United Neighborhood Houses. There was also a sprinkling of consumer cooperatives. With such disparate groups there was inevitably much tugging and pulling, but early in March, 1937, at a two-day session in the then Hotel Pennsylvania, a "Consumers Emergency Council" was formed with a common program of action so that federal, state, and local agencies would have a recognized, broad-based organization to turn to when questions relating to consumer representation and other consumer problems arose. As one of the advertising media put it, in writing up the conference, "And the silent, curious handful of men, who'd come from the ranks of business to watch, knew that was news."

I became chairman of this organization-in-process, a role that, I was amused to find, led to my being designated as "Consumers' Helen Hall" on the cover of a leading advertising monthly, *Tide*, with a warning signal to the advertising fraternity enclosed.

I had long ago decided that a strong, widespread consumer movement was essential to get the government protection necessary to improve the living standards of low-income families. I had also come to feel that activities around consumer issues were basic and stimulating to all kinds of neighborhood groups. There was infinite variety in the subject matter, most of which related directly to the problems the housewife faced each day.

As I look back over these preliminary phases of our consumer work at Henry Street, I know that cooperative buying, from milk to sneakers, from the Housewives Milk League to our Henry Street Credit Union and our Home Planning Workshops, have proved stimulating and fun, while they have added some understanding and some dignity to the job of the low-income housewife. Local leadership sprang up as women became aware that they could play some part in changing their conditions of life.

However, the Consumers Emergency Council had been organized on a temporary basis. It soon became evident that continuing consumer representation on a national as well as a local level was needed. Closer contacts were being established with consumer leaders in Washington and with officials of federal regulatory agencies that affected the consumer interest. Responses to our press releases were coming in from all over the country. Wider interest had developed in working for a federal Department of the Consumer, to be on a par with the departments representing Labor, Commerce, and Agriculture. Bills had been introduced in Congress to implement such a department and a number of congressmen were interested. Also, efforts were being made by certain chainstore organizations to form phony "consumer groups" to offset an attack on chainstore expansion by competitive interests. This attack included legislative efforts to impose a special tax on the "chains."

We therefore reshaped the structure of the New York Consumers Emergency Council into the Consumers National Federation, with the following Executive Committee:

> Helen Hall, chairman, president of National Federation of Settlements; administrator of Henry Street Settlement, New York City.
>
> Robert Lynd, vice-chairman, professor of Sociology at Columbia University; author of *Middletown* and *Middletown in Transition*.
>
> Benson T. Landis, treasurer; author of consumer and cooperative pamphlets.
>
> Persia Campbell, executive secretary; economist; author of *American Agricultural Policy*.

Ruth W. Ayres, economist; former Consumer Advisor with Consumers Advisory Board, NHA; New York director, National Survey of Consumer Purchases.

R. N. Benjamin, secretary, Pennsylvania Farm Bureau Federation.

Paul Douglas, professor of Economics, University of Chicago.

Andree Emery, chairman, Consumer Section, New York League of Women Voters.

Herbert E. Evans, vice-president, Consumer Distribution Corporation.

Mildred Gutwillig, director, Recreation Rooms and Settlement, New York City.

Susan Jenkins Brown, field secretary of Consumers' Union of United States, Inc.

Felice Louria, executive secretary, New York Consumers League.

Fanny Moskin, temporary chairman, Council of Women's Auxiliaries of Women's Trade Union League.

Rolf Nugent, research economist, authority on consumer credit.

Meyer Parodneck, president of Consumer–Farmer Milk Cooperative.

Mary Simkhovitch, director of Greenwich House Settlement and Member of the New York City Housing Authority.

Anna Lord Strauss, civic leader.

The objectives of the Consumers National Federation were to encourage consumer groups all over the country to organize and be articulate in their communities, and to join in a national effort to make themselves felt on important issues. These objectives were partially spelled out in the first issue of our bulletin, *The Consumer*, which appeared in June, 1937:

> The Consumers National Federation, an outgrowth of the Consumers Emergency Council, seeks to give coherence and focus to this consumer movement by providing centralized services of information and education. . . .
>
> . . . One of the main weaknesses of the consumer movement in the past has been the want of leaders able to explain the processes of industry and finance to consumers and at the same time effectively to represent the consumer point of view in public councils. Plans have accordingly been made by the Consumers National Federation to set up a series of expert committees on a nation-wide basis to follow and interpret developments in different fields of interest to the consumer—cost of living, price and production policies, standards, housing, cooperatives. . . .

> The Federation will also . . . encourage the formation of legitimate consumer groups and . . . work out criteria by which bona fide consumer organizations can be identified. The latter function becomes the more important now that various business interests are working actively, openly or behind the scenes, to set up "captive" consumer groups. Professor Robert Lynd, vice-chairman of the Federation, drew attention to this development in a recent article in *The New York Sunday Times.* . . .

Toward the end of the thirties, the federation was confronted by a mean problem—reactionary elements in the community that saw communist influence in every progressive undertaking. These elements were led by Congressman Dies, chairman of the House Un-American Activities Committee. The Dies Committee first focused its attention mainly on segments of organized labor, on supporters of the Spanish Loyalists, and on demonstrations of the unemployed. But in December of 1938 Congressman Dies took an unprecedented action. Sitting as a committee of one, without summoning other committee members, he received a report on the consumer movement from his recently appointed chief investigator and, without submitting it to his other committee members, released it to the press. Of course it made national headlines. Individuals connected with Consumers Union, the Milk Consumers Protective Committee, and even the Consumers National Federation were singled out for attack. A quote from a letter written to Dies by Morris Ernst, as counsel for the Consumers National Federation, gives a sense of our indignation at the time:

> These charges, and the other multifarious charges made against the Federation in the Matthews report, are false and do not have a shred of credible evidence to support them. What is to me, however, utterly shocking and revolting, is that you, a Congressman professing to believe in the American system of fair play, should have permitted these charges to be broadcast publicly without affording the Federation any hearing whatever. Such a tactic seems to me indecent no matter who is affected by it; it is particularly so when it affects men and women of the calibre of those who sponsor the Consumers National Federation.
>
> It is requested that this letter of protest be added to the record of the Committee and printed as part thereof. Certainly this is

the least you can do to repair the injury you have wilfully inflicted on the Consumers National Federation.

Very truly yours,

Morris L. Ernst,

for Consumers National Federation

Meanwhile, Congressman Jerry Vorhees of California, at that
time a member of the Dies Committee, issued a release stating
that the Consumer Report was not an official Dies Committee
release, that he had never seen the report nor been summoned
to a meeting to consider it. Mr. Vorhees had been a consumer
cooperator of long standing, and was, later on, head of the
Cooperative League of the U.S.A. He was indignant at the
implications in the Dies report that advocacy of the principles
of consumer cooperation meant advocacy of the political and
economic structure of the U.S.S.R.

Following the Dies attack, *The New York Times* ran a favorable article on the Consumers National Federation, giving a
description of its work and listing members of the board.

I remember being pretty mad at the thought that the Consumers National Federation, which had been such a struggle to
start and to support, might in any way be hurt by this un-
founded attack. It was hard enough, and still is, to raise money
for consumer work of any kind without this kind of slander
which was bound to worry some people. I remember Paul
Kellogg's pointing out the inevitability of conflicts of interest as
humanity struggles to improve its lot—but I didn't feel very
philosophical at the moment.

Meanwhile the federation, with office space and limited clerical help provided by the Henry Street Settlement, had, through
Persia Campbell, its volunteer executive secretary, and its competent volunteer committees, been carrying forward an impressive
program. One of the highlights had been the organization of a
delegation to Washington in an effort to mobilize national
opinion on particular consumer problems through two days of
conferences and an appointment with President Roosevelt.

The list of delegates was a Who's Who of leaders, not only
in the consumer movement, but of forward-looking trade union
representatives, and members of the National Parents Association, the American Association of University Women, the National Council of Jewish Women, the National Urban League,

and the Congregational Christian Women. During our two days in Washington we lunched with twenty administrative officials of the government; met with leaders of both the American Federation of Labor and the Congress of Industrial Organizations; with the progressive bloc of congressmen who had recently presented their legislative program to the President; and with senators LaFollette, Wagner, Thomas, Hill, and Schwellenbach. On the second day, while a committee of five of us conferred with the President with respect to a consumer department in the federal government, other delegates visited the large women's and other socially oriented organizations with headquarters in Washington.

In January, 1940, after World War II broke out in Europe, a conference was arranged with Mrs. Roosevelt at the White House to solicit her continuing support for consumer protective action. A press release from the federation summarized this conference:

> Leaders of consumer organizations with several million members throughout the nation were guests of Mrs. Franklin D. Roosevelt at the White House this afternoon when they discussed with her the need for expanding and coordinating the government's services for consumers, and plans for a conference, to be called later, on Government and the Consumer.

Among its other activities the federation had set up a pioneering "Prices and Products" service reported in a series of special fortnightly bulletins, intended to alert consumers to price trends for selected consumer products. This service was continued until 1940 when Harriet Elliott, Consumer Commissioner of the Defense Advisory Commission, undertook a somewhat similar activity.

The federation, always short of funds, and dependent on competent volunteers, became a war casualty as the demands of war absorbed the energies of its volunteer personnel; many of them became involved in the War Price Control and Rationing programs. Persia Campbell, our very expert volunteer executive secretary, who had carried the real weight of organizing and developing the National Consumers Federation and without whom it would have been impossible, became head of the Consumer Program of New York City's Civilian Defense Operation.

XXXVI

Consumers in World War II —
Price Control and Rationing

Many of us had urged price control and rationing programs before our entry into World War II on December 7, 1941, and continued to press for them until they were instituted.

In New York, as the Office of Price Administration organized its Consumer Division, with neighborhood women on local price and rationing committees, the United Neighborhood Houses' Consumer Committee went into action, channeling OPA literature through the adult divisions of all the settlements and undertaking various OPA related programs. Mildred Gutwillig, chairman of the committee, who had put her drive and organizing ability into the cause of the consumers, became chairman of a New York City Consumer Council, which worked outside the OPA to be free to criticize and press for its own policies as well as to cooperate. Henry Street Settlement played an active role in this over-all program under the experienced leadership of Susan Jenkins Brown, who at the time was in charge of our community studies.

By the time I returned from the South Pacific early in 1943, the OPA, under Chester Bowles, had appointed a Consumer Relations Adviser to his staff and created a National Consumer Advisory Board, of which I became vice-chairman. Consumer information with respect to the importance of price control and rationing was being distributed by the OPA through its local offices and various agencies, including the schools. But there was much resistance from certain interests to many of the OPA's policies and their strict enforcement. The legislation providing for price control and rationing was constantly under congressional fire.

Finally, as the war drew to a close, the pressure to remove controls became politically irresistible, despite efforts by consumer-oriented groups to maintain them.

On March 9, 1945, I testified before the U.S. Senate Banking and Currency Committee in support of the continuation and strengthening of the Price Stabilization Act. I spoke for the National Federation of Settlements and the New York City Consumer Council, and used material from a study Henry Street had made of "wartime savings."

Statisticians, I noted, had presented evidence to the committee proving the country-wide need of continued controls. I spoke "from the standpoint of close-in living in industrial neighborhoods—my own on the Lower East Side of New York—and in the sixty-two cities where the 178 settlements of the National Federation of Settlements carry on their work."

But we needed not only the renewal of the Price Control Act but a much greater appropriation for its enforcement. The New York City Consumers Council, which is made up of seventy-two widely different groups, has asked me to speak especially for them today in urging that the OPA be given a higher appropriation for enforcement at the consumer level. We have a Price Control Act, but the appropriation cannot begin to do the job at any one of the levels of control. . . .

The black market in meat, to give but one example, has been so difficult to handle that a group of our Consumer Council women in the Bronx have organized a "Come and shop with us" tour, shopping en masse in a determined effort to secure meat at ceiling prices. Another group has had deputies from the Department of Markets stand all day in neighborhood stores to enforce sales at ceiling prices because the OPA is not granted sufficient funds to have enough inspectors of their own. Another group is discussing starting a cooperative store for meat and groceries in the neighborhood to force prices in nearby stores back to ceilings. . . .

I had also been asked to stress to the committee the problem of quality deterioration.

> When it starts in materials, it cannot always be detected by consumers. But nowadays it has reached the stage in cloth where you can almost see it in the dark. We need quality standards and grading all along the line. Quality deterioration is a direct outcome of restrictions passed by Congress which prevent the OPA from giving consumers proper safeguards in the grading of goods. This ought to be remedied this year. It is one of the sorest points in the whole picture. . . .
>
> War is so terrible that any domestic gain seems small when stacked up against the tears and hard-won victories. But here on the home front there has been a great understanding by many of the women of the country of their responsibilities as buyers and of how their spending affects the standard of living. Long since, they had to transmute much of the pioneering women's household enterprise into ability to bargain well in the modern marketplace.
>
> But they have only gradually become aware of how helpless they are as individuals, and what kinds of protection they should have at their elbows. That is what they are asking you to supply them, in an Office of Price Administration which is implemented with powers of grading that make price ceilings mean what they say and an appropriation of sufficient funds to enforce these ceilings.

When the war ended, the Office of Price Administration and its Consumer Advisory Board were gradually closed down. Piece by piece, controls came to an end; though rent control survived in New York City, where it still survives on a limited scale under municipal control and great duress.

Through membership on the national, regional, and local OPA Consumer Advisory boards and committees, many people had become convinced of the need for continuing consumer organization. Members of the OPA National Consumer Advisory Board and others tried to hold an informal group together. On November 14, 1945, spokesmen for fifteen national organizations appeared before the House Labor Committee as a Committee for the Protection of the Consumer, on the invitation of Congresswoman Chase Going Woodhouse, Democrat of Connecticut.

Mrs. Woodhouse later presented the testimony of our new Consumer Committee to the House of Representatives.

Appearing before the House Labor Committee as a spokesman for the National Federation of Settlements, I had summarized reports coming into the settlement houses throughout the country on the concerns of low-income families and returning veterans with respect to postwar conditions. My testimony follows:

> After VE Day, the fear of unemployment began to creep back into the conversation. Settlement leaders from many parts of the country—meeting last weekend at Niagara Falls—reported the change this winter was bringing. Their neighbors feel deep fear of both unemployment and inflation. They have just seen the cost of butter go up 6½ ¢ with the removal of the butter subsidies. They have already seen the buying up of small homes by real estate people, to sell at inflationary prices. They are wondering where their sons are going to live, and whether ceilings on building materials will hold down the cost of the necessary new houses. They are wondering whether their representatives in Congress will see that a law is passed putting a ceiling on the sale price of new and old houses; whether the OPA will be able to keep the rent ceilings.
>
> In other words, they are wondering whether real estate interests are stronger than the interests of the soldiers who are just coming home.
>
> There is much confusion among working people and the newly returned veterans and their families, but it is beginning to crystallize into a feeling that while they seem to have won a war in Europe and the Pacific, they are certainly losing one in Washington. The *Full Employment Bill* is held in committee. The *Unemployment Insurance Bill* is held in committee. The *Wagner Health Bill* is held in committee. The *Wagner–Ellender Housing Bill* has had no hearing yet. There is no bill as yet to protect the ceiling on new and old houses. Subsidies are being removed with an inevitable rise in food costs. Unemployment is increasing and pay envelopes are thinner. Families are doubling up to make room for a soldier son and his new wife. This is the way it looks to the people in hundreds of industrial neighborhoods in the United States, and it does not seem to add up to what they fought for.

On March 22, 1946, an "Anti-Inflation Rally" was held in New York City, at which I had been asked by a number of the national organizations to speak for them in urging retention of price controls. I said, in part:

> . . . There would be less danger of inflation now if all the women of America who plan and buy for their homes were conscious of their responsibility to do something in this crisis. . . .
> . . . We women buyers need to realize that not only have we a stake in protecting our living standards when we go to market; but we have one when we go to the ballot box. And we don't need to wait for Election Day but can let our representatives at Washington know right now how we feel about their responsibility in keeping household costs down and in preventing inflation.
> . . . The presidents of twenty-nine national women's organizations have issued a call to action which asks for the immediate extension of the Price Control Act.

To illustrate for the reader how widespread the interest was, the American Association of University Women, the National Council of Catholic Women, the National Council of Negro Women, and the National Council of Jewish Women were some that took part in the rally.

After the war consumer leaders, particularly those who had been members of the OPA Consumer Advisory Board, felt the time had come to try again to establish another national consumer organization. We felt that so much interest had been engendered through price control activities of various kinds, with consumer advisory committees all over the country, that it would be a shame not to use some of this increased awareness to again get consumers together nationally and at once. So, on February 18, 1947, following the last formal session of the OPA National Consumer Advisory Board, an organizational meeting was held in Washington to establish what was to be called the National Association of Consumers. Members of the organizing committee included: Mary Dublin Keyserling, who at one time had been executive director of the National Consumers League; Persia Campbell, then in the Department of Economics at Queens College; Ella Baker, of the National Association for the Advancement of Colored People; Caroline Ware, of the National

Association of University Women; Colston Warne, of Consumers Union; Esther Cole Franklin, who had served as Consumer Relations Adviser with the OPA; Clara Hardin, of the National Board of the YWCA; and former Congresswoman Chase Going Woodhouse. Representatives of the St. Louis Consumer Federation and of the Cincinnati Consumer Conference were on the executive board.

We also assembled an advisory council, including Leon Henderson, the first OPA administrator; Professor Hartley Cross, an officer of the Eastern Cooperative Wholesale; and Donald Montgomery, former Consumer Counsel with the U.S. Department of Agriculture, and now Consumer Counsel to the United Auto Workers Union. And, once more, I became chairman of a new consumer organization which had to face the difficult problem of fund-raising for the unpopular job among foundations and such sources of support of consumer protection. Chase Going Woodhouse accepted the position of executive vice-president, with headquarters in Washington.

During the following summer and fall, I was especially involved with other responsibilities, having accepted an invitation to serve as consumer representative on the U.S. delegation to the United Nations Food and Agriculture Organization's Conference in Geneva.

On my return home I found that the hoped-for financing for the National Association of Consumers (NAC) had not been forthcoming. So we decided in October, 1947, that the headquarters should be moved to the Henry Street Settlement, partly to conserve funds so that we could afford at least one professional executive staff member. Clifford W. Patton was engaged as NAC's executive secretary in December, 1947, and carried on ably and devotedly until June, 1949, when shortage of funds again forced a reorganization.

In April, 1947, the NAC had launched its monthly bulletin, *Consumers on the March*, which was to be the main vehicle for its information-education service to group and individual members for a number of years, supplemented by special releases. A major legislative issue in the postwar period related to housing, including the preservation and strengthening of rent control and the provision of new housing for low-income families, together with slum clearance.

The NAC was also much concerned with high postwar prices and tried various techniques to exert pressure against them. For one thing, on June 10, 1947, it cooperated with the New York City Consumer Council in a public "trial"—"The People of the State of New York against High Prices"—before the Court of Public Opinion of the City of New York, with the support of Mayor William O'Dwyer. Among the association's other activities were training courses in consumer problems, led by Persia Campbell, which aimed at developing leadership for the consumer movement. Certain research projects were also undertaken as a basis for legislative and other programs.

After Clifford Patton left the NAC as executive director, his assistant, Mrs. Rose Kerber, carried on the work of the office. A three-member editorial board, consisting of Felice Louria of the Henry Street staff; Persia Campbell, again volunteering her time and skill to the consumer cause; and Sidney Margolius, a well-known reporter and writer on consumer affairs, continued publication of *Consumers on the March*. More responsibility for program had to be taken by members of our volunteer board in view of our limited financial resources, but the dislocations and pressures caused by the Korean War encroached heavily on time and energy.

I appeared at a number of congressional hearings during this period on behalf of the NAC and the National Federation of Settlements jointly, and the NAC participated in other ways in national programs to bring to Congress the consumer's viewpoint.

We were struggling to keep our national consumers organization going, but, sadly enough, the last issue of *Consumers on the March* appeared in July, 1954. Organization and individual membership dues were still being paid but it did not seem possible to raise enough funds to keep the organization viable.

Consumers Union made some contributions for educational programs, and Henry Street Settlement, in addition to providing space and staff help, arranged benefits through its Drama and Music Departments. Foundations were unwilling to give support, since the NAC had been set up as an action organization and was not tax exempt. Toward the end of 1954, the NAC board began to consider a basic change in the organization, confining its scope to consumer education and guidance, on a tax-exempt basis. Colston Warne, president of Consumers Union, offered to provide a headquarters office for NAC at Amherst. He also enlisted the interest of William Haller, Jr., of the Amherst Economics Faculty, to take over the job of executive secretary on a volunteer basis. The transfer was made in March, 1955. *Consumer News* began to appear in May, 1955, but it was not possible to keep it going for long. Even the change to tax-free status had not succeeded in bringing foundation or other substantial support. "Indigenous" people were not as popular in those days with foundations as they later became, and consumer education among neighborhood groups is costly.

However, the basis for a consumer movement had already been laid and helped to form a foundation for the new experiments in consumer representation in government.

The National Association of Consumers had consistently given such support as we could to the principle (and practice) of consumer representation at all levels of government. So we were gratified when, in July, 1951, Senator Guy M. Gillette, Democrat of Iowa, backed by a bipartisan group of senators, introduced Senate Resolution #169 which provided for a Committee on Consumer Interests as part of the Senate's committee structure. Since this seemed an important step forward, I made a statement when the resolution came before the Subcommittee on Rules of the Senate Rules and Administration Committee, on April 18, 1952.

In the first place, I urged that the Consumer Committee—if it was to function in the economy to protect the ultimate buyer—be given the status of a separate committee, like the Small Business Committee. "I do not need to point out," I said, "that there are a lot more consumers than there are small businessmen."

Answering the oft-repeated argument against giving the consumer special attention inasmuch as "we are all consumers," I conceded that we are, in the literal sense of consuming food and using goods. "However, we would have to admit that the meat packer, while he consumes meat, does not represent the consumer interest in meat when he comes before Congress.

"That literal use of the word," I continued,

> seems like an escape from economic reality. For our economy consists, broadly speaking, of producers, manufacturers, whole-

salers, retailers, labor, and the final buyer who is the official consumer, so to speak. While the interests of these groups converge at some points, on the whole they often conflict, and it is at the points where they conflict that the consumer is most helpless.

Take a loaf of bread. The whole drama of production, manufacturing, distribution, and retailing lead up to the final moment when the housewife puts her money down on the counter for that loaf of bread. But she has had mighty little to say about the product she is buying, what goes into it, what is written on the label, its flavor, etc. She can read or listen to advertisements, but they are directed naturally to the business, not of protecting her family, which is her job, but of selling one kind of bread or another at the greatest profit. Her right to choose and her power of refusal have been said to serve her sufficiently, but both may be weakened by isolation and lack of knowledge and confused by advertising. It has taken us a long time to realize that the perhaps once most informed member of our economy—the mother or housewife—is now the most helpless. Her grandmother knew what went into a loaf of bread because she had kneaded it and baked it; what went into a can of beans because she put them up. Even how good the cloth was going to be, because she or some other member of the family may have woven it.

We have traveled a long way from this kind of economy, to one where a housewife is the end buyer, as she faces the shelves of a supermarket, or the intricacies of a department store. This is not a plea to turn backward, but to give more protection to the modern housewife, upon whose success in the marketplace must in no small measure depend her family's health and welfare.

I suggested to the committee that if they were to study the lists of people who spoke at the hearings before the Committee on Banking and Currency of the Senate on the Defense Production Act, they would see how overweighted they were with other interests. Speaking specifically, I said:

It would be hard, by any stretch of the imagination, to feel that the National Cotton Council represented the housekeeper who is interested in an inexpensive, good-wearing housedress. Or that the American Butter Institute, the Wholesale Grocers Association, the National Cheese Importers Association, the National Auto Dealers Association, the National Association of Manufacturers, the National Milk Producers Association, the

United States Chamber of Commerce, the Texas and South Eastern Cattle Raisers Association, the Cornbelt Livestock Feeders Association, the National Association of Food Chains, or the National Canners Association, each and all were representing consumers. Quite naturally they were speaking from their own standpoint and for the benefit of their own industries and they came equipped to do so.

Commenting on the fact that out of the eighty-eight persons testifying on the Defense Production Act Amendments of 1952, there were only five consumers representing national organizations who had had the hardihood to speak. "Business can afford to be represented by economists and experts whose job is to prepare and present their viewpoint where it will count for most. Voluntary organizations, on the other hand, are usually supported by small dues and gifts. And the economists whom they may be able to call upon most often give volunteer time to prepare testimony and present it."

Housewives, however deeply concerned, hesitate to appear where so much of the testimony must involve technical problems. They have, too, to get away from their family responsibilities and perhaps also a job, and have to consider the train fare and the cost of hotel accommodations. I continued:

> The best person to make a presentation for consumers may live in the South or St. Louis or further west, but it is expensive to bring anyone from a distance. Then, too, if we were to do a thoroughgoing job and answer many of the arguments presented by industry, consumers would need an expert from each field to do it well.
>
> It has certainly made the average housewife uneasy to see by the papers that the "Meat Lobby," or the "Real Estate Lobby," or some other powerful economic group is in Washington, and know at the same time that nowhere are there groups as powerful and as persuasive representing their interests and the interests of their families. It has been disheartening to have coffee prices race upward for no understandable reason; to have sugar jump at the mention of war; and it has been dismaying to face daily, shelves of rising prices. A Consumer Interest Committee in the Senate would go far to give the housekeepers of America a sense that their particular interests are being studied, interpreted and protected.

Resolution #169 was reported out by the Senate Rules Committee, but too late for action in the 82nd Congress. It was introduced in the next Congress as Senate Resolution #38 by Senator Gillette and his backers on January 16, 1953. Meanwhile, Jacob Javits, then a member of the House of Representatives, had introduced concurrent Resolution #32 in the House, calling for a joint Congressional Committee on Consumers, to consist of seven representatives and seven senators. However, following the Republican victory at the polls in November, 1952, the climate of opinion did not favor any significant action for consumer protection at the national level for a number of years.

In New York State, at least, consumers fared better. Averell Harriman, during his campaign for governor in the fall of 1954, promised to provide a means through which the consumer voice could be heard directly in the executive office of the governor if he were elected. This promise he carried out with the appointment of Persia Campbell, then vice-chairman of the National Association of Consumers, as his Consumer Counsel. This was an extraordinarily fortunate choice for the consumer, since Persia Campbell had not only the knowledge and skills needed for this job, but a creative mind along with unusual wisdom. She had not only contributed generously of her time and skill to the National Association of Consumers, but, as I have said, she had been the volunter executive secretary of the Consumers National Federation.

From 1955 to 1958 I was a member of the new Consumer Counsel's advisory committee, set up by Persia Campbell in the governor's office, and as such participated in the development of policy and functions of this innovative office. The functions can be briefly described as: advising the governor on all matters affecting the interests of people as consumers; developing and recommending consumer legislation and warning against legislation harmful to consumers; studying and reporting on consumer problems; appearing before governmental agencies in support of the consumer interest, and facilitating the appearance of consumers and consumer representatives. These four functions can be further condensed as: to advise, to recommend, to study, to appear. And the last of these is by no means the least. To those of us who had struggled so long to do these jobs ourselves on a voluntary basis, this New York State program sounded like heaven. The governor's generous appreciation of the work of his Consumer Counsel was expressed in a letter to me when I retired in June, 1967.

To the dismay of all consumer leaders, Governor Rockefeller abolished the Office of Consumer Counsel when he took over the State Administration in January, 1959, though he continued to support the Consumer Frauds Division in the New York State Department of Law, in which the State Attorney-General, Louis Lefkowitz, was personally involved, and on whose Consumer Advisory Committee I have served for many years.

As Governor Harriman pointed out, certain other states subsequently adopted the principle of consumer representation through various arrangements, and President Kennedy established it formally at the federal level.

In writing of the consumer movement from the thirties on, there is no question that the success of Consumer's Union has played an extremely important, if not the most important, part in the development of the movement as a whole. It has not only been successful in its central function of testing consumer goods for *Consumer Reports** with over a million and a half circulation, but Consumers Union has been able to bring technical skill, financial help, and visibility to the consumer movement in a way no other organization has succeeded in doing. It has had a profound effect, not only in helping the movement in this country, but abroad as well. The development and work of Consumers Union, under the vigorous and courageous leadership of Colston Warne is a story in itself—one of extraordinary interest, which he himself, I hope, will tell.

I cannot think of the consumer's movement at the present time without being grateful for what Ralph Nader has contributed to it in brilliance, drama, youth, and determination—and added to this his ability to inspire other young people to work for the same cause. It has given a real lift to the burdensome fight for consumer protection.

* 1970 circulation.

XXXVII

Low-Income Study
and the Poor Pay More

In 1950, through the offices of the National Social Welfare Assembly, a group of nine national welfare organizations cooperated in gathering human evidence supporting the report entitled *Low-Income Families and Economic Stability*, which was prepared in 1949–50 by the Subcommittee on Low-Income Families of the Congressional Joint Committee on the Economic Report. This Conference Group, of which I was chairman, was convened to bring the subcommittee's findings, which had shown that a fourth of all families in the U.S. were living on incomes of less than $2,000 a year, "down to earth—or rather to human clay." To do this, we collected case studies of one hundred families to present to Senator John Sparkman, chairman of the congressional subcommittee. From his committee it went to the Joint Committee on the Economic Report. We felt that one of the reasons our report might prove useful was that it illustrated, very graphically, what an economic waste, as well as human misery, poverty can be. The typical cases pointed to the forty million American families who wanted refrigerators, washing machines, all down the list of family conveniences, if only they had the money to buy them—and this was our point—if this potential buying power was released, how good for all concerned!

Senator Sparkman sent an editorial assistant to Henry Street to help prepare our report, and the report of our low-income study, entitled *Making Ends Meet on less than $2,000 a Year*, was used on many subsequent occasions to support our consumer programs. It illustrated in concrete terms the Joint Committee's Report which had referred to low-income families as an "economic frontier for American business," pointing out the size of the potential market if their income was increased by various amounts. The case studies also illustrated the struggles these families went through and the sort of things they went without. Of course the one hundred stories were by no means a statistical cross-section, but they did give a glimpse behind the anonymous curtain of statistics. Their significance lies in the fact that they fell into widespread patterns with which all of the social agencies were familiar.

I would like to quote directly here from my letter to Senator Sparkman, submitting this material:

> We have been glad to cooperate with the Sub-Committee in collecting these stories for we like to think that as wide an audience as possible shares with us our own intimate knowledge of how American families in this income group manage. Most of all we hope that more people will share our admiration for their sturdiness and courage and their determination to have their children get a better chance than they had. We hope, also, that the American bent to get on in life shows through these written stories as it does in the lives of the men, women and children as we know them.

There were things in common which stood out in these families that seemed worth emphasizing. First, there was an unmistakable upward trend in educational goals for today's children—as compared with those of their parents, who in turn had had more education than their grandparents. This upward trend held in very large part also for living standards, however inadequate they still were.

As the one hundred stories showed, the close-in hazards of individual households fall into recurring patterns of low wages, part-time work, accidents or illness, death of the breadwinner, handicaps in education and skills, bad housing. And, of course, along with economic handicaps go often serious personal inadequacies with which the community as well as the family must deal.

Approximately one-third of our urban family breadwinners had worked a full year before the date they were interviewed—without earning as much as $2,000. Among them were truck-drivers for small retail establishments, an ash collection contractor, hotel employees (not the waiters who receive the tips, but the men who work behind the scenes). There were also those who were doing unskilled tasks in factories, domestic servants, laundry workers, clerks in stores.

We had always been concerned with the problem of installment buying as it affected low-income families in our neighborhoods, but with the advent of public housing it became a major problem. The tenants in the new projects were sitting ducks for the "peddler" salesman, who, with the lure of "new furniture at nothing down," called on the new families side by side, floor by floor, all eager to have a pretty home—pretty to the children, a source of pride to the husband, pretty to the mother's own eyes, and with plenty of status thrown in. One of the most touching experiences I have known is being shown homes all fixed up, with the children trailing mama, watching her face and your face, to make sure you are really appreciating—and all the time in the back of your mind you are fretting, not about the aesthetics, but about the economics of installment buying.

William Kirk, the director of Union Settlement, and Mildred Zucker, director of James Welden Johnson Community Center, and I got together in July, 1959, to propose to the Fred L. Lavenburg Foundation a consumer education and action project for both the Upper and Lower East Side on which we would work jointly.

The Lavenburg Foundation had recently made a grant to Henry Street for an experiment in intensive organization of the tenants in La Guardia Houses, of which I have written. The foundation had also funded projects of a similar nature under the direction of William Kirk and Mildred Zucker.

William Kirk served as our chairman as we proceeded to outline our plans to Mr. Carl S. Stern, at that time vice-chairman of the foundation. We wanted to investigate the installment credit situation and to get the material with which to fight some of the devastating aspects of it. And we planned to follow the study with a program of education suitable for our neighborhood. We knew only too well that while families may have left bugs and rats behind them when they entered the housing project, they were often taking on new unmanageable debts of a corroding kind and furniture which went to pieces before they had finished paying for it.

The Lavenburg Foundation was already committed to an interest in new housing and how low-income families fitted into it, so they were interested. We also drew in Colston Warne, as Consumers Union had an education fund which fitted into our needs. Mrs. Henry H. Villard, president of the boards of the James Welden Johnson Community Center and of the Flagg Fund, was on our committee, and Mr. Stern asked Dr. Robert K. Merton of the Columbia University Department of Sociology to lend his interest and advice.

A grant from these three sources enabled us to start a study of installment buying in the housing developments in which the three settlements were working. Dr. Merton suggested that the Bureau of Applied Social Research of Columbia University do the research, with David Caplovitz as director of the study.

The staffs of the three settlements arranged meetings of the tenants in La Guardia and Vladeck Houses, opposite Henry Street, and uptown in Jefferson and Washington Houses, to enlist their participation in the study and to introduce David Caplovitz and his assistant, Louis Lieberman, to our consumers and their problems.

To my mind all such studies should have a double purpose: to get neighbors involved in the purposes of the study as well as to gather information that will help do battle! As we said in our introduction to the final report, "In this study our neighbors gave as much time as the interviewer needed to complete a complex, long, and intimate review of their personal economic circumstances."

Dr. Caplovitz writes of the methods employed:

> When the study was ready to move into the phase of the formal interviews, the families with whom the settlement had established relations were again called upon for assistance. In Washington Houses and in La Guardia Houses, the volunteers helped first by distributing copies of the project's newsletter that announced the study and, again, by introducing the interviewers to the families in the sample.

The report was finally published in 1963 by the Free Press of Glencoe under the title, *The Poor Pay More*; and a paperback edition was issued in 1967.

We feel that the report served its purpose well, reaching to President Johnson's desk by way of Esther Petersen, to public hearings, to universities, and perhaps in the use of the title, which, I am told, became a sort of slogan in Washington, "The Poor Pay More."

That the poor pay more is what it is all about. Again their standard of living lies between the two ends of the pay envelope —what goes in and what they get for what goes out. What goes in may be protected by labor organizations, but what goes out is still not protected by the government in the same way that commerce and labor and agriculture are from the federal government on down to city hall. Nor are our schools sufficiently directed toward making intelligent and conscientious spenders out of our children as they grow up. Until this is done, the consumer story will still be a very unfinished piece of business!

Last Word

There have been such swift changes and tragic events during the time I have been working on this book that the temptation to add a postscript, good or bad, to different chapters has been almost irresistible; but it seemed like writing another book, so the reader will have to get the latest word for himself. But as a last word, I do want to say that in spite of all the struggles I have lived through and the intense problems we face today, I am grateful to have had a share in the work I have written of; and I am also grateful indeed for the friends and neighbors and fellow workers with whom I have shared the satisfactions and disappointments, the pain and the fun all along the way. I have to admit that I envy the younger ones who, I know, will continue to help turn confrontations in neighborhoods, in the nation, and the world into communications; for my experience tells me that in spite of everything, it can be done.

Acknowledgments

So many people have helped me in the writing of this book that I almost gave up trying to make the acknowledgments, about which I feel so deeply. Many of my friends have listened to particular chapters. Many have supplied technical advice. Some have edited certain sections of the book. Persia Campbell, for instance, gave me a great deal of help with the consumer chapter and, in the process, took out the good things I had said about her so I had to do it over again! Susan Jenkins Brown brought her memory of the years she worked with us at Henry Street, as well as her editorial skill. It was a comfort to have Margaret Berry and Helen Harris see it from the Settlement standpoint. Simon Slavin, Director of the School of Social Work at Temple University, looked at it as a teacher of social work, as well as from his years on the lower east side as head of the Educational Alliance. Readers should be grateful to Dorothy Dunbar Bromley for her professional skills so often applied in condensing. Clarke Chambers, Paul Kellogg's biographer at the University of Minnesota, was very generous in reading it with his historian's eye. Leon and Mary Keyserling brought technical advice to bear, and much more, when it was needed. A number of my Board and many of the staff at Henry Street supplied memory, accuracy, and encouragement. I was not able to turn to the Teffertellers, as they were in Vietnam building a settlement and training center in Saigon. Bert Beck, however, helped with both criticism and encouragement. Mary Conway Kohler, Fonrose Condict, poet Margaret Ogden and Dorothy Buel all helped with understanding and enthusiasm. Juliette Clark, Ruth Scherer, Sylvia Berkowitz took part in putting together this manuscript and in keeping me going. As a matter of fact, any friend who visited me was pretty apt to have to listen to some portion of this book while in the making, and I want to thank all those patient listeners and sometimes critics.

Index

Aaron E. Norman Fund, 247
Abbott, Grace, 54
Abrons, Herbert, 62
Abrons, Louis, 62
Addams, Jane, 31 43, 173, 174
Addict in the Street (Larner),
    249–52
Advertising Council, Public
    Policy Committee of, 178
Advisory Council on Economic
    Security, 53
Advisory Council on Old Age In-
    surance, 55
Aldrich, Alexander, 248
Altmeyer, Arthur J., 57, 58
Amalgamated Clothing Workers
    Union, 237
American Chamber Orchestra,
    122
American Medical Association,
    55
Anderson, Christine, 26
Ardrey, Robert, 220
Armstrong, Barbara, 55
Arnstein, Leo, 208
Art classes, 125–38
Ascoli, Mrs. Max, 177
Askin, Mrs. Arnold, 87
Association of Neighborhood
    Workers, 20
Astor Foundation, 228
Ayres, Ruth W., 333

Babcock, Kenneth B., 295–96
Bacon, Betty, 210
Baehr, George, 285
Baker, Ella, 341
Balfior, Joe, 94
Bar, Alfred H., Jr., 127
Barley, Ann, 215
Barnes, Harry Elmer, 251
Batista, Fulgencio, 80
Beck, Bertram, *xv–xvi*, 77, 100,
    274
Beck, Deborah, *xvi*
Becker, Florence, 169
Becker, John 224
Beekman, William, 18
Behrend, Louise, 123
Benjamin, R. N., 333
Berger, Victor, 169
Berry, George, 54, 331
Berry, Margaret, 175
Billikopf, Jacob, 11
Bluestone, H. M., 297
Bonynge, Paul, Jr., 74
Bowles, Chester, 337
Brager, George, 273
Brandeis, Louis, 43
Brewster, Mary, 6, 61
British Women's Voluntary Serv-
    ices, 187
Brooks, Marshall, 115
Brophy, Alice, 243
Brown, Edward, 246

Brown, Howard J., 81, 246, 249, 289, 311, 312, 314–17
Brown, Susan Jenkins, 183, 187–88, 270, 333, 337
Brudney, Juliet, 163
Bruere, Henry, 149
Bustamente, Luz, 97–98
Buying clubs, 143
Bynanek, Everett, 18

Calise, William, 89, 123, 168, 248, 255, 265, 266
Calkins, Clinch, 42
Campbell, Persia, 332, 335, 341, 343, 347
Can We Renovate the Slums (study), 151–52
Caplovitz, David, 352
Carlton, Winslow, 85, 88, 140, 248, 271, 272, 285
    Gouverneur Hospital and, 291, 298, 300–1, 317
Carlton, Mrs. Winslow, 87
Carter, Elmer, 224
Case Studies of Unemployment (book), 43
Charity Organization Society, 19
Chicago Commons, 77, 174
Children, 100–7
    psychiatric treatment for, 110–13
Children Make Murals and Sculpture (Rosenberg), 128
Christodora House, 82
Citizens Committee for Children, 177–78, 275
Citizens of the World, 211–13
Civil Service Commission, 27
Civil Works Administration, 30
Clark, Bradford M., 313
Cloward, Richard, 272, 273
Cohen, Sadie, 150
Coit, Stanton, 19
Colbern, Fern, 176
Colvin, Woolf, 295

Commission on the Health Needs of the Nation, 285
Committee on Economic Security, 53, 55
Community Council, 223
Community studies, 144–57
Condict, Fonrose Wainwright, 22
Consumer-Farmer Milk Cooperative, 81, 326–28
Consumers
    problems of, 318–36
    during World War II, 337–48
Consumers National Federation, 333–34
Consumers Union, 324, 334, 343–44, 348
Consumers Emergency Council, 332
Cook, Charles, 128, 245–46
Cooper, Charles, 77, 174, 177
Copeland, Aaron, 122
Corlear's Hook Medical Association, 285, 291
Council Against Intolerance, 224
Council of Economic Advisors, 231
Cross, Hartley, 342
Crowley, Alice Lewisohn, *see* Lewisohn, Alice
Credit Union, 139–41
Cummings, Homer, 53
Currier, Audrey, 88
Currier, Stephen, 88, 272

Dana, Fairfield, 86, 247
Davis, Alwin, 267
Davis, Michael, 280
Davis, Preston, 243
Day care centers, 38, 177
Dewson, Mary, 54
Dies, Congressman, 334
Dingle, Congressman, 283
Dodge, Sally, 189
Dole, Vincent, 249
Dollars and Sense (play), 116
Dominic, Frankie, 229–30

Dorsey, Ora, 90
Douglas, Paul, 43, 52, 330, 333
Doyle, Frank, 303
Drunkenness, 103–7
Dublin, Louis, 89
Dudley, Edward H., 293, 313
DuMois, Ana, 267
Dutchman's Farm (play), 116
Dutchman's Farm (study), 15–21, 147
Dyer, Chouteau, 115

Educational Alliance, 151, 163, 239, 271, 296, 313
Egan, Robert, 120–24
Eisenhower, Dwight D., 54
Elderly Helping the Elderly project, 162–63
Elliott, Harriet, 336
Elliott, John Lovejoy, 31, 174, 327
Emery, Andree, 333
Engels, Lehman, 122
Ernst, Morris, 334
Ethical Culture Society, 31
European Recovery Program, 216
Evans, Herbert E., 333

Family Society, 11
Farbstein, Leonard, 280, 301–2
Federal Housing Act (1937), 148
Federation of East Side Clubs, 153–54
Felt, James, 88, 100, 297
Fernando, Anthony, 18
Fisher, Winifred, 208
Folsom, Marion B., 54
Fogarty, John, 272
Food and Agriculture Organization, 215
Foreign Policy Commission to Cuba, 80
Foster, Victoria, 98
Fox, Esther Tabor, 208

Fox, Mary, 5
Frankel, Milton, 162
Franklin, Esther Cole, 342
Frazer, Hannah More, 202
Frazier, Benjamin West, 14, 85
Frazier, Winifred, 326
Fred L. Lavenburg Foundation, 240, 351
Free, Montague, 189
Freedman, George, 294
Full Employment Bill (1945), 231
Fulton, Robert, 18
Fund-raising, 87, 88, 90
Furman, Sylvan, 270

Gallico, Paul W., 63–64
Gamble, Charles, 201–3
Gang warfare, 219–30
predelinquent gang project and, 226–30
Gannon, Frances Foley, 329, 330
Garfield, Goodwin, 229
Gaston, Herbert E., 210
Gebiner, Marie, 97
Gelber, "Chesty," 141
Gillette, Guy M., 344, 347
Ginsberg, Mitchell, 39, 240
Goetschius, George, 286
Gold, Leona, 98
Goldberg, Jack, 243
Goldberg, Joe, 141
Good Companions project, 98, 125, 161–66, 239
Gosselin, Grace, 30, 34
Gouverneur Hospital, 81, 115–16, 164, 246, 280, 288–317
Graham, Frank P., 53, 55, 56
Grand Street Settlement, 163, 271
Greater New York Fund, 85
Green, William, 54, 56
Greene, Felix, 140
Greenwich House, 77, 174, 324
Gross, Leon, 141

Group Health Insurance, 88, 247, 285, 291
Gulick, Luther H., 207
Guttman, Charles, 73, 75
Guttman, Renee, 203
Gutwillig, Mildred, 326, 329, 333, 337

Hainey, Jimmy, 159–60
Hainey, Katie, 159–60
Haldeman, J. C., 316
Halleck, Dede, 138
Haller, William, Jr., 344
Hamilton, Evelyn, 109
Hamilton-Madison House, 267, 271
Harbach, Franklin, 8, 139, 141, 222
Hardin, Clara, 342
Harlem School of the Arts, 123
Harlow, Arthur, 88, 247
Harriman, Averell, 347, 348
Harris, Helen M., 176–77, 229, 270, 321
Harrison, George M., 54
Head Start, 171, 172
Health and Hospital Planning Council of Southern New York, 294
Health care, 108–13, 277–87
    Gouverneur Hospital and, 288–317
Health Insurance Plan of Greater New York, 291, 295
Health Insurance with Medical Care—The British Experience (Orr), 281
Henderson, Leon, 342
Henry Street Dance School, 117
Henry Street Music School, 117, 120–24
Henry Street Playhouse, 114–19
Hentoff, Nat, 251
Hesley, Karl, 7
Heyman, David, 285
Hill, Senator, 336

Holm, Hanya, 117
Honest Ballot Association, 25
Home Planning Workshops, 98, 125, 162, 183, 185, 187–89
Hoover, Herbert, 23, 41
Hopkins, Harry L., 13, 53
Hospital Council of Greater New York, 289
House of Representatives
    Appropriations Subcommittee of, 272
    Labor Committee of, 339
    Un-American Activities Committee of, 334
    Ways and Means Committee of, 56
Housing, 15–21
    public, 181–89, 235–44
    studies on, 147–52
Houston Settlement Association, 222
Howe, Fred, 321
Hudson Guild, 31, 151, 174
Hull House, 81, 173
Hunter, Joel T., 54
Hunter, Kent, 42

Impelliteri, Vincent, 168, 292
International Conference of Social Work, 216
International Settlement Conference, 190
International Ladies Garment Workers Union, 237
Isaacs, Stanley M., 23–25, 324

Jack, Hulan E., 293, 297
Jacobson, Harry S., 269
James, Anna, 288
James, George, 313
Javits, Jacob, 251, 347
Jenkins, Susan, *see* Brown, Susan Jenkins
Jewish Family Service, 182
Jewish Social Service Society, 11

Job Corps, 81
Johnson, Lyndon Baines, 277, 287, 353
Joint Commission on Accreditation of Hospitals, 295–96
Jones, Alfred Winslow, 269, 270
Jones, E. Claude, 326
Jones, Nellie, 112
Jungle Mission (play), 215

Kahn, Alfred, 272
Kaplan Foundation, 271
Kaplan, Jacob M., 269, 270
Katz, Mike, 141
Kelley, Florence, 86, 174, 318
Kelley, Joseph P., 322
Kelley, Nicholas, 86, 322
Kellogg, Paul, *x*, 11–12, 23, 27, 31, 61, 78, 207, 215–16, 224, 226
  on Advisory Commission on Economic Security, 53, 55, 56
  consumers, problems and, 325
  Henry Street Playhouse and, 116
  in National Federation of Settlements, 40, 174
Kelly, Leota, 204
Kempel, Leslie, 208
Kennedy, Albert J., 77, 79, 174, 175, 256
Kennedy, John Fitzgerald, 273, 348
Kennedy, Robert F., 273
Kerber, Rose, 343
Keyserling, Leon, 89, 234
Keyserling, Mary Dublin, 89, 341
Kingsley House, 174, 177
Kirk, William, 351
Kogel, Marcus, 292
Korn, Richard, 123
Kroeger, William, 268
Kron, Maria, 98, 161–63, 165
Kurtagh, Emerich, 34, 153
Kurzman, Paul, 267

La Guardia, Fiorello, 13, 21, 22–28, 86
  consumer problems and, 319–22
  Day Care Centers supported by, 177
  public housing and, 181
LaFollette, Philip, 56
LaFollette, Robert, 42, 336
Landau, Jack, 141
Landis, Benson T., 332
Lane, Esther, 117, 119
Larner, Jeremy, 249, 250
Lash, Trude, 177
Lazrus, Jay Kay, 127
League for Industrial Democracy, 5
League of Mothers' Clubs, 326
League of Nations, 191, 192
Lee, Isabel, 203
Leeds, Morris E., 54
Lefkowitz, Louis, 348
Legal Aid Society, 98
Lehman, Herbert, 64–65, 89, 164, 227, 237
Lehman, Mrs. Herbert, 64, 89, 227
Levine, Rachel, 110, 111, 113
Levy, Mrs. David, 177
Levy, Harry, 149
Lewisohn, Alice, 62, 114–15
Lewisohn, Irene, 62, 114, 115
Lewisohn, Samuel, 54
Liberty League, 84
Lieberman, Louis, 352
Liese, Sylvia, 270
Lillian Wald Settlement, 113, 271
Lillienthal, Mrs. Joseph, 87
Lindeman, Eduard, 208
Lindsay, John, 314, 317
Lippman, Ralph, 62, 121
Living Newspaper, 115–16
Livingston, Martin, 267
Lloyd George, David, 281–82
Lockwood, Douglas, 126, 182, 186

Loftus, Sally, 81
Lord, Betty, 115
Louis, Murray, 117–18
Louria, Felice, 333, 343
Lovejoy, Owen, 31
Lower East Side Citizens Committee on World Organization, 209
Lower East Side Public Housing Conference, 148–49
Lower Eastside Economic Planning and Development Coalition, 268
Lower Eastside Neighborhoods Association (LENA), 81, 169, 237, 270–71
  concert series of, 122
  founding of, 254–68
  Gouverneur Hospital and, 291, 296–99, 304–5, 307–11, 315–17
  Narcotics Information Center of, 246–47
Low-Income Families and Economic Stability (study), 349
Lynd, Robert, 332, 334

MacArthur, Douglas, 201, 202, 204
McBride, Mary Margaret, 185
McCarthy, James E., 223, 227, 270, 271–73
McCarthy, Joseph, 89
McCloskey, Mark, 177
McCormick, Austin, 228
McDowell, John, 175
McGowan, Frank J., 291
MacIver, Robert M., 270
McLean, Basil, 294, 295
McNichols, Dorothy, 225
McNichols, Vera, 225
Madigan, Francis V., 243
Making Ends Meet on less than $2,000 a Year (study), 349

Maloff, Saul, 250
Margolius, Sidney, 343
Marill, Edward, 17
Markowitz, Jacob, 89, 168, 191, 248, 255, 298
Marshall, Agnes, 101
Marshall, James, 168, 210
Maynor, Dorothy, 122
Medicare, 287
Medicine Show (play), 115–16, 283
Mental Hygiene Clinic, 109–13, 169
Merton, Robert K., 352
Methadone, 249, 252
Milk Consumers Protection Committee, 323–26, 334
Mills, Vincent M., 58
Mobilization for Youth, *xvi*, 62, 81, 247, 268, 317
  community studies by, 145
  founding of, 269–76
  legal services of, 98
  LENA and, 265
  planning of, 169, 223
  survey of television watching by, 221
Moley, Raymond, 54
Montgomery, Donald G., 331, 342
Morgenthau, Henry, Jr., 53
Morgenthau, Rita Wallach, 8, 114, 115
Morris, Newbold, 86, 126, 266
Morrissey, Elizabeth, 54
Moses, Robert, 24
Moskin, Fanny, 333
Moskovitz, Benamin, 128, 137
Motley, Constance Baker, 293
Mural on Our Street (film), 128, 138
Murray, Clyde, 77
Murray, Senator, 283
Murrow, Mrs. Edward, 87
Musicians union, 266
Myers, Kilmer, 255, 265, 269

Narcotics abuse, 245–53
National Association of Consumers, 210, 342–44
National Association of Manufacturers, 52
National Child Labor Committee, 31
National Conference of Social Work, 43
National Consumers League, 85, 318
National Federation of Settlements, 43, 56, 78–79, 154, 173–176, 207, 210, 215, 231, 233
health care and, 278, 280, 282, 283, 285, 286
study of unemployment by, 145
Unemployment Committee of, 40
National Institute for Mental Health, 169, 271–72
National Resources Planning Board, 207
National Youth Administration, 177, 186
Neighborhood disruption, 219–25
Neighborhood Guild, 19
Neighborhood Playhouse, The (Crowley), 115
Neighborhood Playhouse School of Theater, 115
Neuberger, Roy, 127–28
New Deal, 29–39
New York Association for Improving the Condition of the Poor, 18
New York Consumers League, 318
New York Fund for Children, 228
Nikolais, Alwin, 117–19
Nordlin, George H., 54
North East Neighborhood Association, 267
Nugent, Rolf, 333

O'Dwyer, William, 292, 343
O'Malley, Nora, 81
Ohl, Henry, Jr., 54
Ohlin, Lloyd, 272, 273
Old peoples' programs, 158–66
Ortoff, Murray, 240
Orr, Douglass W., 280–82, 286
Orr, Jean Walker, 280

Pandit, Madame, 214–15
Paperno, Lloyd, 315
Parodneck, Meyer, 324, 326, 328, 333
Patton, Clifford W., 342, 343
Peck, Lillie, 78–79, 175, 207, 208, 210
Perera, Mrs. Lionel, 123
Perkins, Frances, 53, 56
Personal service, 96–99
Peterfy, Karin, 183
Peterson, Esther, 353
Philadelphia Association of Settlements, 173
Pinchot, Gifford, 43
Pollack, Louis, 141
Pollack, Molly, 141
Polony, Elemer, 128
Poor Pay More, The (study), 353
Porter, Rose, 256, 270
Potter, Mrs. Robert, 87, 248
Predelinquent gang project, 226–30
President's Committee on Juvenile Delinquency, 273
Price control, 337–48
Pryce-Jones, Alan, 251
Psychiatric treatment, 110–13
Public relief, 10–14
Public schools, cooperation with, 167–72
Public Works and Economic Development Act (1969), 268

Quinn, Lillian, 38

Rabinowitz, Aaron, 237
Raddick, L. D., 224
Raemer, Jennie, 140
Rafterman, Nat, 141
Ramsey, Duane, 15
Rationing, 337–48
Recreation Rooms and Settlement, 181
Rector, Milton, 228
Red Cross, 191–206
Reid, William, 140, 243
Reiss, Winold, 224
Riessman, Frank, 273
Relocation, 235–36
Rice, John L., 319
Richmond, Mary, 10
Riis, Jacob, 19
Robbins, Ira, 128, 156, 243
Rockefeller, Nelson, 348
Rodriguez, Carmen, 161
Romig, David, 247
Rooms of Their Own (study), 152–54
Roosevelt, Eleanor, 33, 209, 210–11, 266, 336
Roosevelt, Franklin, 29, 30, 151, 210, 277, 319, 331, 335
Roosevelt, Theodore, 41, 173
Rosenberg, Lilli Ann Killen, 127, 128, 255
Rosenfield, Sidney, 291
Rothschild Foundation, 127
Rumsay, Mary, 319, 330
Russell, Walter, 20
Ryan, John A., 54

St. James Community Center School of the Arts, 123
Scandrett, Richard, 28
Schalk, Dorothy, 123
Scharrenberg, Paul, 54
Schierer, Lillie, 90
Schiff, Jacob, 61
Schlein, Stanley, 6
Schneeweiss, Samuel, 89, 141
Schoenfein, Benjamin, 86

Schoeni, Helen, 116, 204
Scholz, Robert, 122
Schroeder, Hyman, 8, 89
Schuyler, Bess, 126, 127
Schweinitz, Karl de, 11
Schwellenbach, Senator, 336
Senate, U.S.
    Banking and Currency Committee of, 231–32, 338, 345
    Rules and Administration Committee of, 344
Sergie, Lisa, 210
Shah, Romesh, 236
Shahn, Ben, 127
Sharkey-Brown-Isaacs Bill, 24
Sheps, Cecil, 316, 317
Sherwin, Bell, 54
"Short Story on the Long Waiting List, A" (Levine), 113
Silber, Matty, 90
Simkhovitch, Mary, 36, 77, 174, 324, 333
Slavin, Simon, 249, 296
Sloan, Berkeley, 199
Smallman, Kirk, 138
Smith, Al, 84
Smith, Josephine, 161
Social action, 144–57
Social Security, 52, 53–58
    average payments under, 165
Social Security Act (1935), 58
Soho House, 175
Some Folks Won't Work (Calkins), 42, 43
Sommer, Stan, 202
South End House, 77, 175
Sparkman, John, 349
Spiegel, Samuel, 298
Spofford, Grace, 117, 120
Staff of settlements, 92–95
"Stand-Patism Versus Change in Psychiatric Clinic Practice" (Levine), 113
Staunton, Peggy, 81
Steinholtz, Dr., 295

Stern, Carl S., 351
Stewart, Bryce, 43, 55
Stoney, George, 153
Stoutenburgh, Isaac, 18
Strauss, Anna Lord, 333
Sutton, Percy E., 293, 316
Suzuki, Shinichi, 123
Swap shops, 186–87
Swope, Gerard, 54
Synanon, 248–49

Taber, Louis J., 54
Tannenbaum, Dora, 290, 291, 298
Taylor, Graham, 77, 174
Taylor, Lea, 174
Taylor, Ruth, 38
Teagle, Walter C., 54
Teamsters union, 328
Tefferteller, Ralph, 88, 92–93, 101, 165, 223, 245, 247, 255, 265, 269
Tefferteller, Ruth, 75, 92–94, 164, 211–13, 223, 227, 229, 236
Thieman, Annelise, 110
Thomas, Norman, 28
Thomas, Senator, 336
Tobias, Max, 164–65
Tompkins, B. A., 86
Trager, Betty, 90
"Treatment in the Home" (Levine), 113
Trumall, Dr., 249
Truman, Harry S, 234, 277, 285
Trussell, Ray E. 302–4, 307, 311, 313, 315
Tweed, Bill, 18
Two Bridges Neighborhood Council, 267

Unemployed Councils, 5
Unemployment, 40–52
    LaGuardia and, 22
    New Deal and, 32–33
    postwar, 231–34

UNICEF, 213–14
Union Settlement, 77, 81, 151, 177
United Housing Corporation, 237
United Nations, 207–16
United Nations Relief and Rehabilitation Administration (UNRR), 177
United Neighborhood Houses, 20, 23, 176, 177, 208, 215, 229
    community studies by, 154
    Consumer Committee of, 329, 337
    League of Mothers' Clubs of, 151
    Unemployment Committee of, 14, 36
University House, 4, 9, 13–14, 29, 84
    arts program at, 125
    Board of, 85
    drama program at, 176
    fund raising by, 11
    health care at, 277, 278
    nursery school of, 109–10, 169
    old-age programs, at, 165
University Settlement, 19, 79, 245, 271

Van Cortlandt, Philip, 18
Van Curler, Jacobus, 16, 17
Valle, Marta, 267
Villard, Mrs. Henry, H., 352
Villegas, José, 97, 240
Visiting Nurse Service, 6, 19, 108
    housing study by, 149
Volunteers in Service to America (VISTA), 78, 164
Vorhees, Jerry, 335

Wagner, Robert, Sr., 42, 231–33, 283, 336
Wagner, Robert F., Jr., 22, 168
    Gouverneur Hospital and, 289, 293, 297, 298, 301–2, 312, 315

Wagner-Daughton Bill, 58
Wagner-Lewis Bill, 56
Wainwright, Fonrose, 176
Wainwright, J. Mayhew, 22, 23,
    41–42
Wald, Lillian D., 6–8, 19–20, 31,
    61, 89, 108, 114, 174, 237,
    256
Wales, Margaret, 7
Wallace, Henry A., 53
Walsh, J. Raymond, 210
War Mobilization and Reconver-
    sion Act (1944), 232
Warburg, Mrs. Edward M. M.,
    88
Warburg, Felix, 88
Warburg, Mrs. Frederick, 88
Ware, Caroline, 341–42
Warne, Colston, 342, 344, 352
Washington, George, 17
Wasserman, Rose, 224
Weddin, Asta, 139
Weinfeld, Edward, 122
Weinfeld, Lillian, 122
Welfare Council, 36
Welfare Rights Organization, 273
*What Some Slum Dwellers Want
    in Housing* (study), 152
White, Frank, 121
White, Gaylord, 77
Whitney, Caroline, 324, 326–27
Widows' Pensions and Boarding
    Homes, 38
Wiener, Geoffrey, 267
Williams, Albert Rhys, 210
Wilson, Woodrow, 191

Winant, John G., 58
Wisconsin Industrial Commission,
    58
Wise, Stephen S., 210
Witte, Edwin E., 55
Wittenberg, Kenneth, 314
Women's suffrage, 38
Woodhouse, Chase Going, 339–
    40, 342
Woods, Robert A., 175
Worker's Education project, 34,
    89
Works Progress Administration,
    4–5, 20, 30–32, 34–35
    art program of, 126
    Federal Theater Project of, 115
World Food Council, 215
World War I, 190–92
World War II, 190–206
    Advertising Council during,
    178
    rationing and price control dur-
    ing, 337–48

Yale, Milton, 255
Yerby, Alonzo, S., 313
Young, Betty, 117–19, 122
Young Women's Christian As-
    sociation, Industrial Divi-
    sion of, 43
Young people's cooperatives, 141–
    43

Ziprin, Sheba, 149
Zucker, Mildred, 351